NICE WORK
IF YOU CAN
GET IT

NICE WORK IF YOU CAN GET IT

The True Adventures of a Costa Del Sol gigolo

Dean Saunders

JOHN BLAKE

Published by John Blake Publishing Ltd,
3 Bramber Court, 2 Bramber Road,
London W14 9PB, England

www.blake.co.uk

First published in paperback in 2008

ISBN: 978-1-84454-509-4

British Library Cataloguing-in-Publication Data:

A catalogue record for this book is available from the British Library.

Design by www.envydesign.co.uk

Printed in Great Britain by Creative Print & Design, Ebbw Vale, Wales

1 3 5 7 9 10 8 6 4 2

Papers used by John Blake Publishing are natural, recyclable products made from
wood grown in sustainable forests. The manufacturing processes conform to the
environmental regulations of the country of origin.

To Grunger Bird
Love always,
Biker Boy

Acknowledgements

No words, written or spoken, will ever express how grateful I am to have a family like mine.

Thank you, Mum and Dad, for being so encouraging when I'm doing the right thing and so forgiving when I've done wrong. When the difference between the two was blurry, that was not your fault.

And thank you Neil 'Boycey' Saunders. We may be chalk and cheese, but we're still blood. Remember, bruv, this time next year...

I have been blessed with so many good friends, but some were more involved in the making of this book in various ways, so I would like to thank them especially: Darren Crome, Danny Dudley, Leigh Coupland, Chris Woods and Marissa.

I would also like to say a special thank you to the Dudley family and Maria del Mar for looking after me in Spain. Also to Simon, Rachel and family. You all have my undying loyalty and affection.

To my best friend, LDC, thank you for being so understanding throughout the writing of this book and, believe me, time spent with you is never a waste.

Thanks to everyone at Yanx, Bubbles, Stars, The Old Bailey and Jimmy Tramps.

With regard to my career change, this would have been a much slower process without the help of Alex Nicoll and Harvey Platt. Thank you for your time, your constructive criticism and the words I needed to hear from someone other than family, before I could believe I had any talent.

Last but not least, I wish to thank Wensley Clarkson and Tammy Cohen for helping me tell this story. It has been a valuable learning experience and you have made it a positive one – so, thank you.

Thank you all,
Deano

Deano can be contacted at: www.deanosaunders.co.uk

Contents

Introduction

This was not your average job interview.

Am I qualified? That would have been the first thing I'd have asked myself before going for any normal job. But this was hardly an ordinary nine-to-five. And, let's be honest, my third-rate degree in psychology was not going to impress this particular interviewer.

What experience have I got? Plenty, I thought, although not all good. I could always just leave out the sexual disasters, I told myself. After all, it wasn't as if he was going to ask me for references.

'So, what can I do for you?' Andy's voice was deep and resonant, and soothing to my jangling nerves. His Armani suit was made to measure, and his shoes shone as brightly as the Rolex on his wrist.

Sitting across from him in the swanky casino, I felt overcome with self-consciousness as I tried to work out what to say.

'You want to be a gigolo, right?' he said, his perfectly tanned features arranged into a scowl as he cocked his head to one side, sleek black ponytail resting on his left shoulder.

'Yeah, that's right,' I said, irritated at how weak my voice sounded, and how full of doubt. In an attempt to disguise my crisis of confidence, I'd started trying to mirror Andy's body language, one of the few useful pieces of information I'd actually retained from my three years at university. His dark eyes watched as my hands changed position and he didn't bother to hide his smirk. This man knew full well what I was doing.

'So, what do you want to know, Deano?' he asked, leaning back into his chair and forming his fingers into a steeple, like one of those Derren Brown-type celebrity mind-readers.

'Everything,' I replied idiotically. I then proceeded to further demonstrate my lack of sophistication by blurting out what I thought I already knew about being a gigolo, based entirely on films I'd seen (you know the one I'm talking about, featuring Richard Gere and an assortment of startlingly white shirts). Andy seemed displeased, or at least unimpressed, with my response. He inhaled as if preparing himself to be patient with me, while glancing over behind him to make me aware he needed to get back to his client. As his eyes scanned me, I began to question what on earth had made me think I could cut it as a male escort. What did I have to offer women? Why would they willingly pay for my company when they could have someone like Andy? Or just go to a bar and pick someone up for free?

'I hope you like a challenge,' Andy sighed, 'because you have a long way to go...' As he continued, his bored tone combined with his 'who do you think you are?' body language made everything inside me shrivel into a small, insignificant blob of self-doubt. I must have been mad to think I could do this. Me? A naive Essex lad with a recently broken heart and a history of bungled sexual relationships.

But as Andy's words came back into focus I started picking up something positive behind them. The criticism had been replaced by a glimmer of encouragement (just a glimmer, mind – he was still the King of Cool), and it seemed as if he was no longer judging me, but offering me something instead.

'...So, listen, pay attention and this'll get you started,' he said, and something very close to a real smile played across his lips.

What followed was a list of rules. Gigolo rules. They might not be perfect, he warned. They might not even work for me. But they'd kept him in business. And, crucially, they'd kept him alive. Marbella, capital of what had been renamed the Costa Del Crime, was a dangerous place to mess around with wealthy, bored housewives – or their daughters or, more importantly, their husbands.

I listened attentively as Andy, who could have been only a few years older than me, explained the basics of life as a Costa gigolo. The more he spoke, the more I warmed to him. OK, scratch that. The more he spoke, the more I wanted to *be* him. To a pathologically shallow, hot-blooded 22-year-old, he was everything I aspired to. And he had everything I wanted. One day, I vowed to myself, I'm going to be sitting where he is now. One day, I'm going to have women queuing to pay me for my company. One day, my mobile is going to be bursting with the numbers of some of the richest, best-connected women on the coast.

Ever heard the saying 'Be careful what you wish for'? If someone had said that to me at that moment, with my bright new future as a handsomely paid escort glittering tantalisingly ahead of me, you know what my response would have been?

Bollocks to that.

CHAPTER ONE

Jeana

'If you don't believe in you, nor will your client. The size of your ego is as important as the size of your equipment.' ANDY

I woke up in unusual comfort, wrapped in a duvet, spread-eagled across a king-size four-poster bed. January was a bleak time to be waking up alone in a fifth-floor apartment overlooking a grey, comfortless Med. But on that particular morning in 2003, something felt different. The smell of my flatmate's first cigarette had been replaced by soap and perfume; the usual harsh glare flooding in through the curtainless window had given way to a soft, subtle light. The sudden realisation that I wasn't actually at home jolted me abruptly from my semi-sleep.

Sitting bolt upright, I scanned the room for anything that would trigger my memory, and remind me of where I was or how I had got there. Everything was white, peach or gold. Typical Marbella *Footballers' Wives* taste, but, compared to my own dark, damp room, this was heaven. I took in my work uniform, folded up on a chair in the corner. Normally, my clothes landed wherever I took them off, and I hadn't seen them so neatly folded since leaving my parents' house to come to Spain six long months before.

Fuzzy images of making love began to flicker in the back of my mind. Sure, it could just have been the vestiges of last night's dream, but one thing made me doubt it. Unlike my regular dreams, I had woken from this one in someone else's bed. Naked. The chain flushed and suddenly she appeared from the en-suite bathroom in a pinstriped trouser suit, which hugged her curves as she sat down and fiddled with her earrings at the dressing table. Her blonde, shoulder-length hair was tied up and her professional garb made me suddenly feel very conscious of my age. I was only 22 and she had to be about twice that. But, from the memories that had begun filtering back into my mind, that hadn't been a problem for either of us the night before.

The lines on her face were more noticeable in this light than they'd appeared when I first met her, and she was doing her best to conceal them with the finishing touches of her make-up. I sat up and watched her paint on her outside face until she caught me staring in the mirror, and her features softened into a smile. Looking into her blue eyes brought everything back to me and I was relieved to see that, although they were not as hungry as they had been the night before, they were still warm and friendly. I had a sudden flashback of flirting with her at the restaurant where I worked. Then an image flickered through my mind of her

passing me her number and address and offering to 'make it worth my while' to go back to her villa. As more memories rushed back, one phrase kept rebounding around my head: 'I must be dreaming!'

'Morning, handsome,' she said in the Canadian accent that had made the previous evening's events seem even more surreal. I've always had a problem believing that accents from the other side of the Atlantic are actually real, and not put on – probably the result of watching far too many American films and sitcoms.

But, this was *not* a screenplay. She came over and sat on the edge of the bed, placing a hand on my leg before breaking into the same warm smile.

'Morning,' I replied, pinning my morning glory down under the duvet with one hand and raising the other to give a short wave. I stopped short as I realised I had no idea what her name was.

This was not the first time I had woken up next to an anonymous female, but her being older than my usual quarry somehow made my amnesia seem less excusable. I felt like it should earn me a detention, or at least a few dozen lines.

'Deano must remember the names of women he sleeps with.

Deano must remember the names of women he sleeps with...'

She picked up her Prada bag and produced a 20-euro note from the matching purse inside. She passed it to me between her index and middle finger.

'This is for your cab.' She grabbed her watch and checked the time, her eyes widening in alarm as she saw the hour. 'I have to be someplace, so just show yourself out, OK?' she said, patting my thigh through the duvet.

Standing up, she brushed down her trousers, smoothing out the non-existent creases. Then she sashayed across the room. As I watched her prominent bum sway and jiggle just beneath the hem of her jacket, I remembered what she'd looked like naked and felt myself becoming aroused. She was nearly through the bedroom door when she turned and looked at me again.

'There's a cleaner in, OK, so don't run around nude or anything.' She looked over pointedly at my white Calvin Kleins resting on top of my black uniform.

All of a sudden, I wondered if she knew me better than I thought she did, because my immediate reaction normally would have been to dance around the house celebrating my first shag in ages, then ring round and talk about it to anyone who'd listen. Or was telling me that someone was in the house just her way of warning me not to steal anything? I just smiled and nodded to her, looking up to the ceiling as she turned to walk out.

'Oh,' I heard, and then suddenly her head popped back around the edge of the door, 'the envelope on the bedside table is yours.' Her heels clattered on the marble of the spiral staircase as she called out, 'Bye, then.'

'Bye!' I shouted back, and then waited for the sound of the front door closing.

For a while, I lay motionless in bed, just staring at the long white envelope, which rested against the lamp on the small table. It wasn't sealed, and, if she knew my name, she hadn't written it on the outside. But it was obvious what was in it.

Money.

So it was real then. It hadn't all been a product of my feverish, sex-starved imagination. This woman really had paid me to sleep with her.

I decided against the dance or the phone calls and put my clothes on quickly, keeping my eye on the envelope but lacking the courage to go and see what was inside. What if it just contained a fiver? To be honest, judging by my last few largely rushed sexual encounters, that would probably have been on the generous side. I tried to reason that, no matter how much there was, it was all a bonus. After all, I'd got the chance to make love to an attractive woman, so just the taxi fare would have been more than enough.

But part of me still felt as though the contents of that envelope would determine the course of my life, just like school, college or university, and I was worried about not making the grade. Just how much was I worth? I picked up the envelope without opening it and stuffed it into my pocket, disappointed at how light it was and how easily it folded up.

Glancing through the window, I caught sight of the maid in the garden, dressed in her blue chequered uniform, and quickly pulled back into the room. Feeling suddenly like an intruder, I just wanted to get out of there as quickly as possible. I mean, I didn't know anything about this woman. What if there was a jealous husband about to arrive home from a business trip? I'd seen all the movies. I knew all the plots.

To my relief, I got to the front gate without being spotted and managed to open it before realising, as it clanged shut behind me, that I'd left my mobile phone in the bedroom.

Twat!

I had no idea where I was and no way of calling a taxi. After about ten minutes of sitting on the kerb calling myself every name in the book, I rang the buzzer. When the gate opened, I had the embarrassing task of having to explain the situation to the maid, who eventually accompanied me up to the bedroom to retrieve my phone and even phoned a taxi for me.

Just how smooth was that? Eat your heart out, Richard Gere.

The moment I stepped into the taxi I had to fight an urge to tell the driver all about the night I'd just had but – owing to my somewhat limited grasp of Spanish – I contented myself to humming along to Kiss FM. The driver must have taken exception to my humming, or the fact that the Spanish radio station was playing only English music, because he started twiddling the radio dial furiously, stopping only when he'd managed to locate the Gipsy Kings.

I closed my eyes and started reflecting on this latest twist to my love life. Since arriving in Spain, my heart in tatters from breaking up with Chloe – my long-term girlfriend and one true love – life hadn't exactly been a non-stop sex-fest.

I knew I wasn't bad-looking, and didn't have major problems talking to girls, but for some reason I just couldn't seem to crack the One-Night Stand etiquette. Come too soon, can't come at all, can't get it up or, on one occasion, 'don't put it up there!' I cringed as I thought about some of those encounters. But my trouble was that I needed to feel comfortable with a woman in order to perform properly and, until now, I hadn't been able to allow myself to get comfortable with any woman who wasn't Chloe. Catch 22.

However, the previous night's events had changed all that. In a weird way, I felt like I'd lost my virginity all over again. As the Gipsy Kings blared, I tried to put together in my mind exactly how I'd ended up there, and exactly what it all meant...

I'd met her at work a couple of weeks before. I'd been at the American restaurant for only a short time and, already, bar work was boring me. I was a terrible waiter. I was too shy for the meeting and greeting, so if I was going to talk to anyone there had to be a bar between us; then I felt more comfortable, but bored nonetheless. I liked to pass this shyness off as reserve – a throwback from my days as a bouncer in a rough Romford nightclub. But, to be honest, I'd always been shy – at least until I'd had a drink.

People tend not to think about what places such as Marbella are like in January, when the summer crowds have gone. This restaurant was busier compared to most, but hardly buzzing. On the plus side, there was still a fair amount of eye candy, even in January, and this woman was a prime example. The birds my age seemed to fly elsewhere for the winter, but there were still a healthy number of attractive, mature women at any time of year in Marbella.

She took my fancy right away, and I already knew she liked

me. I'd been working there just a few days when she asked me if I had a girlfriend. Shocked by her forwardness, and conditioned by four years of being with Chloe, I foolishly replied, 'Yes,' then spent the rest of the evening mentally kicking myself.

The next time she came in, she was wearing a red roll-neck sweater and blue jeans. Her blonde hair was loose around her shoulders. The smile she flashed at me revealed no trace of lingering resentment at the way I'd rebuffed her the last time, and I was determined to let her know I wasn't in fact attached.

As I said, I am a useless waiter, but, taking a deep breath, I seized the first opportunity I could to leave the bar and take her a menu.

'Well, hello.' She shot me a mischievous look. 'You're not always this quick to come over.'

'You looked thirsty,' I said, matching her with a cheeky smile.

'I am, and starving!' she replied, looking down at the menu. Then she sat back and looked me up and down. 'Will you be serving me all night?'

'Well... your wish is my command,' I said with a little bow.

'Hmmm, I don't think what I want is on the menu any more. I'll have to get back to you.'

'And to drink? Water? Wine? Cocktail?'

'Yeah, why not? But I'm not sure which cocktail.'

'I'll get a menu...'

'Don't bother, just surprise me, OK?'

'Fruity or creamy?'

'I think, tonight, I'm in the mood for something... creamy.' She smiled suggestively at me as I returned to the bar to mix her a cocktail.

I noticed my drinks tickets for the other tables seemed to be mounting up rather alarmingly, so I didn't have time to do more than race over with her drink before getting back to work and appease the impatient waitresses.

Looking over to her table, I saw her full lips wrapped around the straw, clearly savouring the drink I'd mixed her. She glanced my way, eyebrows raised and nodded. Phew, I'd impressed her.

Everything seemed to move in slow motion as I continued to watch her licking her straw, playing with her hair. Yes, she probably was old enough to be my mother, but she was incredible. The food waiter arrived and, even while he was taking her order, her eyes continued to dart back to me, teasingly. Maybe I had done the right thing by telling her I was taken, because she seemed to want me even more than before.

She had just finished a huge steak, but she still looked hungry. Smiling, she beckoned me over with her finger. Confident I was definitely in there with her at this point, I threw the bar towel over my shoulder and swaggered up to her table smirking.

'I'm very disappointed,' she said, her smile fading instantly, 'you said *you* would be serving me all night.'

I could feel my head and neck shrinking into my shoulders as I tried to escape into my shell. I thought that I was being punished for rejecting her the other night.

'You've been in Spain too long, having two men do a one-man job.'

Her face was still humourless. I wanted to run back to the bar and hide until she had left, but she was still talking. I didn't want to leave and be thought of as rude as well as inadequate.

'You shouldn't say you can do a job and not do it properly, it's very frustrating for a woman.' Her frown really screwed up her face and it pained me that I had disappointed such a beautiful woman. Just as I was about to apologise, she grabbed my wrist and slapped the back of my hand, breaking into a smile again. 'I'll forgive you, just this once.'

I sighed in relief as I realised she had been joking.

'What is this?' she asked, lifting her empty cocktail glass.

'It's a Multiple Screaming Orgasm.'

'Well, you make those well,' she told me.

I laughed and returned to the bar, even more attracted to this stunning woman. She was fun and feisty, and I knew I wanted to sleep with her – not that that put her in a particularly exclusive group, mind. I also knew that she knew it too – and, if she didn't, she was doing a bloody good impression of someone who did!

I started to make her another cocktail. Not that I was trying to get her drunk – I just needed time to build up the confidence to go and ask her out. But, just as I was about to pour it, she stood up and made her way to the bar with her credit card in her hand.

'I only take cash, sorry. But you can have a free cocktail.'

She gasped theatrically and took a seat, so I passed her the drink. 'What else can I get for free?' She began playing with her straw again.

I smiled and carried on drying glasses.

'How's the lucky girl?'

'Who's that?'

'Your girlfriend.'

'Oh, we split up.'

'That's too bad. Her loss, right?' she said with a sympathetic smile.

She'd ordered a couple of carrot cakes to go and, when they arrived, she stood up to leave without finishing her cocktail. Suddenly panicked, I wanted to say something, anything to keep her there, but she'd already started towards the door.

Then she hesitated, as if weighing something up. Turning back into the room, her expression was less playful, as if she had grown tired of the games. 'You got any plans for after you get off?' she asked.

'Bed, sleep... why?'

In answer, she stopped a passing waiter and asked him for his pen and a sheet of paper and scribbled something down. Then she pressed the note into my hand and left.

What she'd written would change my life. There was an address and a phone number. And scrawled across the bottom was a message: 'Get a taxi. I'll make it worth your while. I tip well.'

I was naive and I certainly couldn't claim to be an expert when it came to sex, but even I knew what this meant.

Not only was I going to sleep with her; she was going to pay me for doing it!

For the next hour, I was giddy with excitement, not letting go of the crumpled piece of paper. I couldn't believe my luck, but at the same time I felt incredibly nervous, so I had a few beers. Not enough to get any normal full-blooded male even tipsy, but for me it was more than enough to calm my nerves. My alcohol tolerance is legendarily pitiful; I am the original lightweight and even the last seven months in training had failed to turn me into a drinker.

When I finally finished work, I took my San Miguel-sponsored courage in my hands and hailed a taxi, reading to the driver the address written on the note. After a bit of head scratching, followed by a phone call to a fellow taxi driver, we set off inland, down roads that became increasingly exclusive.

The villas scattered along these unlit lanes were inhabited by the people who really did have money, although at this time of year many of them were empty rentals, waiting for the next bunch of wealthy short-term tenants.

The further we drove and the quieter it became, the less confident I felt. Maybe it was just that I had seen one too many horror films, or maybe it was my Catholic upbringing, but the overwhelming lust I felt and the ease with which this was all happening made me nervous. I had been with a few girls during my time in Spain, but one thing was for sure, I had worked for them. Bought them drinks, made them laugh, pretended to be listening and even interested, convinced them that their boyfriends were cheating on them back home, or whatever else did the trick. But, at the end of the night, I knew that I had worked for it and I had no reason to worry or feel guilty. No girl, and certainly no woman, had ever walked up to me and given me her address, let alone told me she would 'make it worth my while'. It was ludicrous.

She had seemed like such an ordinary woman, besides the possible symptoms of nymphomania. Maybe that's how she traps all her victims, I thought. By the time the taxi reached the villa, lust had been replaced by fear. The same fear that had stood in my way all my life and kept me from having what I wanted.

I resisted asking the taxi driver to take me home to Marbella, and got out into the crisp night. Days were still bright and warm at this time of year, but at night I would always wear a sweater over my polo shirt. I forced myself to push the button on the intercom, and waited for a reply.

The intercom sounded, then there was a click and the security gate hummed and slid open. I wandered in and saw the silhouette of the mostly unlit villa. Single palm trees marked each corner, towering over the garden. I could hear water trickling as I made my way along the stone path. The security light flicked on and blinded me momentarily, revealing the large swimming pool in the near corner of the garden, bordered by a small wall. Hearing the gate lock behind me, I stopped. I saw a Mercedes parked by the wall under a shelter, and hoped it belonged to her rather than to a jealous, axe-wielding husband. Although she'd taken a taxi from the restaurant on both the occasions I'd seen her, I had just assumed that had been because she was drinking.

I continued towards the house and then, emerging from the rays of the light, I saw her. She stood at the door in a white towelling robe, hugging herself and not daring to step outside into the chilly air. She smiled and beckoned me in, before locking the door behind her. I tried not to think about whether the locked door was to keep intruders out, or me in.

I noticed she was barefoot and that the few inches in height she'd lost made her seem more vulnerable, less in control. As we strolled through the hallway to the living room, she turned, looked down and stopped me with a raised finger. She pointed down at my shoes and then walked through into the living room, eyeing me kicking them off and leaving them where they were.

'You really should hide them,' she advised me sincerely. 'My husband might come home and find them.'

My mouth fell open and I considered putting the shoes back on and running, until she laughed hysterically.

'I'm just kidding!'

But about what, I thought, being married or the possibility that he could come home?

She patted the sofa next to her. 'I won't hurt you, I promise.'

I smiled and left the shoes where they were, going into the living room to join her on one of the many sofas.

The room contained two three-piece suites and a glass dining table with six places. In each corner was a large Persian rug, and the subdued lighting came from square-shaded lamps positioned on glass coffee tables. In front of our sofa was another glass table with drinks coasters on it, and a giant plasma-screen TV fixed to the wall. I surveyed the room and noticed the free corner, where of course I would have had a pool table. Then I considered the possibility of there being a games room with one in already.

'Dance floor?' I asked, nodding to the rug in the spacious but empty corner.

'On occasion. But not tonight. I've been on my feet all day.' She edged closer to me and brushed her hair behind her ear, then she pulled her legs up on to the sofa.

'You look tired,' she said, but before I had a chance to reply she had sat up and swung her knee over my lap to straddle me. She kissed me softly and held my face in her hands. Her hands wandered down my chest and then finally ended up at the throbbing bulge in my black jeans. 'Not *that* tired, I see.'

We laughed and at last I began to really relax. We kissed again, but then she stood up. I was used to my cold apartment, so in this heated villa my sweater was too much.

'It's really warm in here,' I told her as I removed my sweater and put it down beside the sofa. My eyes lit up as she undid her robe belt, only to meet with disappointment when she tucked the robe in and tightened it again. As she walked away, I sat up, unsure of whether or not to follow her.

She turned and asked, 'If I offer you a beer, will you think I'm trying to get you drunk and take advantage?' She wore that devilish grin as she went to the kitchen to fetch the drinks. 'You'd be right,' she called in as she prepared the drinks.

'No servants tonight?' I was only half-joking. The villa was too big for anyone to manage without help, and it was doubtful that she lived here alone.

'Why do you think you're here? I'm just showing you where they are for next time.'

We joked and chatted for a while, and I found out that she was actually Canadian, not American, as I'd thought. It felt strange being asked questions by someone twice my age, like I was being interviewed or counselled for something. Maybe this *is* an interview, I thought, to see if I can get past first base.

I felt quite drunk by then and was more than willing to say whatever I thought she wanted to hear to seal the deal. I asked her similar questions just so I could hear that accent some more. I'd found her attractive from the start, but then, after she had made her proposition and I knew that she was interested in me, she'd gone up a few notches. Now, under the effects of alcohol, the boundaries between reasonably attractive and stunningly beautiful were completely blurred. I had to have at least one night with her and I felt confident that she wanted the same thing.

'Are you in the habit of inviting strange men back to your villa?' By this point I'd relaxed enough to be enjoying myself.

'You don't strike me as strange.' She put her drink on the table and eyed me up and down. 'And as for a man...'

I feigned feeling hurt by grabbing my chest, but she laughed and sat on my lap again, facing me. She kissed me once more and sighed mockingly. 'I don't mind being in charge for a while.'

She sat on me and we kissed passionately, our hands caressing each other, but over our clothes. Then she undid the belt of her robe and slipped it off, letting it slide down her toned arms and exposing herself to me. Any possibility of respectful eye contact went out of the window as I encountered her curvaceous body. Then she took hold of my face and started to kiss me again. This time, my hands were not hampered by clothing, and I stroked and squeezed as I pleased.

She pinned my shoulders to the sofa and kissed my neck before yanking my polo shirt from my waistband and peeling it off me. My arms were still in the air and she held them there as she kissed my chest and worked her way down to my abdomen. She dismounted and then knelt on the floor between my legs, tugging at my belt with one hand and undoing my fly with the other. I sighed, relieved to be getting out of those tight jeans. Not that they were usually that tight, but then usually I didn't have a woman gyrating on my lap. She threw me another cheeky smile, as, in one gradual continuous motion, she stripped me of my jeans, boxer shorts and socks.

Then she buried her head in my lap. After the initial shock, I was torn between ecstasy – a blow job! Without having to work for it! What a result! – and worry. What was in it for her? What if I shot my load and failed to get going again?

I tried to slow myself down by thinking about work, but then I just imagined her coming in and us doing it on the bar, which didn't exactly have the desired dampening effect! In the end, I took her hand from where it was and held it as I joined her on the floor. It was my turn to repay the favour and anyway I needed a break.

She had bathed recently and smelled like vanilla. Her skin was fair and smooth and waxed to within an inch of its life. With my lips and tongue I probed every bit of her, working my way down, while surreptitiously searching for my trousers and my condoms.

My clothes were scattered all around us between the sofa and the glass table. The size of the room and amount of comfortable sofas available made our lovemaking on the floor, in such a cramped space, seem perverse. It was all so unreal. Everything, from her leaving the note at the restaurant up to this moment on the floor, suggested that this was a dream. A dream I had no intention of waking from.

Even so, I kept my eyes open as we made love, watching her face and her chest closely as her breathing became irregular. It seemed like an eternity before her grip on my hair tightened and her back arched. I didn't need any further invitation – I'd been ready and waiting for what seemed like years. As I came to my climax, I remember thinking that, with my tongue still aching from its recent workout, I was glad she wasn't asking me to talk dirty!

The rest of the night passed in an alcohol-soaked blur. I vaguely remembered making love in the kitchen and then somehow making it up to her bedroom, where we made love at least a couple more times. And the next thing I knew was waking up in that four-poster bed and realising that, from now on, *everything* in my life was different.

The taxi pulled up outside my apartment and, with the Gipsy Kings still echoing in my head, I reached into my pocket and

extracted the 20-euro note and the folded white envelope. As the driver searched his leather money pouch for my change, I looked down at the envelope and said to myself, 'Fuck it, just look and get it over with.' I unfolded it and hooked my thumb inside to pull it open, holding my breath as I did.

For a while, I just stared at the contents, then I raced up the five flights of stairs to my apartment, still clutching the white envelope, too impatient to wait for the lift. I needed to tell someone about it before I exploded, and it was a safe bet that my flatmate, Wayne, was still at home in bed. As I fumbled with my keys, I had a sudden attack of doubt. What if he didn't believe me? What if by talking about it I was jinxing myself and it would never happen again?

Boasting had never got me anywhere before. Always better to play it cool, answer when asked, even when you do feel like you are about to burst. So, as I walked in and saw Wayne's wiry frame slouched at the computer putting out his first cigarette, I forced myself to slow down. Nodding a 'hello', I walked straight down the hallway to my room without a word about the previous evening. Cool, hey? And I would have made it to my room had he not called out, 'Where d'you sleep last night?'

Wayne didn't raise his eyes from the computer screen as I walked back in, still debating what to tell him.

I had known Wayne for six months, and already he had got me the job at the restaurant he worked in and convinced his girlfriend to rent out their spare room to me. He had witnessed the take-offs to most of my sexual crashes and not only joined me in drowning any sorrows, but also ensured

that I made it back to the apartment and got up in time for work the next day. But, despite how grateful I was and how much I liked the guy, he did have a tendency to gossip after a few beers. He just seemed to know everything about everyone and, if you asked, or sometimes even if you didn't ask, he would have a story about someone. I don't mean that in a nasty way; he never had a bad word for anyone. In fact, it was hard to work out what his opinion was on anything because he'd normally begin his conversations, 'I heard that so and so...' and then he'd always say, 'But whether that's true or not...?' before shrugging.

I realised that, if I told him what had happened, within a week everyone in Marbella would have heard about it and retold their version to someone else. But before I could fully appreciate the consequences of that, Wayne had peeled his eyes from the screen and spotted the money in my hand.

'What's that?' he asked.

'Four hundred euros,' I said, feeling the same need again to run around and shout about being valued at half my monthly salary.

'Where d'you get 400 euros?' he asked, knowing full well that I had not been paid at the restaurant yet, nor been out since New Year's Eve due to lack of funds.

'Some woman came into work and paid me to go home with her.' I laughed as I said it because I knew how ridiculous it sounded.

But Wayne raised his eyebrow doubtfully and his head just nodded and returned to the computer screen. If he had thought I was lying, he would have said, 'BOLLOCKS!' but, come to think of it, if he had believed me, he would have said, 'BOLLOCKS!'

But, whether he believed me or not, the story was as good as public the moment it left my lips. I hadn't seen anyone in Marbella since New Year's Eve, except for Wayne, but I knew the very next person I saw would already have heard his latest bit of news.

A week passed and I promised myself I would not blow the money I had earned. But I wanted to go out with my mates now that I could afford it again. I was also determined not to leave it too long before my next sexual encounter, in case my magic wore off. I decided against phoning the Canadian for a repeat performance, even if it was a freebie, on the grounds that I had no idea what her name was and dreaded the thought of her asking me only to receive the sound of silence or an incorrect guess.

With my newfound wealth, I'd bought a few books on building confidence, in the hope of reading something that would turn me into the suave man-of-the-world I wanted to be. I wanted what had happened the other night with the Canadian woman to be a regular occurrence, paid or not. I knew I could pick up girls and, if I wanted, maintain a relationship. But for some reason, as soon as it became clear it was a one-night stand, the sex bit went out of the window.

But the more I read the same old advice, the worse it made me feel about being single. In the end, I got dressed and headed into town. I no longer cared what anyone was going to say to me. It was Friday night and I just wanted some company – preferably female.

Saturday mornings at the bullring were crazy, as busloads of tourists arrived for the market and stopped at the restaurant where I worked, hungry for breakfast and lunch. Pickpockets, buskers, market traders and Gypsies were everywhere, practising their trades as I arrived late to practise mine. Fish, the restaurant manager, gave me a disapproving grimace and looked pointedly at his watch, before leaving me with Wayne to make the rest of the coffee orders.

Despite being late and the workload being close to unbearable, I was in good spirits as I relived my second successful sexual encounter in a week, which had ended less than one hour before I arrived at work. Once again, I wanted to share this piece of news with Wayne, or any waiter who would listen, but this time I decided to keep it to myself. Anyway, I had not been paid for my latest conquest and the girl was about my age, so I felt it was hardly a story worth telling.

It was great having such pleasant memories so fresh in my mind and I replayed the whole experience over, so lost in my own little fantasy world that I failed to notice the woman standing at the bar, waiting to catch my attention.

'Two pieces of carrot cake please,' came the Canadian accent, instantly jolting me out of my daydream and bringing back another set of positive associations.

She laughed as I did a double take, half shocked that she had come to speak to me again, half worried that she was going to ask me if I remembered her name.

'Hi, how's things?' I said smiling, stopping my work so I could give her my full attention.

'What are you doing later?' she asked, tilting her head to one side and brushing her hair back off her face.

She was wearing a cardigan over a white T-shirt, blue jeans and trainers and, unlike the last time I had seen her, I felt a lot less intimidated. She looked younger in casual clothes and her eyes looked eager again, not just friendly. I decided to play it cool and shrug. After all, Christine, the previous night's conquest, may have wanted me to come round again.

'My place at eight?' She smiled at me over her shoulder as she strutted out of the restaurant, her thumbs in her back jean pockets, drawing attention to that peach of an arse of hers.

Who was I trying to kid? I knew where I was going to be at eight o'clock and it was not at Christine's.

'Who was that?' asked Wayne, smiling as he caught a final glimpse of the Canadian disappearing into the crowd.

I ignored him and just smiled, so he whipped my arm with a bar towel.

'No one… anyway, you should have seen who I went home with last night,' I said, with no intention of sharing that information. There was no need, as word always seemed to travel fast enough without my help. Wayne knew that, too, which was why he didn't ask again.

At precisely eight o'clock, I was standing outside the gates of the enormous villa. I had taken a siesta after work to make sure I had the energy to keep my sexual roll going. My hair was slicked back with wax and I wore my only clean shirt and trousers. I'm a jeans, T-shirt and trainers bloke, so, to me, I had made a big effort just to go to some woman's house. But, then again, she was not just some woman. She was a mature woman, who not only wanted to have sex with me, but also appeared to have money to burn!

On the taxi ride over, I'd spent most of the journey telling myself that the hard part was out of the way now; I could relax and be myself. I had already impressed her enough for a second invite so, theoretically, the pressure was off. But there was something about the idea of being with an older woman that made my heart pound and my palms sweat. I kept repeating to myself, 'You're not anxious, you're excited!' – a mantra I had borrowed from one of those confidence books.

The security gate clicked and hummed, and I slipped in as soon as the gap was big enough. Again, the sudden floodlights startled me. I half expected guard dogs to appear from nowhere at any moment. By the time I reached the steps to the veranda, she was at the door in jogging bottoms and the same T-shirt and cardigan she had been wearing earlier.

'Well, look at you! All dressed up!' she said, looking me up and down before giving me a kiss on each cheek.

'Shall I get us some drinks?' I asked, once we were inside.

'Remember where everything is?' she replied, sinking into the sofa, brushing her hair back. I looked towards the kitchen and nodded, although what came back to me most vividly about that particular room was taking her from behind over the breakfast counter. The smirk on her face as I left her to go and make the drinks suggested that she was thinking about the same incident, or at least she knew I was thinking about it.

'Hey, I've got beer, but if you want wine or anything it's all there,' she called from the living room as I poured her Baileys and then wasted a few moments looking for a bottle opener to open what turned out to be a screw-top bottle of San Miguel.

'I've gotta tell ya, I'm no cook, so, if Chinese is OK with you, we'll get a take-out.' She had already started dialling for the takeaway so the choice had been made.

I loved Chinese food – or at least I had done until a few weeks earlier, when a story had come out about a woman nearly choking to death on a dog's identity chip, which had somehow managed to make its way into her Peking duck.

It seemed strange to be sitting there talking about random rubbish like how busy the market had been earlier, when a week ago she had paid me to stay the night. I wanted to talk about that. I wanted to know why. Was it any good? Was I going to get paid the same again? I felt a bit guilty about having slept with Christine the previous night, but then I told myself that, if she'd contacted me before that morning, I might not have ended up with Christine at all. So it was her fault. Very mature, I know.

When the food arrived, she laid out the steaming silver trays in the centre of her dining-room table and brought in two plates from the kitchen. As she scooped generous servings of Peking duck, rice and sweet and sour pork balls on to our plates, I chose not to share my story and instead reminded myself to chew carefully.

'Mmm, this is so good!' she said, closing her eyes and shutting off all her other senses to fully appreciate the flavoured pork-like dish. I had never understood people's fascination with food and my associations to it were quite different. As a boy, as long as I ate everything on my plate (even the greens) I was a good boy, so, always eager to please, I would eat anything. As a teenager, whatever I could wolf down the quickest in between studying, working and socialising was the order of the day. By the time I got to university, I was eating food for whatever it had to offer. Carbohydrates (and caffeine) for energy, protein for brain and muscles and a vitamin pill a day just in case. But the way some people 'oohed' and 'aahed' over food was beyond me – to me, it was just food. Get it down ya and get on with something important! I used to think.

'You gotta enjoy the simple things in life,' she said, after I had shared my lack of food appreciation with her. 'Food, drink, breathing, sex... it's all so basic, but so important to enjoy.'

I agreed with her on the drinking and sex part; these were definitely two things I could not live without. I'm also a big fan of breathing, and had decided long ago to keep that up for as long as possible, but food? Well, if I could take a pill three times a day with all the nutrients I needed in it, that would suit me down to the ground, I thought.

'Slow down,' she urged.

Automatically, I feared that this was a sexual complaint hidden in her discussion on food.

'Have you read the *Kama Sutra*?' she asked, bringing the conversation back to a more interesting topic but reaffirming my fears that her 'slow down' comment was sex-related.

'Well, I mostly just looked at the pictures,' I replied with an apologetic grin.

She brought the back of her hand up to her mouth as she laughed. She rolled her eyes and smiled. 'It's not just about sex, it's about getting pleasure from all your senses. Music, smells, food...' She stopped as she put another forkful of sauce-covered rice into her mouth and sighed at how delicious she thought it was.

I speared another pork ball with my fork and dipped it in the sweet and sour sauce, before putting it into my mouth and hesitantly closing my eyes. The crispy battered shell began to soften and roll about on my tongue as my mouth watered uncontrollably. My jaw shook with the effort of chewing slower than I could ever remember having chewed, and I tried to savour the pork and occasional piece of rice that had stuck to the sauce. Before I was ready to admit to myself that she had been right, I was smiling and my head was gently nodding.

'I told you!' she said victoriously, making me aware of my other senses again.

Our conversation moved from food to music, and rapidly went from music to ex-lovers. I had always considered past lovers a taboo topic with new lovers. But that was obviously not the first taboo area we had touched on or talked about.

'So you were married?' I said, trying to confirm that her marital status was now divorced or separated, and that there really was no need to hide my shoes.

'Yes, I was married for 12 years. We've been divorced for ten,' she said, spooning out another helping of rice, 'and I can't listen to Simon and Garfunkel and not think of him.' She shook her head and smiled, before looking at me with narrowing eyes. 'And you? You seem more like the heartbreaker than the heartbroken. Like most guys!' She reached over and touched my arm to let me know she was just teasing.

'No, I'm still getting over a girl. We weren't married, but we were together a long time.'

'It's all relative. Kids?' she asked, seeming more serious and concerned.

'No, no way. Much too careful for that,' I said, shaking off the idea of being tied down with children at 22, even if I did love the girl.

'You?'

'Uh-huh. I have the most beautiful daughter in the world,' she said, bringing her hand to her heart. 'She's smart, too. She's here in Europe studying. In fact, she's why I'm here.'

I looked around and thought it strange that a woman who loved her daughter so much wouldn't keep any photos of her in frames around the villa. Maybe it's a Canadian thing, I thought.

'My place in Vancouver's a shrine to her – it kinda creeps her out! She's grateful I'm just renting this place so when she stays she doesn't have to see herself on every wall!' she said, explaining the lack of personal items adorning the walls of the villa, as if she had read my mind.

'Does she know about her mother's seduction technique?' I asked, hoping she wouldn't take offence.

'If she did, I think she'd freak out. She keeps trying to set me up with her professors and her older friends. She's kinda

ageist! Thinks we oldies should stick together!' She laughed, and pretended to shrivel and use her fork as a walking stick.

'You don't like men your own age?'

'There are some, but they're mostly married or seriously screwed up. I've tried dating. That's how I met my first male escort,' she explained, raising her eyebrows. 'I'd seen about a dozen guys, all about my age, and then this next guy, although he was younger than the others, he was just the perfect gentleman.' She put her elbow on the table and rested her chin on the palm of her hand.

'And he tried to charge you for the date?' I asked, not believing anyone could have the balls to do that.

'Not for the date, but what he thought I wanted to do afterwards.' She laughed and shook her head. 'I threw my wine over him and left. Which felt great at the time, but then later when I was alone in bed, wondering what it would have been like, I regretted it. Can you believe that?' She indicated how big her regret was with her thumb and her index finger, before shrugging.

'So did you call him back?'

'I didn't get his number and he stopped emailing after that, understandably. But, the idea stuck in my mind. Hiring a man to meet my every want and need, hmmm...'

'So now you're an escort junkie?'

'Hey! I don't always pay. It makes sense right now. My daughter vacations here. I don't want young guys running up to me in the port, or worse, running up to her and asking if she's as wild as her mom!' She covered her eyes and shook her head.

'So I'll never meet your daughter?' I pouted, pretending to be disappointed, although in reality, if she was as smart and beautiful as she was supposed to be, I would probably have been completely intimidated.

'Maybe by chance. But I think I've bought your loyalty.'

I finally realised that the sum she had paid had not indicated what I was worth. It was for my discretion, so she could have her fun without hurting her daughter's feelings.

'You've never wanted to remarry?'

'Not yet. I like it this way. I get a man when I need one – a good one, not just whoever is left at the bar.'

'Thanks. I'll take that as a compliment.'

'You should. So what about you? Are you looking for another girlfriend?'

'Are you asking?'

'I'm flattered but, like I said, my daughter would chase you off.'

I took this as an easy let-down, not that I had thought for one moment she would actually say 'yes', or that I wanted another girlfriend. It wasn't that having one twice my age would have been that big a deal. I just could not allow myself to ever feel for someone else what I had felt for Chloe. At that particular point in time, I would have preferred a bout with Tyson. 'Actually, I'm determined to stay single, at least for a few years.'

'Well, that's good news... for both of us.' She gave me a crafty smile and sipped her Baileys.

'Anyway, we barely even know each other's names,' I said, taking the chance and hoping to be reintroduced.

'Did I tell you my name? Oh, well, what's yours?'

'I'm Deano. And you? I don't remember.'

'You shit. I didn't tell you. OK, guess.'

'We could be here some time. Can you give me a clue?'

'It's Jeana. There. Feel better?' she asked.

I nodded and put down my fork in defeat, giving up trying to finish the Chinese food on my plate. There were just juices and grease and the odd piece of rice or veg floating in the foil trays, so we cleared the table together and then made our way back to the sofa.

'I got us a movie. I remembered you saying how much you liked this guy.' She handed me the DVD box and I smiled as I saw the Adam Sandler film.

'Yeah, great. He's hilarious.' I was stunned that she had remembered something like that – something as personal as one of my favourites. I had friends I'd known for years and I found it hard enough work to remember their birthdays, let alone their favourite colour or their favourite comedian.

'I don't think I've seen him in anything. But then I'm a bit out of touch now my daughter's not always around to watch these with me. I just don't seem to laugh as much on my own, so I don't bother. That sounds foolish, I know.'

But I knew exactly how she felt. Chloe and I used to go to the cinema every Sunday or we would get a video from Blockbuster and laugh ourselves silly. I could count on two hands the times I had laughed without the aid of alcohol since splitting up with her. It was probably the thing I missed most about being with her, even more than the sex.

We sat at opposite ends of the couch, Jeana's legs outstretched and resting on my lap.

'Hey, do you mind if we see the previews? I wanna see what else looks good.'

She chose the option on the menu, extending her arm when the remote batteries seemed to be dying. Then she flinched and retracted her feet as I reached down for my beer.

'What?' I asked, confused.

'I thought you were going to tickle my feet. It drives me... I can't handle it,' she confessed, evoking in me the irresistible urge to do just that to her.

I slowly put my beer down and then grabbed her ankle, ignoring her cries as they were still as playful as they were urgent. I rubbed my fingertips lightly and quickly over the sole of her foot and she screamed, laughing uncontrollably. She writhed and tried her hardest to pull me off and I was just about to stop when her other foot appeared out of nowhere and kicked me in the head. I was stunned and stopped automatically. So did she, gasping and bringing her hand up to her mouth.

'My God, I'm so sorry,' she begged my forgiveness and, although she continued laughing hysterically straight afterwards, I knew she meant it.

I laughed as well as soon as I had got over the shock of the knock to the head.

She moved to my corner of the sofa to stroke the spot she had accidentally kicked and I thought for a second that we were not going to watch the film. But then she kissed my head and snuggled up to me, resting my head on my shoulder.

After 90 minutes of laughing and the occasional question/ answer session – 'Why'd he do that? Who's she?' – the film ended with Jeana wiping the tears from her eyes before they rolled down her cheeks and on to my shoulder.

'That was so sweet. You're right, he's so goofy!' she said, still laughing. She stood up and held out her hand. 'Come on. I wanna show you this.'

She led me outside to the veranda at the back. It had a below-ground Jacuzzi, which was surrounded by a raised circular platform covered by similar wood to the floor. She knelt down and pushed in a button, starting the bubbles. She took off her cardigan and whipped her T-shirt over her head, her full breasts bouncing without the support of a bra. I had seen a million pairs of boobs before, strolling along the beach, but knowing that I would soon be pressed up against hers was an instant turn-on. I unbuttoned my shirt and dropped it to the floor, then I hesitated and waited to see if she was going to keep anything on or go commando. She pulled down her jogging bottoms and walked out of them, so I copied her, leaving my boxers on. Then she turned and signalled to me to turn around, removing her final item of clothing before getting into the warm tub. I dropped my boxers and got in quickly, the cold air giving me goose bumps and affecting other body parts in non-flattering ways, despite my feeling desperately horny.

'There's someone I want you to meet,' she said.

I furrowed my brow and looked down into the water, jokingly searching for whoever she wanted to introduce me to.

She laughed and splashed me with water. 'No, silly. He's a hustler, a gigolo in the port. He could give you some advice if you wanted.' She seemed more excited than I was about the idea.

'Me? A gigolo?' I laughed off the idea. But, somewhere deep inside, a seed was planted. Could I really do that? No, it was ridiculous. But surely she wouldn't suggest it if she didn't think I had what it took?

'Well, an escort then. I could give him a call and we could all meet up. If you're seriously going to stay single, you may as well make some money while you're playing the field.' She tilted her head back and exhaled as any tension was massaged away by the jet streams and bubbles.

'So then, while you're a gi– escort, you just have to make sure you have a good think about what you wanna be when you're older!' she laughed.

I was touched both that she cared enough to think about my future and that she already knew enough about me to sense that becoming a male escort might just strike me as a great way of helping postpone making any grown-up decisions about my life.

'And what are *you* going to be when you're older?' I knew it was a cheeky question but, hey, we had already laughed, she had cried, we were naked in her Jacuzzi, so I decided, if I couldn't be cheeky then, when could I be?

'Well, as long as there are plenty of available young men, I won't ever get any older.' She smiled at me and I half-expected her to grow fangs and dive at my neck.

I was warm, relaxed and painfully erect, eagerly awaiting

any signal from her that she wanted sex there and then. I had held off making any moves until that point for fear of being rejected and made to feel like an impatient schoolboy, so instead I was deliberately playing it cool until I got a definite green light.

'You can come closer – I didn't bite you last time, did I?' She smiled, tilted her head back and dipped her hair in the water as I made my way towards her. Green light, I thought as I waded over and then, smooth as ever, slipped and fell towards her. My arms flew out and grabbed the tub either side of her, only just stopping me from crashing into her and causing major injury. Her legs were open and as I positioned myself on my knees between them, she wrapped them around me.

'Mmm, not so cold now, hey?' She felt me pressed against her, and we were so close, I felt a rush of excitement at holding off from kissing her.

But then she brought her hands to my face and planted her lips on mine. Our kissing became more and more passionate, our tongues deep in each other's mouths as she grabbed the hair of the scruff of my neck. Our hands massaged each other and we continued to kiss, every kiss and touch wet and slippery.

She raised herself up and sat on the edge of the tub, beckoning me first with her finger and then gently grabbing my head with both hands and bringing me down towards her groin. While I went down on her, I tried to position myself over one of the jets, but concentrating on the two activities proved too difficult. This was mainly due to the threat of slipping again, which, in that position, might have resulted in injuries as embarrassing as they were painful.

After a while, she slipped back into the tub and we went back to kissing and caressing each other. I thought about sitting myself on the edge of the tub and pulling her head towards my groin, but not wanting to push my luck I let her lead things. She continued to masturbate me till I came, and then we felt it was probably best if we got out of the Jacuzzi. She had put towels there for us in advance, so we wrapped ourselves up and ran back into the villa to get warm and dry.

'It's so freeing, don't you think? Being naked.' She was asking a young man who at that point would have agreed with her that black was white, or vice versa. The whole experience was incredible, but I held back from saying so because I knew how stupid and immature it would sound.

We took more drinks upstairs and made love in the bedroom, on the bed, in the missionary position. Quite conventional in comparison to my memories of our first night and hardly worth paying me for, but who was I to argue?

I was back in the saddle, the force was, once again, with me and I was enjoying every minute of it. I had missed the regular sex that came with having a girlfriend and at one point it had seemed that, in order to avoid the heartache of break-ups, I was going to have to sacrifice my favourite pastime as well. But not any more! All of a sudden, it seemed to me that there would always be older women out there dying to get their hands on a young stud like me, and some of them were willing to pay for it!

After a short rest, during which I cuddled her from

behind and enjoyed the warmth and comfort of having a full-bodied woman in my arms, I began to feel aroused again. One thing that had usually saved me from feeling completely sexually inadequate was the short recovery period I appeared to require. With my first few girlfriends, the first time may have usually taken only a few minutes, but then I would go down on the girl for a while and be rock solid and ready for round two, which would always last longer. It would usually be my muscles that tired before my cock's fourth or fifth time.

But, as had happened with girls in the past, Jeana had had enough and just wanted to cuddle and sleep. As she drifted off, I had no option other than to lie there awake and pray that the urge and my erection went away. I couldn't even go and relieve myself as she had specifically requested that she wanted me to cuddle her until she was fast asleep.

I stared at the back of her head and waited for the first signs that I could slip off to the bathroom but, by the time they finally came, the urge had passed and I had started to fall asleep myself. What alerted me to the fact that she was sleeping was her twitching and then calling her ex-husband's name. How depressing, I thought. Ten years on and she was still dreaming about her ex like I still dreamed about Chloe – how beautiful she was, and how she was, even now, probably asleep with some idiot next to her.

For a moment, I felt a stab of sadness. Jeana had given me plenty of encouraging advice about Chloe, but suddenly I realised why she'd never trotted out that 'you'll get over her' line other people are so fond of. A full decade after splitting up, Jeana was still not over her husband, despite all the lovers she'd had in the meantime.

Love, in my opinion, had been very unfair to both of us. Sex, on the other hand, was suiting us very well for the time being.

'Where are you?' Jeana sounded agitated, but I was the one who had been standing there on the street corner like some rent boy for the last 20 minutes.

'I'm in the port like you said, by Coyote. Why do I need my passport?' I was concerned that she had asked me to bring that particular item out with me. Was she going to check my age? Were we leaving the country? If we are, I thought, Fish is not going to be happy when I don't turn up at the restaurant tomorrow.

'I can't see you – oh, wait...' The line beeped and went dead and a taxi pulled up at the bus stop where I had been waiting. The back door swung open and Jeana called out. 'Get in!'

I climbed in and kissed Jeana straight on the lips. It was nice being able to do that, as cheeks were all I had kissed for quite a while before meeting her.

'I thought we were going to the port for a drink.'

'Maybe later. There's someone I want you to meet first. Andy, remember?'

It suddenly came back to me, the gigolo she had mentioned in the Jacuzzi. She had phoned him earlier that night and he had just called back to say that he would be working at the casino in Gibraltar – hence the need for the passport.

'I thought you said he was a full-time gigolo?' I said, dubious already.

'He's with a client. He said he can give you ten minutes, but then he has to get back to her.'

'Ten minutes?'

'That's it. Time's money, honey. Make sure you ask him what you want to know.'

'What do I...?'

'And you can thank me later, properly.'

I felt like Dorothy going to see the Wizard of Oz, or more accurately her other three loser sidekicks rolled into one. My heart was in a terrible state, my brain was a mess after having endured my seven-month bender in Marbella and I really doubted I had the balls – second thoughts, better rephrase that – the courage to go through with being a gigolo. But, as we walked up the steps and entered the casino, I decided that it was worth listening to what the man had to say.

I had no way of knowing that this meeting would shape the next four years of my life.

CHAPTER TWO

Andy

*'If they won't pay your rate, walk away.
There's nothing more attractive than a man who
knows what he's worth.'* ANDY

A crowd of people was gravitating across the casino floor towards the far roulette table. I could sense the buzz of excitement even from where I was standing. Evidently, Jeana could feel it too, and she drifted away across the floor as if drawn by the same magnetic force. I prowled round the outside of the knot of people, positioning myself at the furthest end from the crowd's focal point. Unable to see the wheel or the table, I couldn't appreciate the looks of surprise, amusement and envy that the pack were all throwing in the same direction. Finally, giving into my own curiosity, I edged my way through the mass of players and spectators.

A grey-haired lady sat and concentrated as the croupier spun the wheel and called 'last bets'. Her liver-spotted hands trembled as she clenched them and her eyes became savage as she tried to visualise the little white ball selecting her number from the dizzying black and red pattern on the wheel. The sound of the wheel's spin slowing was followed by the bouncing of the ball, before it finally did lodge in the lady's number as with all those times before. She gasped and brought her claw-like hands up to her chest, diamond-covered fingers clasped in prayer below a diamond necklace.

A hand appeared on her right shoulder and she automatically reached for it and brought it to her lips. I followed the arm up to the suited young man who stood behind her and saw that Jeana had wormed her way through the attentive crowd. She was whispering to him.

At that moment I realised who he was. He bent down to the older woman's ear and whispered something, before leaving the table with Jeana and heading over to me. He swaggered with the confidence of a professional criminal who knows he's untouchable, retying his ponytail and then brushing down his Armani suit jacket as he approached. Jeana put a hand on my shoulder as I extended my hand to meet his. He gripped my right hand firmly and then cupped it with his left, exposing his Rolex as his sleeve rose.

'Andy, Deano. Deano, Andy.' She kissed me on the cheek, making me feel as if I was being dropped off at school. 'I'll see you guys in a while,' she said, smiling back over her shoulder and returning to the table to congratulate the old lady on her winning streak.

'Shall we?' Andy said, nodding towards the bar.

I followed, suddenly feeling very self-conscious and inadequate. Everything about him said that he was the cool kid at school or, more likely, that he was too cool for school. You know the type. The one who got on with everyone; the one all the girls fancied but none of the bullies messed with either. Dressed impeccably, he walked with such confidence that I was willing to bet even his trips and falls were graceful. But then I thought about it and reasoned: people like Andy never trip.

And then there was me. I looked smart by my own standards, but my Hugo Boss still didn't feel like the second skin his suit appeared to be on him. He was born for the part, while I barely knew the lines.

So who better to instruct me than he?

'Drink?' he said, as he struck a pose at the bar.

Jeana had told me that he was a model and now I could see it. Apart from the clothes and his ease of movement, his face was chiselled and his hair perfect. His frame looked more athletic than muscular, but anything less than a six-pack below his shirt would have been a surprise.

'Yeah, a beer please,' I said, and was momentarily confused when he ordered two whisky and cokes and gave no explanation. I thought for a moment that maybe he had misheard me or misunderstood, but the quietness of the small casino and his command of English made either of those unlikely. Like many South Americans, he had a slight American brogue, probably having learned much of his English from films. Like Jeana's Canadian accent, it made the situation quite movie-like and surreal.

We left the bar and he directed me towards a table on the gaming floor. I sat straight down, while he unbuttoned his suit jacket and pulled at his trousers before sinking into his own seat. Looking me up and down, he took a sip of his drink and then nodded, before sitting back and sighing softly.

'What do you want to know?'

When I told him I wanted to know everything there was to know about being a gigolo, his reactions passed from scorn to amusement. Finally, when I'd convinced myself he was about to do a Simon Cowell and tell me to go away and do something else because I obviously didn't have what it took, he softened.

'Well, in order to have all the answers, you need to know the right questions,' Andy drawled, taking another sip of his drink. 'Do you want to know the right questions?' he continued, his intense gaze never wavering. Looking at this guy who seemed to have everything I wanted, to be everything I aspired to, I suddenly felt I would have done a Churchill the nodding dog impression to anything he'd said.

Andy signalled with his hand for me to ask him a question. I wanted to think of something profound that would show him I wasn't a young pretender trying to hang out with the big boys. But, instead, the first question that came blurting out of my mouth was straight from the kindergarten.

'How much do you charge?'

It might have been a crass question, but it was something I needed to know. What was the going rate for a gigolo? Mind you, I could forgive any woman for only wanting to give me half of what they'd give Andy. Maybe there was a kind of gigolo discount rail somewhere...

Andy shook his head in mild irritation. 'How much do I

charge? Don't judge yourself by other people's sticks,' he said, staring pointedly at my crotch. 'You may be disappointed.'

Sitting there and taking a comment like that in Romford in front of my mates would have been reason enough to go into immediate hibernation. But I wasn't in Romford and none of my mates was there to hear his dig, so I chuckled and held my tongue.

'Joke,' he said, raising his hand to apologise, as if he had read my mind and doubted how much longer I would remain civilised. He'd obviously made some internal decision, because his tone became much less patronising after that.

'When you're working as a rent boy in Torremolinos, then you worry about the going rate, trying to undercut everyone.' He waved his hand in disgust. 'But, if you are going to be with clients like Jeana, you see what they're willing to pay.'

'And if I don't like how much they offer?'

'Ask them. They may go higher than what you had in mind. They may go lower. Then walk away. Simple.'

Walk away! I thought. I'd never in my life turned down a chance to have sex and doubted I'd ever be in a position to do so. Yet here he was talking about turning down an offer of sex for money – the whole thing was sounding more and more surreal.

'People want what they can't have, so be prepared to walk away and watch them chase you,' he said, with the smile of someone who'd never had to try too hard.

'How can you be so confident?' I said, not sure whether to admire him or feel aggravated by his arrogance.

'That, I can see, is your biggest problem. You lack

confidence, and that's fatal, gigolo or not. You can dress up in your fake Hugo Boss suit...'

I sat up, mouth open, about to protest, but he dismissed my half-hearted attempt at outrage with a brief movement of his hand.

'...Yes, it's a fake. The lapel is all wrong. Anyway, you can wear a crown, but, if you're not a king underneath it, it'll show.

'Lack of confidence means you're afraid. Maybe of success, maybe of failure. And your fear may be justified. But eliminate the fears one by one, and your confidence will come.' His pride was obvious as he spoke, implying that he too had faced his fears – and conquered them.

'Eliminate my fears?' I repeated, confused as to how to tackle that mountainous task.

'Protection and practice,' he said, bending back his index and middle finger.

'Protection? Oh, you mean condoms.'

One look at Andy's long-suffering expression revealed I'd said the wrong thing.

'If STDs were all you thought you had to worry about, you're in for a shock.' He shook his head and then sipped at his whisky.

'What else? Husbands, I suppose.'

'Right. So always be prepared. It's hard to carry in places like this, but I've got my protection in the car.' As he said that, I could tell he was waiting for a reaction from me.

'What else?' I said quickly, letting him know that, whatever his protection was, it was of no interest to me.

'Well, apart from your weapon,' he laughed and looked at

my crotch again, 'you'll need one of these.' He leaned towards me and opened his suit jacket, revealing the Dictaphone and the small microphone pinned to the inside of his lapel. My first thought was, why the fuck would I want to play back the recording of some woman's husband beating the crap out of me? My second guess was that Andy was a raving pervert and loved himself so much that he just wanted to listen to himself at work once he got home. I suggested as much in an attempt to lighten the atmosphere. 'So this is what you do when you get home,' I said, making a charming wanking gesture with my hand.

Again, the rolling of the eyes. 'No. This is to make sure no one screams *rape* at the end of the night and you have to leave penniless, or in the back of a police car.' His face was serious, he did not break eye contact with me and the mood was once again heavy.

Whatever else it was, it was evident that being a gigolo was not going to be an easy option.

I was silent, thinking over the unforeseen difficulties of becoming a professional escort. Previously, my main concerns had been about getting it up and not coming too soon, but now I had a host of other fears to get over.

'No, when I get home, all I want to do is be alone and read. Being sociable takes it out of me.' He sighed and glanced at his watch. 'By the way, are you bi?' he asked in the same bored tone as if he was asking if I was cold or tired.

'You're not my type, mate,' I joked, trying to cover up my discomfort.

He shook his head and leaned in again. 'You'll double your

work if you do both. And couples, they're another big market now.' Seeing that I had switched off and wasn't interested in those kinds of jobs, he shrugged before looking again at his watch and then over to where his client was sitting. Catching his meaning, I stood up and we shook hands again.

'Get my number from Jeana if you need to chat again. We'll talk over a beer.' From his sly smile, I gathered that he'd heard me perfectly when I'd first asked for a beer at the bar, and the whole charade of getting me the same drink as him was just some sort of power trip. Or maybe a test.

'Oh, by the way,' he asked, 'how much is she paying you?'

'Four hundred euros,' I replied, interested to see his response.

Andy's bottom lip poked out and he raised his eyebrows, obviously impressed at the sum. 'Not bad, for someone with your experience. Anyway, good luck.'

His final words were whispered as he had seen Jeana approaching behind me. I felt her hand on my shoulder as she appeared at my side.

'Well?' she asked, her eyes bright with interest.

'Well what?' I shrugged.

'Come on, you gotta tell me what you guys said to each other. That had to be an interesting conversation.' She could hardly disguise her impatience and scowled and pouted playfully when I chose not to say anything. 'What's that?' she asked looking at my drink.

'Whisky. Did you wanna stay and have a flutter?'

'Mmm. A flutter. I like the sound of that. Can we have a flutter back at the villa instead?'

I downed my whisky and left the glass in the holder of the

nearest roulette table. In the taxi on the way home I took out my notepad and pen to write down some of Andy's pearls of wisdom – three years of college had left me very well trained. Jeana found this very amusing and deliberately rubbed my leg and nibbled on my ear to try to break my concentration.

'You swot!' she exclaimed when I refused to be distracted. 'Well, no... it's a good thing I guess. There's gonna be a test when we get in, OK?'

Hmmm... now that was just the kind of test I liked.

The next time I met Andy was purely by accident while I was at Plaza Beach in Puerto Banus. The summer beach parties there were not as luxurious as the ones at Nikki Beach, but most people preferred it because it was so close to the port and its clubs. I had just arrived with one of my best mates, Frank Chapman, on our way to meet some people we had been out with in Marbella the night before.

Let me tell you about Frank. He's tall, skinny and apart from his dodgy teeth (his words, not mine) he's a good-looking bloke – always smartly dressed. We've been friends since we were four, although as he keeps changing the age I can never keep up with how long we're supposed to have known each other.

My original plan in coming to Spain, apart from getting over Chloe, had been to see Frank. So I wasn't best pleased to arrive here and find he'd buggered off somewhere else. This was a devastating blow as Frank is the ultimate pulling machine, exactly who I needed with me to help me get over my heartbreak.

Frank's success with women lies in the fact that he is the funniest bloke who has ever walked the planet – not to big him up too much, but it's true. He's the sort of bloke that, with a single look or word, can have a bunch of girls laughing themselves silly. And, while he'd have them laughing, I would just sit there and smile quietly until I was drunk enough to be as loud as him. Sad, but true.

My confidence peaked at age 12, when we used to go to the cinema and dare each other to go up to girls and offer them a chewing gum while the Wrigley's advert was on. I was fearless in my approach, but clueless when it came to conversation. Very sad but, again, very true.

Apart from when Frank was there, my only luck seemed to be in loud nightclubs or on holiday with foreign girls, as neither of these required too much talking. I was a listener, not a speaker. But Frank, well, he spoke loud enough for the two of us. So I was relieved when he eventually found his way back to Spain and we could become, once again, the dream pulling machine. Mind you, as I was eyeing all the beautiful, scantily clad women on the dance floor at Plaza Beach, it did occur to me that we might be just slightly outclassed here.

A team of girls dressed in white T-shirts and tight pink hot pants were doing a dance routine, seemingly oblivious to all the drooling men who surrounded them. Then, out of nowhere, a man appeared and walked up to the girl closest to the bar. He was cool, suave and had a dark ponytail. Andy.

He was trying to join in with this girl's dancing and, as you'd expect, was doing a pretty good job, but for some

reason she was having none of it. The girl called out to the huge security guy, who rolled his eyes and unfolded his arms as soon as he saw Andy.

'Andy! Fuck off, leave the poor girl alone!' came the booming voice of the Mr T lookalike, before he refolded his arms and settled his features back into their customary scowling expression.

'It's OK, I'm trying to apologise,' Andy shouted back.

Obviously, he wasn't making too good a job of it because the girl suddenly slapped him across the face and stormed off the stage. The crowd cheered, booed and clapped at the spectacle and Andy turned to everyone holding his face. 'Oops!' he said, before bursting into laughter himself.

I made my way over to him and his friends at the bar, unsure of what sort of reception I was going to get. When Andy saw me, he hid his face in mock shame.

'You saw that? God! Yeah, well, there's personal and professional lives. One of them has to be successful!' He turned to his friends and they all laughed. Introductions were made, but there were only two of us and about ten of them, so I didn't expect to remember anyone's name.

'What was that all about?' I asked.

'I slept with her sister. I tried to say sorry, that's all. Truthfully, I wouldn't have slept with her, had I known it was her sister. I told her that, and you saw what happened after.'

We all laughed at the innocence of his explanation and he offered to buy us both a beer. Frank declined and said he had to go and meet some girls further down the beach, and that he would see us later, which left Andy and me to talk.

'I'll get these. Payment for the advice.'

'You need more – of course, on professional matters only,' he said, gesturing to the dance floor, as if I needed a reminder of his disastrous apology.

When the beach party ended, everyone went over to Linekers Bar in the second strip of Puerto Banus. Most of the strip was full of well-dressed clubbers, but on Sundays Linekers filled up with the hardcore few from the beach party, still in their T-shirts, shorts and bikinis with sarongs wrapped around them.

I had originally planned on an early night, to be fresh for work on Monday morning. But I never knew when Andy was going to be available and, despite the fact that in large doses his arrogance would have got my back right up, his advice was invaluable. Frank had pulled a girl on the beach and taken her back to Marbella on the back of his moped, leaving me to make my own way home. The more I drank, the more the thought of going home alone didn't appeal to me. After all, I was drunk, surrounded by beautiful women and I had a professional gigolo as a pulling partner. What could go wrong?

The seal on my bladder had been well and truly broken hours ago and I had been slowing down, sipping the same beer for an hour in an attempt to make my trips to the toilet less frequent. I looked like I had a serious coke problem the amount I was up and down those stairs. I'm sure the bouncers were waiting for me to drop dead of heart failure. Eventually, while we were talking, Andy also felt the call of nature and, so as not to interrupt the flow of the conversation, I went with him. OK, in fact, I was ready to burst again and I had been trying to get away for the last five minutes.

South American urinal etiquette is quite different from its European equivalent, I discovered as, while we were pissing beside each other, he leaned over and had a good gander.

'I hope you're a grower,' he said, shaking off, 'because you ain't no show-er!' He zipped up his shorts and went to the mirror to check his hair.

'Seven inches... I read that's about average. But it's meaty,' I said, looking down and understanding how easily that could have been doubted from its current shrivelled condition. I'd had no complaints in the past and a fair few compliments – but I still hadn't been able to resist finding out how I measured up to the UK average.

'You got staying power?' he said, reluctantly tearing himself away from his own reflection in the mirror.

'Varies,' I confessed. 'I'm young and highly strung – it's normal...' These were, in fact, the words of a young nurse I had met during my first few months in Marbella.

'You're wanking too quick,' he said matter-of-factly, ignoring the smirks of the passing clubbers as they went to use the urinal. 'Take your time. Come on, I'll show you something,' he said, waving me over to the sinks.

I panicked for a moment, thinking he was going to give me a wanking demonstration in the middle of Linekers toilets.

He gripped the edge of the marble surface with his thumb, held on to the sink bowl with his fingers and positioned himself about a foot away. 'You can do these like this, or lying down. I'll show you this way – I don't wanna lie down in piss,' he said, curling his lip as he looked at the state of the floor. He bent his knees and then thrust his pelvis forwards, tensing as he held it there and then brought it back to his resting position again, talking me through the whole movement. 'So you clench your arse, two, three, four, then relax. Then you do your pissy muscles.' He thrust again, this time not as far. 'Two, three, four...'

'Pissy muscles?' I asked, with an eyebrow raised.

'You know, the ones you use to stop yourself pissing. Pissy muscles! Squeeze, two, three, four.'

He pulled my arm and the two of us exercised our glutes and our 'pissy' muscles (only later did I discover he meant PC muscles), while people queued to use the sink. Andy just laughed and looked at them.

'You wanna try?' he asked, but the huge guys just raised their hands and left without washing them, leaving us to do a few more repetitions before we went back downstairs to continue the hunt.

By now, my speech had started to slur and even the roughest of the girls that Andy and I had joked about earlier were looking damn fine. When I said this to Andy, he nodded knowingly and pulled me by the arm to say something to me. 'That's one of the secrets of being a great escort. You need to learn to blur your perception, like you're doing now. Every woman's beautiful if you can do that.'

'What d'you mean? Get drunk before every job?'

'No. Accentuate the positive – ignore the negative. Close your eyes and visualise.'

I understood what he was saying, but how was I going to

get permanent beer goggles? I thought. I had to visualise every day to make myself feel better about me, so how could I do that with a woman during the course of a brief encounter? I knew that, if I asked him how to get good at visualising while I was with my clients, his answer would have been 'practise', so I didn't bother.

We were up on one of the podiums dancing, or at least I was doing my best impression of it, when a vertically challenged bodybuilder started shouting up at Andy. I thought for a moment that Andy was in trouble and instantly I was on the defensive. Even though Andy looked fit enough to handle himself, he was a bit of a pretty boy and it was easier to imagine him running out of the club screaming and leaving me to deal with the pit bull than to imagine him actually throwing a punch.

Andy jumped down from the podium and the short-arse pushed him. I jumped down and walked behind the short guy, ready to leap to the aid of my mentor and new friend. But as Andy walked back towards the guy his arms were out wide and, instead of throwing punches, they dived into a hug. I exhaled, the adrenaline still rushing through my veins and preparing my body for a fight.

'Deano, this is Freddie,' said Andy, his arm still around Freddie's shoulders.

Freddie grabbed my hand, pulled me towards him so he could reach up and put his bulging arm around my shoulders. 'You having a good time?'

I was, I thought, and I would be again if you let me out from under your sweaty pit.

'Freddie's from the gym,' Andy explained.

'You should get yourself up there, put a bit more meat on those bones!' was Freddie's verdict, after releasing his grip on me so he could squeeze my arms.

'Yeah, maybe,' I said, squeezing my own arm and agreeing that I could do with getting a bit pumped up.

'It's great for "work". There are a lot of rich women there,' said Andy, winking.

They were talking about training or something when I tuned out. The music was so loud and I was too drunk to concentrate on anything except the three girls dancing on the podium in front of us. Stunning at the time, through the haze of the smoky club, all concern for what they'd look like in the morning had been drowned long ago. I watched them dancing and started to show off some moves of my own – until they started looking over at me and laughing.

I didn't care if my dancing was bad at that point, such was the optimism of my drunken state. In my mind, I had made them laugh and that was going to make things easier for the three of us to go over and talk to them. But, when I turned to inform Andy and Freddie of my next move, I was suddenly shocked into sobriety. They were kissing. Each other.

'No way!' I mouthed, shocked at what I was witnessing. Another hero bites the dust, or rather Freddie's bottom lip, I thought. I knew I should have stuck with Frank. He might have stripped on the podium, or maybe even the bar, but play tonsil tennis with a dwarf bodybuilder? Never. No way. But then I would have missed out on learning the 'gigolo flexes' Andy had shown me. I shrugged it off and kept on dancing. Maybe Freddie was a client and Andy was earning out of it? He had told me that most escorts make extra money doing that sort of work. Or maybe he was just bisexual. Either way, he was kissing a bloke and for neither love, nor money, could I do the same. Not like that anyway. I had given blokes pecks for a dare or to make two girls do the same and maybe more, but not the full Frenchie like they were.

For some reason, I felt that my chances of success with any of the three girls on the podium had gone down and so I decided to leave. I didn't want to be rude and leave without saying goodbye to Andy and Freddie, but there was no way I was going to interrupt them. So guess who ended up going home alone? And it had all started so promisingly!

A few weeks later, I was given flyers to the opening night of a new strip club in Puerto Banus. I took my friends Frank and Wayne to have a look, but we had to be back for midnight to meet some girls on a language exchange who we'd hooked up with the night before. As we had only an hour, we wasted no time and decided to have a lap dance each straight away.

Frank was first, asking the girl with the biggest tits and choosing to have the dance in front of everyone instead of in the back room. I chose a petite blonde with a perfect bottom and decided to go in the back instead. After seeing Frank's face as his girl danced for him, I knew he wouldn't be standing up and coming back to the bar for a while afterwards.

I sat back in the armchair, my hands resting on the arms,

ready and waiting for the show. She slowly began to twist and turn, making waves with her body that pinned me to the back of the chair. Piece by piece her clothing came off until she was down to her thong and high heels. Then, unexpectedly, she started to undo my shirt and pull it out from my trousers. What had been an entirely pleasurable experience until that point lost some of its magic as I looked down at my bloated belly. I really do need to start doing some running and sit-ups again, I thought, as she continued her performance.

I snapped back to the present as she placed her hands on the back of the chair either side of my head, and slowly dropped her head to my groin. Her legs locked and her arse was still up in the air, swaying from side to side as her hair tickled my 'Stella six-pack' stomach. She moved her head slowly up my torso, her hair stroking me till she got to my face. She rubbed her cheek against mine, rubbing her nose on mine as she changed cheeks, her lips so close to mine that my mouth watered. She continue to arch back until her nipple was in my mouth, then she grabbed my head and cradled it against her chest before pulling away and ending the dance.

I thanked her as I buttoned up my shirt and she kissed me on both cheeks and went to sit with some of the other girls in the corner. Wayne had decided to save his money for the girls we were meeting later on and Frank had no more money to spend so we drank up and left the club. As we were walking down the steps, someone was making his way up with his head down.

'That's your mate, ain't it?' said Frank as he got closer.

I looked down and saw that Andy had recognised me first.

'Hey, man! Where did you get to the other night?' he said, genuinely surprised that I had left.

'Sorry, Andy. Emergency. Had to be somewhere.' Yeah, somewhere else, I thought.

'Where are you guys off to now?'

From being the king of cool, he had gone down in my estimation. Not because there's anything wrong with homosexuality, but because my respect and admiration for him was born of that urge to be just like him. As soon as I'd witnessed what I had, I saw him in a different light – no longer as Andy, my mentor and inspiration, but just another guy I'd met.

'Marbella. We're meeting some girls,' I said, feeling like I was back at school when everyone knows you're having a party, but there are just some kids you don't want to invite.

'Great. D'you mind if I tag along?'

'Well...'

'There's plenty of room in the car. Anyway, there's five of them, so it'll even up the numbers,' said Frank, who I had forgotten to share the Linekers incident with.

Andy looked at me awaiting my final decision, as if I had a real choice. I spent the entire car journey wishing I had told at least one of my two friends about the other night in Linekers. When we got to Puerto Deportivo, I kept trying to warn them, just in case he made a move on one of them. They would have been all right about it, I'm sure, but where I come from it's just good manners to warn them first.

By the time the girls arrived, I had forgotten all about it and Andy was once again the babe magnet he was reputed to be, well aware that he could have had his pick of any of them. They were all well spoken and fashionably dressed, but there was something a bit teeny-bopperish about them. They were all giggling and flirting with Andy, and the three of us took a back seat for a while. When we finally did get to speak to them, another friend of ours, Chad, walked in and our hearts sank when we saw he was accompanied by the girls' dragon-like teacher, flapping her wings and blowing smoke, demanding that they went back to their respective host families. Chad had happened upon her wandering aimlessly in the port and, like the good Samaritan he is, showed her the way to the bar, not knowing that the girls were hiding from her there.

'You're a fucking jinx, you know that!' Frank growled at Chad, who laughed off his comments like he laughed off everything.

Things just didn't seem to register half the time with Chad. In one ear, out the other – his brain permanently alternating between two edicts: 'be helpful' and 'pull birds'. His hair was bleached blond – well, what there was of it after he had shaved it – and he was always dressed impeccably.

Andy looked at me, and then back at the cranky old woman, and I guessed what he was thinking. But, as she grabbed a couple of the girls by the wrists and started to lead them out of the bar, I turned to him and said, 'I can see you getting slapped again!'

'Yeah, second thoughts. I'll stay here.'

We laughed and watched the comical scene, hoping that a couple of the girls would have the guts to sneak back out.

'Seventeen years old and being kept under lock and key. It's not right,' said Frank, as we all sat there and stared into our pint glasses.

As far as we were concerned, our wild night was pretty much over. There were no English-speaking girls around with whom: 1) we hadn't already slept; 2) we hadn't already tried to sleep, and failed miserably; or 3) we wouldn't have slept, even if you had paid us. Admittedly, we couldn't name one girl from category three.

Our other option was the Old Town, which I enjoyed but my friends weren't so keen on due to their Spanish (or lack of). We had tried it before with me being the translator for a while, but it got boring and so to liven things up I didn't translate as accurately as I could have done.

'Tell her she's gorgeous and I want her number,' one friend had hissed, which, with his best interests at heart, I had translated as, 'My friend says your boobs aren't real, so can he feel them to make sure?'

Apart from getting drunk now, there was little else to do, besides sing karaoke until the pool table was free, which wouldn't be in the next couple of hours.

'I'm off after this, lads,' I said, swirling the last of my pint around the bottom of my glass.

'I'm going Expo. Who's up for it?' said Chad, rubbing his hands together.

'Expo?' asked Andy.

'Brothel,' I explained, and Andy nodded, looking Chad up and down.

Seeing the light in Andy's eye as he gave Chad the once-over, I had a sudden premonition of how the evening would go if Andy tagged along with Chad. So sure was I, in fact, that I made my excuses and dropped out of the evening. I just couldn't bear to witness what I was sure was going to happen. But, as Frank and Wayne were going to have a ringside seat, I pre-warned them about the night in Linekers, preparing them for what promised to be an entertaining evening. Apparently, the conversation went something like this:

Chad: Expo, I mean I've never been, but they reckon there's a pool table in there and all these girls and, if you want, you can take the girls upstairs.

Andy: They're prostitutes?

Chad: Well, yeah I suppose. Or they're just really easy.

Andy: Yes, some men like to pay women for sex.

Chad (nodding his head in agreement): Yeah, so do you wanna go?

Andy (staring into Chad's eyes and putting a hand on Chad's thigh): And some men like to pay men for sex as well, yes?

Chad (nodding, smiling and completely oblivious to the come-on): Yeah. So, do you wanna go to Expo then?

Apparently, Andy gave up after a second more blatant attempt, which equally failed to register with Chad.

As Andy walked out, Chad went up to Frank and Wayne

and said, 'Deano's mate's a nice guy, ain't he? A bit touchy-feely though.'

They split their sides laughing, as did Chad, not knowing what he was laughing at, but sure it must be funny, whatever it was.

Waking up, I stumbled into the bathroom. Hmmm. Not exactly a sight for sore eyes, with my 'morning-after' complexion. Taking a long hard look at myself in the mirror, I stepped on to the scales: 73 kilos. Most of which was distributed around my midsection, where all definition was a distant memory. I had never been fat, but this was the most out of shape I had ever felt.

Back in England I played football, lifted weights, ran for miles, cycled – you name it; I did it. But in Spain I had relied on my high metabolism to keep me trim. But, as my alcohol absorption speeded up, my metabolism seemed to slow down and with it the rate at which I burned off the calories. Result? The wobbly mass now known as my belly. I didn't even walk very often as I had the car, so my only exercise was sex – and that was pretty hit-and-miss as an exercise regime.

While I was at the restaurant, the guy who had given me the flyers for the strip club asked me if I wanted to try kickboxing in the gym underneath the restaurant. I'd done a bit before and enjoyed it, but I didn't feel like embarrassing myself so close to work, and so excuses not to train were in plentiful supply. Yet, for some reason, I found myself saying, 'Yeah, I'll give it a go.'

The following day, I crawled out of my kickboxing class a

quivering wreck, unsure I'd make it to the changing room, let alone home. Slumping down in one of the chairs by reception, I scanned the gym for any talent and immediately recognised a couple of the guys training together on the machines. It was Freddie and Andy – the pair of them making a show of checking out girls or each other, but in actual fact the mirrors were getting more attention.

'Fancy seeing you two here!' I said, disturbing their posing.

'Deano, how are you my friend? Decided to get buff?' said Andy, wiping the sweat from his brow.

'Giving it a go.'

Freddie offered me his hand, and this time I felt confident that from where I was there was no danger of ending up under his armpit again. As he shook my hand, his mobile rang.

'Shit, it's him. Gotta go. See you soon.' He ran off to the changing rooms with his phone.

'Boyfriend?'

'Business partner. Money worries. None of our business. Come on, I'll show you a routine,' he said, before showing me a workout for my chest and triceps.

I adjusted the pin to make the bench press machine lighter, and positioned myself for the exercise. I wasn't so bothered any more about impressing Andy, as he never seemed impressed anyway. All I wanted to do in my life, I decided, was to better whatever I had done before. That applied to whatever I was doing, be that escorting or lifting weights. I no longer felt like I was competing against anyone else – only myself. The thought of not having to compare myself to anyone else immediately gave me more confidence.

'Your friends told me you're a graduate, that right?' Andy asked, trying to hide the surprise in his voice.

'Yeah. Psychology. Why?'

'Just strange how someone like you could end up doing what we do. Now I understand about all the moral shit. Bet you're Catholic too, right?'

I gathered that he'd spoken to the others long enough to put together a nice little profile on me. Knowing how manipulative Andy could be, that bothered me.

'What about you? How did you end up doing it?' I asked, taking the spotlight off me for a moment.

'If I told you that, I'd have nothing to write about when I retire.'

I laughed as this 32-year-old in the prime of his life talked about retirement as if it were around the corner for him. 'Give me the short version.'

'Well, I tried more jobs than you've tried positions.' He slid himself under the machine grips and pushed, straining as he continued to talk. 'Waiter, model, actor, singer, journalist!' He finished his reps and sat up, wiping sweat from his brow with the back of his hand. 'You know, I was a butler for three weeks. The little shit was younger than me and he had me doing everything besides wipe his arse. Driving him around, running his errands... oh, but the money!' He grabbed at the air and shook his head as he closed his eyes.

'Why didn't you stay if the money was that good?' I asked, swapping over and getting ready for my turn on the machine.

'You know how it goes. You're the butler. Then someone

gets murdered, and everyone thinks it's you...' He stopped to drink some water, watching me as I froze, unable to start my reps.

'I'm joking. There was no murder,' he laughed, 'no, I got caught with one of my master's girlfriends. In the library, with a candlestick.'

We both laughed as he thrust his hand back and forth with his imaginary candlestick.

'No, seriously though. This is a great job for a while, but it must get in the way of other things,' I said, trying to get to the real Andy.

I was genuinely curious about him. How had he ended up as a gigolo? What did he really want out of life? There were still certain parts of him that I admired and aspired to. I wanted to know the answers to those questions, like I wanted to know about all my friends.

'Like what? Friends? Listen, you came in alone, you're going out alone. Forget friends, forget girlfriends, no one is that special. Life is short and meaningless and before the big blackout I intend to have as much fun as I can. *Y est·!*'

I must have hit a raw nerve, as he'd gone straight from having a laugh to acting affronted without passing 'Go', so I didn't push it any further. I nodded, understanding his outlook a little better, but realising how different it was to mine. The differences between people are what make them interesting, and Andy was without doubt an interesting guy. But when it comes to friends I think like attracts like, and when I realised how different we were I knew that there was little point in pursuing any kind of friendship with him. He would just be one of those acquaintances, one of those people I'd pass in the street and say 'hi' to, but we'd probably never get beyond that. He was not looking to make friends and was suspicious of anyone who wanted to befriend him.

The last time I saw Andy, he was on his way to Mijas for the horseracing and asked me if I wanted to come. I'd heard from a friend that he had run up some serious debts playing poker, and when I questioned him about it he said that he was about to change all that. I wished him luck and turned down his offer. By that stage, I'd been escorting for a while and my whole life seemed more and more like a gamble. The last thing I needed was to throw more uncertainty into the mix.

'OK,' Andy called. 'Your loss.'

Andy had taught me a lot, but the one thing he never seemed to learn was that there are many different ways of losing – and even people who seem to have it all can end up losers if they don't, or won't, let themselves be vulnerable every now and again.

'See you 'round,' I said. But I never did.

CHAPTER THREE

Louise

*'Love's a mental illness, an evolutionary throwback,
and some clients are just too susceptible. If you see one
falling too fast, get out of there.'* ANDY

The more flexible you are in terms of what turns you on,
the greater success you'll have as an escort. Andy had
advised me to practise 'visualising' every day – building up
pictures in my mind, rather than relying on what I could see
with my eyes. My practice involved listening to the TV rather
than watching it, and reading erotic stories rather than
watching porn. It was all about being able to use the power
of your imagination to override your natural attraction
strategies. In other words, persuading yourself to fancy
someone, even if she looked like Princess Fiona's less
attractive sister. He told me that once I had discovered the
aspects I liked about a client I was to focus on those to the
point where they blocked out any less attractive qualities.

For me, there are certain accents that will make my ears

prick up immediately. Likewise, there are certain jobs that instinctively have a sexual air to them. One client who possessed both of these qualities was Louise, a 40-something Glaswegian air stewardess. By the time I met Louise, I'd been escorting for a few months, and considered myself quite the consummate actor when it came to feigning sexual attraction. But with her, I didn't have to try.

'It's not that I don't meet anyone – I meet lots of people,' she said. Louise brushed her long dark hair behind her ears and looked down at her square dish, resting her chopsticks on the edge.

She didn't have to justify her actions to me. I wasn't there to judge her, although it did seem strange to me that someone so attractive and unattached couldn't find a man for the evening. Her sleeveless black dress clung tightly to her firm body. Her long slender legs ended at a pair of black high-heeled shoes and her left wrist was decorated by a silver Gucci watch.

'It's just...'

She had a habit of choosing her words carefully, which I was sure a few glasses of wine would have put an end to. Unfortunately, she'd confessed at the beginning of the evening that she never drank, so that particular 'loosening up' avenue was closed, and it made me a little wary of her from the start.

'How do I put this...?'

As I listened, doing the old 'mirroring the body language' trick, I could already feel a connection building. I had gained enough rapport with her to hazard a guess at her next phrase.

'You want to try new things? Experiment?'

Her dark eyes lit up and she nodded emphatically as she chewed her sushi. Finishing people's sentences is usually a big no-no, but in order to fast-track that feeling of connection it is sometimes a worthwhile risk.

'Exactly. Everyone I meet is so...' She waved her chopsticks in the air, hoping to catch the right word.

Again, the opportunity was there to find the word for her and cement those feelings of bonding, so I took it. 'Conventional?'

But as the word sank in she frowned, tilted her head and bit on her chopsticks. Strike one. 'I was going to say "boring",' she said thoughtfully, before pointing at me with the chopsticks and nodding, 'but "conventional" is much better!'

We laughed at the new euphemism she would no doubt be using to describe her friends in future. She paused each time the young Japanese waiter appeared with another platter of delights, and I found myself copying her little bow to him as he left.

'I think it just happens to people as they get older.' She shrugged at her pessimistic observation, and then groaned in mock ecstasy as she tasted her Temaki, a fish-filled seaweed roll.

'I've never had sushi before,' I admitted to her, savouring every tapas-sized morsel. I finally understood why it was so pricey but, Essex boy to the last, I was still firmly in favour of a juicy steak or anything else that would fill me up for the same price. I consoled myself with the thought that I would not be paying for the meal and that, with the money earned that evening, I could well afford to eat what I liked the next.

'Dip it in the wasabi sauce, it's amazing!'

She was right, it was amazing and before the meal was through I was enjoying the food as much as she was.

'I can eat as much of this as I want and I don't gain a pound!'

Her body was incredibly toned and it was only when she smiled and the lines on her face became more apparent that her true age showed. She could easily have passed for early thirties. But it wasn't just her looks; it was her energy, her attitude.

'Seriously, you wait till you're my age; everyone just wants to settle down and do the same thing day after day!'

I thought back to some of my friends in Essex who, even at 22, had fallen into that monotonous rut. Working in banks or insurance brokers and longing for their fortnight's holiday. But my life was different, exciting, interesting... for now at least. I woke up each day and when I looked out of my window I saw the Med. I could walk to work along the seafront and admire the beautiful women as they topped up their tans. Why would I swap that for a ride to the City each day on the District Line?

She went on to criticise her friends and their married or cohabiting lives, but I thought I could sense an underlying envy in her arguments. The sighs of relief at not having to deal with her best friend's brat of a son seemed like a thinly disguised sigh of longing for her own children.

She kept referring back to when single life with her friends had been wonderful. 'Five years – no six, or is it seven...?' Until she realised that ten years had passed since the first of her friends had found Mr Right and settled down. 'And she's

still with him and he still worships the ground she walks on. Sickening really.' She shrugged and rolled her sushi in the dish of soy sauce, before distracting herself with another tasty mouthful.

'Haven't you ever wanted, well, you know... a husband, kids, a home?'

A glazed look came over her, as if all of the above had once been on offer but for some reason she had missed out. I was interested; I wanted to know what had brought her to this. Hiring a stranger to keep her company for the evening. But I was also aware that my role was not as a counsellor or investigator, it was as a companion. A lover. Even if nothing physical happened between us, I was her lover. I was there to listen attentively and pay attention to no one but her. She was the only woman in the world and pleasing her was my sole reason for existing – for as long as she was paying me.

'I'm interested. There must have been someone special, someone who made you feel special.' I watched her eyes soften and a small smile appeared which encouraged me not to change the subject. I could see I had tapped into some pleasant memories, and even if they had ended painfully, they would serve their purpose – to enable me to 'unlock' her. 'Tell me about him. How did he make you feel?'

I prepared myself for the guided tour of her past, ready to pick out any clues that would make the task of pleasing her a little easier. I listened as she talked about her past lovers, how she had worshipped them until they had shown their true colours and become just like all the others. She told me about the things they did that turned her on, but in greater number were the turn-offs. Bad breath, sloppy kisser, hairy back, tiny willy. I worried momentarily that Louise had been spoiled and, maybe, her version of 'tiny' was more like 'average', and I was going to be a disappointment. But when she likened 'tiny' to the last piece of Tamaki, my fears were laid to rest.

We matched each other story for story and from her relaxed posture I could see she was much more comfortable with me now. From what I'd told her, she realised that most of my encounters, apart from with clients, involved alcohol to some extent. Despite not drinking herself, she obviously had no problem with drinkers.

'We could go for a drink if you like? There's a great bar over the road from the hotel. Small... quiet.'

I needed no convincing, although I was a little disappointed when we arrived there and I couldn't persuade her to have even a *chupito* – a tiny shot – while I had a beer.

'No, seriously, I cannot handle it. My body's too pure!' She turned up her nose and then laughed.

After drinking water all night, that bottle of San Miguel was like champagne. I would have killed for a burger, pizza, kebab – anything! But the beer would do and, as I had been hired for the evening, eating light was probably the best idea anyway. No one feels sexy on a bloated stomach.

'So, as you're mine for the evening, can we go back to the hotel now?'

I smiled and stood up, moving my head just out of kissing range. 'I'm yours. We can do anything you want to do.'

Her reply was to wrap her arm around mine and lead me out of the bar, across the street and then over the bridge to

the hotel. She held on to me tightly as we went up the steps and through the revolving door into the four-star hotel. The receptionist mumbled a *buenas noches* as we passed him on our way to the lift. As the lift doors closed, her hand left me only briefly to push the floor number, then both her arms were around my neck and we were kissing. Our first kiss. It may seem ridiculous for someone like me to say, but the first kiss is always an adrenaline rush. I won't claim to remember every first kiss I've ever had, but that feeling – of breaking those rules of proximity – is a buzz. OK, it can be a short-lived buzz, depending on the kiss. Too little or too much tongue, stiff lips, sloppiness, bad breath. So many things can make that first kiss not worth having waited for, but with Louise this was not the case. Her lips and tongue were soft and moist, but her grasp on me was firm and passionate.

We reached the second floor, and she took my hand and led me down the hallway. I stood behind her and pulled her hair to one side so I could kiss her neck, while she searched her bag for the card key. Her free hand reached behind her and stroked the back of my neck as I kissed hers. Inside her room, she closed the door and then disappeared into the bathroom.

'Make yourself comfortable,' I heard through the door.

I knew better than to turn on the TV and get sucked into whatever depressing news was on *CNN*. I took off my jacket and hung it over the chair at the desk, then looked myself up and down in the mirror. I looked a damn sight better than I had done a few months ago, but I still felt like a boy trying to be a man. Staring myself in the eyes, I took a deep breath, trying to exhale self-doubts, just as I'd read in numerous self-help books. This was a good thing I was doing. Giving this lady the pleasure she deserved. Making one more person in the world a little happier and, as far as I could see, hurting no one. What a great job, I reminded myself.

When she reappeared from the bathroom, Louise had taken off her shoes. She loitered awkwardly at the edge of the bed where I was sitting. I pulled her towards me and she stood over me, tilting her head down to kiss me. At first, she seemed reluctant to join me on the bed, so I got up and, as I kissed her, I started to peel off her clothes. I wanted her to do the same to me, but she was shy with where she put her hands, either putting them on my face or at my waist. Eventually, we were both down to our underwear, still standing there, her with her arms wrapped around my neck as we kissed, keeping her body close to mine. She lay down on the bed.

'Lie on your front,' I instructed her, kneeling on the bed.

Obediently, she lay down and I could see that her buttocks were clenched, so I told her softly to relax. I hovered over her body, planting little kisses on the back of her neck and shoulders. Then I slowly worked my way down her whole back, doing the same. When I got to her knickers, I planted a kiss at the base of her spine and then licked and kissed the whole way back up to her neck. As I continued to kiss and stroke her back, she let out little moans and shuddered occasionally, turning me on even more. I removed my boxers and then her knickers, keeping up the kissing while letting her feel my hard dick rubbing over her bottom and back. I massaged all of the way down to her bottom and thighs. Then I wet a finger and, as one hand continued to massage her back and bottom, I slowly put it inside her. As I massaged her g-spot with my finger, I reached for the condom I had left on the side of the bed and started to put it on.

She was excited, her breaths shallow and rapid, and she paused as the head of my dick probed at her entrance. Half an inch in, quarter out, slowly, until I could feel it pressing on the same spot I had been touching with my fingers. I lay on top of her, resting on my elbows, rocking my pelvis and digging my toes into the bed to give me a little more push.

'OK, OK, OK...' she started saying breathlessly, and her hands gripped the bed sheets.

I continued, still unsure if she had come or not and for a moment I thought back to Chloe.

We were only 17 when we first got together and most of my sexual experiences until that point had been judged a success the moment I had convinced the girl to have sex with me. But, with Chloe, I suddenly felt like the pressure was on; I had to impress or I would lose her.

'Is that good? What about this?' I remember saying one night, driving her crazy.

She got quite annoyed with me, not because what I was doing was no good – more because she didn't know the answers to some of my questions herself. She felt terrible when she admitted that, even though we had been going out for a couple of months, she had never had an orgasm, not even by herself. I'd felt a little inadequate at first, but then I saw it as a challenge. Also, I was glad that she hadn't faked it just to please me, which would have been a far worse confession. I wanted to please her as much as she pleased me, so to deny me that pleasure, or to lie to me about it just to make life easier, would have been wrong. So, we tried different positions and oral sex, and our sex life rapidly matured from the fumbling teenage romps that we'd started out with. As everything started to heat up, though, and she started to lose control of herself, she always used to make me stop. She couldn't relax completely and give in to the feeling – until one morning before college.

As usual, I had woken up horny and, after a little convincing, I persuaded her to let me screw her doggy style. While we were doing it, I told her to play with her 'top bit', as it had come to be known during one of our conversations about sex in the college library. At first, when she started moaning I thought I had hurt her and was going to stop, but then she reached behind with her free hand and pulled me harder into her each time I thrusted. Finally, she moaned and shook and had to tell me to stop for a moment, leaving me feeling on top of the world knowing that it had finally been as good for her as it had always been for me.

After we broke up, though, I noticed that not all girls came the same way. While some seemed to tense up and convulse, others just seemed to get faster and harder until they just went all floppy and slow again. Some screamed, some moaned, some whispered and bit their lips or my shoulders (which was a major turn-on). Some dug their nails into my back, another favourite of mine, while others just tried to hide their faces so I couldn't see the expressions they were making.

With Louise, I just couldn't tell, so I kept going. An hour passed and I'd gone from moments of thinking about Chloe to keep me hard to moments of doing algebra sums in my head to stop me from coming (who said algebra would never come in handy once I'd left school?). The sex didn't have to end after a client's first orgasm, but it was a signpost for me, letting me know that I was doing the job properly. Some women were far more verbal – 'Nearly there, harder, faster, up a bit' – whatever, but with Louise I was on my own. Eventually, I came for the first time that evening and she held me tightly before running off to the bathroom.

I lay there, obviously in a better mood for just having had sex, but a little concerned that I was doing a terrible job as a gigolo. But then I decided that the only way I was going to get good at this was if I just kept practising. I looked at it as paid work experience, or vocational training. The whole thing was a learning curve and I had to be prepared to encounter some clients like Louise. But when she came out of the toilet and jumped back into bed I saw a different picture.

'My legs are like jelly!' she said, snuggling up to me, resting her head on my chest.

I smiled and waited for any indication that she wanted to do it again. After all, I had to give her her money's worth. But then her snoring began and I decided it was safe to fall asleep myself. If she woke up horny, I'd be ready.

Our next meeting was two weeks later. She had booked the same hotel and this time she just wanted me to go straight there. We had both enjoyed our first evening together, so I was quite excited at the thought of seeing her again. Especially as sushi, or any other food for that matter, seemed to be far from her mind.

When I arrived at the hotel, she was standing at the reception desk talking to the concierge. She spotted me the moment I emerged from the revolving door. Her eyes lit up and she was smiling excitedly. I checked over my shoulder, just in case Mel Gibson had snuck in behind me. But, no, the welcome was for me.

'I've got something for you upstairs,' she whispered, as we began touching and kissing each other the moment the lift doors closed.

'And I've got something for you downstairs,' I whispered back.

She laughed and moved her hand down to my groin.

I was expecting her to go into the bathroom and come out wearing some sexy lingerie, but when I asked what she had for me she simply told me 'later'. She was much less passive this time, passionately kissing my body all over as I had done to her on our first night together. She even got on top and it was then that she seemed to be having the most pleasure. She just closed her eyes and with one hand on my chest and the other behind her on my thigh, she rocked back and forth until she shuddered and climbed off to lie beside me. We lay in bed and, despite my pleas, she turned on the television. I buried my head under the pillow in order to avoid my attention being monopolised by the 2D visions on the screen.

'Have you got telly-phobia or something? This is what's

happening in the real world!' She rocked me back and forth and finally beat me with her own pillow.

'Life's too short for TV.' I pulled the sheets over my head and pulled her closer to me.

She kicked and screamed, a Glaswegian 'STOP!' breaking into sexy laughter as I pulled her closer. We started kissing again.

'I forgot you're a book not a film man.'

I was more impressed that she had called me a man than with the fact that she had remembered my preference.

'Wannabe writer, remember?' I said as she rolled over, leaving her back exposed for me to kiss. In a drunken moment on our first date, I'd confessed to a secret desire to write a book – something I never normally talked about to anyone.

Louise reached down over the side of the bed and searched in her bag for something. I was confused as the condoms were on the bedside table. But then she reappeared with a small gift-wrapped box. 'This is the something I had upstairs for you.' She handed me the box and propped her head on her hand as I sat up to open the present.

I tore off the navy-blue paper and inside was a tan-coloured box, containing a gold-plated Parker pen.

'I thought this might help things be less of a struggle.'

I looked at her, gobsmacked. It was an incredible gift, so thoughtful, that I was actually lost for words. I thought about giving it back, about not accepting it. But how could I resist such a thoughtful act of kindness? 'I don't know what to say. Thank you. It's beautiful.'

But inside my head faint alarm bells were ringing. I recalled one of Andy's warnings. He had advised me on some dos and don'ts of being a male escort. One of the problem areas was payment and gifts. Andy had told me that some clients would rather pay me in kind, or in gifts such as clothes or holidays, and that this was OK. On the other hand, certain gifts showed that the client was taking a personal interest in you and this could be dangerous. A personal interest could quite easily be mistaken for love, and that's when the problems could really start.

'What the client has to realise from the start is that a male escort cannot be bought. He can only be hired. There is no possessing us. We're theirs for the time allocated but then we're free again. If they think they are in love, or worse, that you love them, things can get messy.'

I remember thinking at the time that Andy just had some serious illusions about how attractive he was and that maybe one or two comments had gone to his head. But now I could see how easily it could happen. One moment you're a free and fun-loving gigolo, the next moment you're being stalked by some crazy woman who wants you (or wants the persona she imagines is you), and, if she can't have you, she'll make sure no one else does either.

I realised that the pen was just a gesture as far as she was concerned and no real cause for alarm, but even so I felt it best to distance myself. I decided that for at least the next month I would have no contact with Louise. After all, I was busy enough with other clients and that provided me with a legitimate excuse for not seeing her. I'd explained at the beginning that our timetables might not always coincide, but that there were plenty of other male escorts available.

So, after our second night together and 'the pen incident', I decided to create a little distance. I didn't want the boundaries to become blurred. She had to be clear that for me it was work. Of course, for her it was romantic and exciting, and I'd made sure of that because that was the fantasy she was paying for. But she had to know that it was purely business. When Louise called for her third appointment, as I'd known she would, I told her that I couldn't make it and that I could arrange for another escort to meet her. By that stage, I knew quite a few escorts and we'd formed a kind of collective where, if one of us couldn't do a job, we'd pass it on to another. We advertised ourselves in the local English-language newspaper and website as an 'agency' called 'Es-sex Boys'.

For a moment, Louise was speechless and then the line went dead. I wanted to phone her back to make sure she was OK, but I reasoned that doing so would have made those boundaries just as blurry again. Moments later, I received a text message which gave me goose bumps.

'DON'T YOU FEEL THE SAME AS ME? AREN'T YOU ATTRACTED TO ME? AM I NOT GOOD ENOUGH FOR YOU?'

What had I done? I had no idea of what state this woman was in or of what she was capable of doing. My first concern was that she might try to commit suicide. After a message like the one I'd just received, it seemed obvious she wasn't the most emotionally stable person in the world. Later, I started to have images of her coming to find me in Marbella, going round the English bars with a photo of me, and asking people like Wayne if he knew me. I panicked as I realised that Wayne would be only too happy to help and would probably lead her straight back to the apartment. She might be there already, waiting for me, dagger in hand, rabbit on the hob... that sort of thing.

A few hours went by. Then my phone rang again. It was Louise. I could tell from her trembling voice that she had been crying. She started apologising for her text message and then asked if she could meet me in a few weeks for a meal. I told her what she wanted to hear; I laughed off the text message and reassured her that, if I were not with another client, I would see her instead. But, really, I had no intention of doing so. I'd had a close call. I wasn't going to let that happen again.

It took two months for the penny to drop for Louise that, whenever she called, I was 'busy with a client'. I know it wasn't the bravest way out of the situation, and I'm not proud of it. But at least I escaped being trapped in a *Fatal Attraction* scenario. And I'd learned a valuable lesson. Lay down the boundaries – and stick to them. Where clients were concerned, I could never be a 'friend', much less a 'boyfriend'.

I was a commodity. I knew it – and it was up to me to make sure they knew it too.

CHAPTER FOUR

Silvia

*'It's just a job. You're you, but a different version of you.
There's no guilt or inhibition. You're being the "you" that
your client wants you to be.'* ANDY

B y our third meeting, it was as if Silvia and I had known each other for years. We'd talked about everything during our first two nights together and, when we met up a few weeks later for our third date, we just picked up from where we'd left off. Like a holiday romance, we crammed as much as we could into our time together and, while we both knew where the limits of our 'relationship' lay, there was nevertheless a strong connection whenever we saw each other.

After an evening at a Thai restaurant, during which there hadn't been one moment's silence, with one conversation flowing seamlessly into the next, we went back to Silvia's hotel in Puerto Banus. Before our first 'date', I'd thought that Silvia, a successful American estate agent, might be nervous about having an escort for the first time, but I later realised that the only time Silvia was quiet was just after sex. Even during sex, she would talk constantly if we weren't kissing or her mouth wasn't otherwise occupied. Telling me how she liked it, telling me what she was imagining, asking me to bite her or slap her lightly on the buttocks.

At a glance, Silvia came across as a middle-aged librarian-type and I'm sure in front of clients she played on that image. After all, who would a family – fresh over from England and looking for someone to guide them through the labyrinthine house-buying process – trust more than a quiet, demure, professional lady?

But, as soon as her work was done, she knew how to let her hair down. If you passed her in the street, you'd never look twice, but my experience has shown me that appearances can be very deceiving. The old adage 'it's the quiet ones you have to watch' has proved to be true on more than one occasion. But even knowing that didn't prepare me for the fantasy Silvia presented to me the third time we slept together.

'Rape?'

'No, "ravish", we don't use the other word in the States.'

'Sounds like rape to me.'

'How can it be if I'm consenting to it?'

'Sounds risky. What if you change your mind and I think it's part of the game?'

'We'll have a safety word. I can shout "TIME" and you stop!'

Eager to please and well aware that she could hire another escort to do it if I wasn't willing, I shrugged and agreed. 'Yeah, sure. When?'

'Tomorrow night. I've got two sets of keys to a show flat. I've been taking people round, thinking about this all day,' she squealed. 'You take the spare set, and the address, and wait for me.'

Part of me was excited about helping make Silvia's fantasy come true, but another part of me was saying that something wasn't quite right about the whole thing. Still, I agreed to do it and, as I got dressed, I put the keys and the address in my pocket.

'Do you have to go? I've got money.' She looked up at me with hurt eyes.

'It's a friend's birthday, I have to go. I hardly see him as it is,' I explained.

'All right, I'll just have to lie here and dream about tomorrow night,' she said, her hand slipping beneath the sheets and heading southwards.

'I'll phone you tomorrow, OK?' I blew her a kiss as I left the hotel room to make my way back to Marbella.

The journey home helped to clear my head and I decided that, if I was going to do this job, I was going to need some insurance. I usually took a Dictaphone with me to protect myself from any rape or prostitution allegations, as Andy had advised. With the number of undercover police around, and the possibility of a shame-ridden client deciding that she had made a mistake, it was a necessary precaution. But only for the first few meetings. Once I had seen a client for the third time, I considered her a regular and I would leave the Dictaphone at home. With Silvia, I had jumped the gun and left it after only the second meeting. If something did go wrong and I had no evidence of her asking me to help her act out this fantasy, I would be in deep doo-doo.

The next day, hungover from having overdone it at my friend's birthday bash, I blindly searched for my mobile as it rang.

'Hey, it's me,' came Silvia's voice from the other end.

I leaped out of the bed and peeled my eyes open, scouting for the Dictaphone. Unable to lay my hands on it, I asked if I could call her back. Once I'd finally found the recorder inside one of my suit jackets, I lay down on the bed and called her back, placing the tiny microphone between my ear and the phone and crossing my fingers that she'd say everything I needed to protect myself.

'What are you doing?' I yawned.

'Waiting for these clients to arrive, bored out of my mind! You?'

'Lying in bed, thinking about tonight. Tell me what you wanna do.'

'Mmmm... I want you to be waiting for me in the dark. And when I come in I don't want you to say a word. I just want you to fuck me. Don't stop. Just tear my panties off and do what you want to me. But I'll try to stop you.'

'You're gonna put up a fight?'

'Oh yeah. You're gonna have to tie me up,' she giggled.

'Mmm... sounds good to me. Now, I know you don't want me to stop...'

'Unless I say "time". If I say "time", the lights go on, your mask comes off and you untie me!'

'Mask? Kinky!'

'Didn't I say that before? Oh, OK, well I don't want you to speak and I don't want to see you, just feel you. Be there before eleven.'

'Got it. What about...'

'Shit, they're here. Gotta go.'

I stopped the recorder and rewound the tape to listen. I had lost count of the times the tape hadn't recorded anything, or the sound was so muffled that, if the shit had hit the fan, I wouldn't have had a leg to stand on. As it played, it sounded distant, but clear enough to give me the peace of mind to do the job. I imagined her there with her clients, distracted by the thought of me lying in bed getting excited about the night to come. The truth, however, was that I was having great difficulty finding the fantasy arousing. It went against everything I had had drummed into me from day one and, no matter how hard I tried to visualise it, I simply couldn't find the image erotic. Power trips were not my thing, so this fantasy lacked the same appeal it might have had for someone else. But, despite not wanting to control other people, being in control of myself was important to me and I was filled with self-doubt. Animal sex was great when there was passion from the other side as well, but the images that kept coming to mind were not like that. They were dark and silent and left me cold.

Finally, I realised that, if thinking about it wasn't arousing me the chances were that, come my curtain call, I'd have stage fright. So, for the first time since I had bought it a month earlier, I got out the packet of little blue diamond pills sitting in my washbag. Now, taking artificial stimulants is not my thing. I love a drink, but I'd never have anything to do with other drugs – not the coke I was constantly offered in the port, nor the steroids shoved under my nose at the gym, and the last drug I thought I'd ever actually need was Viagra. But, 'desperate times' and all that... The current situation demanded that I relaxed my morals so as not to relax other vital bits of me. Or I'd be facing my first unsatisfied client.

I decided to park around the corner from the urban area in which the flat was situated. Already getting into the role of a would-be attacker, I thought it best not to alert her of my presence. Most of the properties were empty, as they hadn't been sold on yet, so only a few lights were on. I watched my shadow circling me as the continuous row of streetlights lit my hesitant approach. I could smell the barbecue coming from the terrace of one of the few inhabited apartments. I felt more like a burglar than a rapist, all dressed in black and clutching the bag of 'goodies' I'd been instructed to bring, which included rope and a balaclava instead of a mask.

After fumbling with the keys, I took one last furtive look around before backing into the show flat. Boy, was I getting into my role – method acting seemed to come easy to me. The unlit entrance hall led through to the minimally furnished apartment, complete with American-style kitchen and huge lounge. I turned the tap, but the water obviously wasn't connected. If this is the show flat, I thought, no wonder no one has bought any of them. It had a distinctly unhomely feel. Spacious, but not comfortable.

I had a look around, wandering into the bedrooms, each with their own en suite. As I entered the first bathroom, a light automatically went on. Now, that is a selling point, I thought, and made a note to myself that I was going to get the same thing as soon as I had my own place. My bag resting in the sink, I pulled out the balaclava and slipped it over my head. I wouldn't have wanted to meet me down a dark alley, and I couldn't help feeling that I was really going to scare Silvia.

Plunging my hand into the bag, I dug out the Viagra packet, popped one out of the foil and put it straight into my mouth. I had no water to wash it down with and was dreading it getting stuck in my throat and ending up with a stiff neck. But, after a few gulps, it had gone down. I imagined it circulating around my body and, hopefully, heading towards one particular part.

I took out the rope and wrapped it around my hands, before reminding myself that it was for tying her up, not garrotting her! I took out the bandana I would be using to blindfold her, just in case she was tempted to peek, and crammed it into my pocket. Seconds after I left the bathroom, the light went out again, which gave me an idea. I went into the kitchen, stood on a chair and unscrewed the bulb. I did the same in the lounge. That way Silvia wouldn't be able to see anything, whereas my eyes were slowly but surely adjusting to the darkness. Then I waited in the corner of the kitchen, glancing nervously at my watch. She was late and I had a fleeting feeling of paranoia that it might have been a set-up.

My mind was put to rest as I heard her old rent-a-car pull up outside and the engine cut out. I closed my eyes and became aware of the approaching footsteps, followed by the familiar rattle of her key ring as she put the key in the door. I took deep, slow, silent breaths as I heard her close the door behind her and play with the light switch. She marched into the lounge and from the silhouette I was relieved to note that it was definitely her, not some poor girl sent in for a set-up as my twisted imagination had feared.

My next thought after recognising her was... shit! Trousers! Couldn't she have worn a skirt to make things easier for me? Still, I'd come this far. Peeling my back from the wall I'd been pressed up against, I crept up behind her as she stumbled blindly towards the bedroom, feeling her way. I didn't want her to get to the bedroom and turn on the light, so, as she was about to leave the dark hallway, I decided to make my move.

My arms simultaneously wrapped around her, my left arm trapping her arms to her sides and my right hand placed over her mouth to stop any screaming. She wriggled and gave a little muffled yelp. I walked her to the bed and forced her to kneel down and bend over it, bringing her arms behind her to tie them up, alternating between tying her hands and forcing her back down on to the bed as she struggled. Once her hands were tied, I took the bandana from my pocket and blindfolded her.

'Stop! Stop! What are you doing?'

I fought to ignore her panicked moans, placing one hand around the back of her neck and pinning her to the bed. My other hand undid her belt and trousers, and pulled them down to her ankles, where I tied the belt up again to make sure she couldn't get loose and kick me. I lifted her on to her feet, turned her round and threw her back down on to the bed. Her hands bound by the rope, her legs bound by her trouser belt and underwear, she lay there helpless, blindfolded and completely lost in her fantasy.

'What are you gonna do to me?' she moaned.

I said nothing but tore open her blouse and put my hand under her bra.

'Don't touch me, get off me!'

I brought my hand to her mouth to silence her and with my other hand I started to stroke her pussy. She moaned at first, but then I took my hand away again and immediately the muffled sounds of her protests stopped. She had become aroused more quickly than ever before and I felt how wet she was as I inserted one finger, noticing how easily it slipped in. My fears about my own inability to rise to the occasion were proving grossly misplaced and I was more than ready to fulfil her fantasy. I rolled her on to her front and then made her kneel, leaving her completely exposed to me. Breathing quickly, I pulled down my trousers and boxers and put on the condom. She sounded like she had had the wind knocked out of her as I slowly put my length in. It was tight where her legs were bound together, which just added to my pleasure. Once everything was nice and lubricated, I started to rock her harder, bringing her towards me as she rocked back and using the spring in the mattress to give us more motion. Thanks to the Viagra, I felt I was so hard I could probably walk around with her still attached.

Halfway through, though, I realised that my mind had

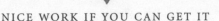

wandered. Bizarrely, I'd caught myself thinking about buying my own place. Maybe I should ask Silvia if she has anything in my price range, I thought, but was suddenly brought back to the present as I thought I heard her say, 'TIME.'

But could I be sure? Cautiously, I slowed down, but continued moving, waiting for her to say it again, if indeed she had said it in the first place. It was hardly one of those moments where I could say, 'Sorry, dear, what was that, I wasn't listening?' so I just carried on and paid more attention from that point on.

A short while later, Silvia shook violently and came. I would have liked to carry on, but not wishing to push my luck by continuing the fantasy for a moment longer than necessary, and realising that, with the Viagra coursing through my system, I could be there for a good while longer, I faked it. I leaned over her back and groaned, twitching before I became a near-lifeless hulk resting inside her. Then I took off all my gear and went into the bathroom, got the bag and threw it all in. Back in the room, I untied her hands and put the rope back in the bag, leaving her blindfold on and her legs still bound by her belt.

I took one last look at her as she lay on the bed, her hands between her legs, and then walked out and back to my car as if nothing had happened. Driving home, my phone began to ring.

'That was amazing. I'm not gonna be able to work tomorrow!' she said.

'Well, I'm glad you enjoyed it,' I said, trying to sound as enthusiastic.

'Hey, listen, I've got a few other ideas. When are you free next?'

'Won't be till next week,' I lied. I needed a little time to prepare myself for whatever she was going to suggest next.

'Shit, I'll be back in Madrid! Are you sure you can't squeeze me in.'

'Commitments. Sorry.'

'So professional. Ah well, I guess I'll see you in a couple of weeks. You take care, babe!'

'You too. Ciao!'

I had nothing planned for the rest of the evening and the effects of the Viagra were still apparent. I needed to go home and have a shower, but I was determined to make the most of the drug before it wore off. So, later that night, I returned home with an Austrian girl I had met in the port. We made love until it was light, and then it was her exhaustion that prevented us from continuing.

It had been a good evening, successful in every way. But, as I slept, the consequences of my actions started to sink in. The effects of the drug were wearing off and, apart from a slight headache, it was well on its way to being eliminated from my body, but the memories of enacting Silvia's fantasy had no intention of leaving me and my sleep was plagued with nightmares. I awoke covered in sweat, relieved that my dream – of being chased by the Guardia Civil for having raped a girl – was just that. A dream. The nightmares continued until the next time I saw Silvia when, as if seeing her had exorcised those demons, I had my first good night's sleep in two weeks.

When I arrived at the hotel Silvia took me straight up to her room. Normally, that would have been fine, but I was starving and had been hoping to go out to eat. On the phone, she'd said we were going to a restaurant first, but had obviously changed her mind.

'OK, my turn to hold the reins,' she said, pulling two sets of handcuffs from her bag.

'Where d'you want me?'

'Strip and get on the bed, slave!'

I laughed and hurried to take my clothes off, but the smile died on my lips as she produced a whip from the same bag. As she came closer, I couldn't take my eyes off the whip, which she patted on the palm of her hand. I stripped completely naked and lay on the bed, waiting for Silvia to handcuff me to the headboard. In spite of the whip, I was excited this time. Unlike her previous fantasy, this one seemed like it could be fun – if a little alarming.

'OK, big boy, what should I start with first?'

She whipped me gently on the thighs and then the stomach. She ran the tassels slowly over my groin and then whipped my chest, harder this time. Then she walked off towards her bag, grabbed it and brought it back with her. From somewhere in its depths, she produced a candle and lit it, before resting it on the nightstand to burn. Next out of the bag was a plastic bottle of chocolate sauce, which she squirted in a thick line from my chest down to my cock.

Covered in chocolate sauce and slightly concerned about the burning candle, I watched her as she stripped naked. She left the whip beside the candle and got on the bed between

my legs. Her head hovered over my dick and I could feel her hair touching my pubic hair.

'Shit!' she said, annoyed.

Suddenly very self-conscious, I tried to sit up. 'What? What is it?'

'I just got chocolate in my hair!' she exclaimed, sitting up with her chocolate-covered strands between her fingers.

I burst out laughing and found it hard to stop, particularly when she started licking the chocolate sauce off my skin. I looked down as she playfully licked around my shaven balls, making me harder and harder. My chocolate-covered cock looked like a king-size Mars bar, as it disappeared and reappeared from her mouth. When she had licked off all the chocolate, she kissed me. To be honest, I was disappointed, not with the kiss, but by the fact that she had used plain instead of milk chocolate. I'm not a fan of dark chocolate – give me milk or white any day! Apparently, chocolate triggers our body to release small amounts of the same chemicals it does naturally when we fall in love. Whoever did that study could not have been talking about dark chocolate.

Silvia got off the bed. I thought she was going to grab the whip again and feared for the state of my erection. But instead she grabbed the giant candle. I tensed up and my eyes never left the candle as she dripped some of the melted wax on to my chest. The heat stung at first but then to my surprise it tingled in a purely pleasurable way. She continued to spill the wax strategically over my body, but the lower she got, the quicker my erection vanished. The last drops of wax hit my balls but, luckily, before I could yell, 'NO MORE!' she had put down the candle and was once more rummaging around in her bag.

'Damn, I forgot the blindfold. Well, we've got time,' she said, grinning, as she came back and put the blindfold on me, leaving me in darkness.

I heard the bag rustle and then felt her weight on the bed again. She sat astride me and leaned to kiss me. Then after a click I heard a high-pitched buzzing, followed, seconds later, by powerful vibrations on my thighs and then up and down my rapidly growing cock. Expertly, Silvia circled the head, making me tingle and writhe with pleasure. She continued to run the vibrator all along my shaft and even down along my sac. All was going well until she tried to move my balls out of the way and put the vibrator where the Costa del Sol never shone.

'Relax,' she whispered, 'I won't put it in.'

I suddenly felt as if this was karmic payback for all of the times I had used that particular line, but I decided to trust her anyway. She placed the toy between my arse and my balls and suddenly, without any warning, I felt the strangest but most pleasurable sensation. My head was tingling and I felt my orgasm coming closer and closer, but she wasn't even touching my dick any more. Finally, taking the vibrator from under my balls and placing it somewhere on her body, she wrapped her mouth around the end of my dick and brought me off as she brought herself off with the vibrator.

I saw Silvia regularly throughout my whole illustrious career as a gigolo, and each time she had another fantasy to fulfil – and each time I was more than happy to help her make that fantasy a reality.

If I hadn't been an escort, and she hadn't been paying me, I'd never have given Silvia the time of day in real life. And I'd have missed out on many truly memorable experiences. It just proved to me what Andy had told me right from the start – if you judge by appearances, you'll only ever skate across the surface of life. Sometimes, if you make yourself dig deep enough, you'll find treasure buried in the most unlikely places.

CHAPTER FIVE

Hayley

'The quiet ones are always hiding something. It could be good, it could be bad, but if you're clever you'll get out before you find out.' ANDY

As with most jobs, there's a kind of camaraderie among escorts, and we'd do each other favours if needed – such as if one of us couldn't do a job we'd pass it on to someone else. But sometimes that backfired. Every now and then, another escort would say that they could do a job only to let me down at the last minute. Sometimes they would get a better offer; sometimes their bottle would just go. But, whatever the reason, it left me with the task of finding somebody else quickly, or doing the job myself.

My evening with Hayley was one such occasion. She had requested a Russian ex-army guy called Luke, who had just had his picture put on the website. He had agreed to do the job, but then phoned me an hour before he was supposed to meet her to tell me he was stuck in Malaga. The guy was twice my size and obviously no stranger to a fight, so even over the telephone my strongest words were along the lines of 'You've really let me down this time, Luke!'

The good news was I was already dressed up as I'd been planning to go out with an Austrian girl I had taken home the week before. The bad news was I didn't have her number to cancel the date. Either way, someone was going to be stood up, so I decided that, as the Austrian girl was going home the following day, I could live with letting her down. I know – not the most gentlemanly thing to do.

As I walked along the front strip of Puerto Banus a short while later, I saw a lone woman seated outside the Havana bar and knew instantly that this was the client. She was exactly as she had described herself: petite, with short dark hair and a cute, Disney-type face. She looked like Snow White but the long puffy, flowing dress had been replaced by a miniskirt and a flowery, transparent silk top. She was pretty and she would have been even prettier if she had smiled, but my arrival barely elicited a 'hello'.

'You're not Luke,' she said, looking up at me straight-faced and then away again.

'Yeah, sorry about that – he had to cancel. I'm Deano.' I pulled myself a bar stool and joined her at the table, not seeing the point in waiting for her to offer me a seat.

A waiter came and asked what I wanted, so I turned to Hayley for confirmation that my services were still required. She gave me a wry smile and said to the waiter, 'I'll have another gin and tonic,' and then she gestured with her hand in my direction.

'*Agua sin gas.*' I looked at her, watching the way she alternated between staring down at her drink and out to the boats in the port. I decided that, despite her attractiveness, this woman definitely needed something, although I wasn't quite sure that an escort was it. She was dressed from head to toe in designer gear, the real thing, and straight from the extortionately priced shops of Puerto Banus – none of your Dagenham market fakes here – so, whatever had removed the smile from her face, it wasn't her financial situation.

'If I'm not what you want...' I was starting to feel uncomfortable with her distance and my confidence was taking a nosedive.

But she sighed and shook her head. She pulled her purse from her Louis Vuitton bag and took out two 100-euro notes, placing them in front of me on the table. 'Two hundred, right? I just want some company – just stay.'

I took the money and felt a little better knowing that, even if her mood stayed that way, at least I'd been paid. I tried my best to make general chit-chat, but got nothing more than a 'yes' or 'no' in response – that's if she answered at all. I began to feel terrible for my parents as I realised that this was how I had communicated with them for years. But that was normal teenage angst. This was something else. It made no sense to me that someone would hire an escort and then give them the cold shoulder. Andy had warned me about that type of client, and his words rang in my ears as I sat there with her.

'Watch out for the quiet ones, Deano, they're the ones with the skeletons in their closet.'

I remember at the time thinking that Andy was doing his best to scare me off becoming an escort. After all, I would eventually be competition for him, unless one of us moved on. Despite what Andy had said, my own experience had shown me that most quiet girls had a lot going on in their heads and they were just dying to share it with someone. I decided to trust my own experience and block out Andy's words, so I stayed.

Hayley seemed determined to drown any anxieties she might have had – preferably in gin. Some clients are like that; they need a good few drinks before they can let go and make the most of me. They're not used to being in control and taking the lead, and it takes some generous measures of Dutch courage to give them the confidence to do so. I can relate. I was exactly the same before I became an escort.

'Are you nervous?' I asked, dipping my head to meet her downward stare.

She nodded slowly and said nothing, keeping her eyes on her drink.

'We could always go somewhere more private if you...'

She shook her head immediately and I knew I had to back off. Despite having witnessed this drowning of inhibitions scenario on numerous occasions, something else seemed to be driving this client and I couldn't put my finger on what it was. Confused, nervous and well aware that any questions would be met by single-word answers, I decided to talk about myself and the surroundings. Yes, I could have sat there in silence, but that role had been taken and to do so would have made it look as if we were having an argument. Not a good advertisement for any passing potential clients.

'Do you always talk this much?' she said, finally breaking away from her thoughts to interrupt my inane chatter.

I decided as always to be completely honest with her. 'Look, I'm sorry, but this has never happened to me before.' I held up my hands to apologise.

'What? What's never happened?' she said, giving me more attention than she had all night.

'Being left to do all the talking. I mean, I love listening – some women pay me to just do that – but you're not giving me much to listen to, so...'

As I carried on waffling, I saw the corner of her mouth turn up and she had to hold in a laugh. But, as quickly as she had taken an interest, she lost it again, returning her focus to the yachts in the port.

'Let's go somewhere else,' she sighed, forcing a smile as she stood up.

We walked along the port and it was buzzing, even though it was still only spring. There were people everywhere having a good time and I wanted to be one of them. I wanted to forget about the car I had parked in the underground car park and have a drink. I wanted to drop this client back at her place and find myself a horny 18-year-old barmaid. But I was a professional. I stayed with my client. I forced my eyes not to wander as scantily clad girls passed us, and I decided that I was definitely having the following night off to make up for what I was missing out on. Then, from out of nowhere, came the first sign of warmth since the start of the job. She took my hand in hers. I'm in there, I thought. Normally, it worked the other way round. I would get the client to open up to me emotionally and then they would be more likely to feel like opening up physically. She had been an ice maiden all night, but, once she had made that physical gesture, I thought at the very least she would be more open to discussing what was on her mind.

'Stay close,' she said to me, as if I was going to wander off and get lost, like a kid in a supermarket.

From the few words she had said to me, I'd already decided that I preferred her when she was silent. The bouncer opened the door for us and, although she was holding my hand, Hayley's expression was still hard and unsmiling.

We walked to the bar together and she whispered in my ear, 'Get me a gin and tonic. I'm just going to powder my nose,' before kissing my cheek and walking off towards the toilet.

Now this woman was a real puzzle and one that, at 22, I lacked the life experience to work out. Hot one minute, cold the next and I saw no connection between any of it. Maybe Andy was right, I thought. Maybe having too many skeletons in the closet really does turn you a bit crazy, and the quietness is just a way of covering that up. I stood at the bar and looked around as I waited for the drinks. It was dark and dingy and full of unsavoury characters, one of which was my client. As I continued my scan of the club, I spotted trouble. Hayley was standing on the other side of the dance floor with a large, bald, suited man and, from the body language, it didn't look like he was asking her the time.

He had one hand around her arm while his free hand jabbed at her face as if he was telling her off for something. The indifferent expression she'd worn all night had been replaced by sheer terror. To my dismay, I realised I had to intervene. I'm five foot eleven and at that point I weighed about 75kg. Hardly the most threatening of characters to look at, but I could handle myself if the situation really required it. I had worked as a bouncer for a short while in the UK and fights had never worried me, but now things were different. I could hardly work as an escort with black eyes or a broken nose. On the other hand, I would have found it harder to look at myself in the mirror had I walked away.

I felt my entire body throb as the adrenaline rushed through my veins and my heart raced. As I approached Hayley, I could see more clearly how scared she was. My plan of action was to try to calm the guy down before any punches were thrown. Thankfully, as I approached, Hayley's companion had obviously finished what he'd wanted to say and walked off, throwing me a mean glance as he did so.

I was about to ask what had happened, but before I even had a chance she grabbed my arm. 'Come on, we'd better fuck off,' she said charmingly, and hauled me back out into the second strip of Puerto Banus, before bursting into tears.

Everyone stared at us as she pulled me through the streets crying, probably jumping to the conclusion that I was the cause of her distress.

'Hayley, what's wrong? What just happened?' I asked, genuinely concerned.

We sat on a metal bench in front of the cinema and I tried to stop her snivelling long enough to get an audible answer from her. But everything I asked was met by a shake of her head and in the end all I could do was offer to take her home.

'Not a good idea. My fella's probably back now, and he'd kill the pair of us!' she said.

My heart sank and, as the situation suddenly started becoming clearer, I was struck by the unfairness of it all. I would have been eating a nice meal with a gorgeous Austrian girl right now if Luke had not got stuck in Malaga. This would be *his* problem, not mine.

'Hayley, who was the man at the club?' I asked, not sure if I really wanted to stick around for the answer.

'That's my fella's best mate and his partner.'

Partner in crime, no doubt. What sort of crime, I had no idea, but I got the impression from Hayley's jewellery, clothes and purse bulging with cash that it was a bit more than fiddling the electricity meter.

'If it's not the strippers, it's those whores. Throwing his money at them, thinking he's Billy Big Bollocks,' she sobbed, dabbing her eyes with a tissue. 'I just thought I'd make him jealous – piss him off by walking in with someone.'

Great. Never mind what happened to the poor sod she walked in with. I got the distinct feeling that if Hayley's 'fella' had been in the club as well as his mate, an evil look would have been the least of my worries. I asked her if she was OK to make her way to the taxi rank, and she nodded. I was too numb from shock to be angry with her for putting me in such danger, and I knew the best thing I could do was to get away from the port. Fast.

I walked away, paranoid that I now had a price on my head. Despite its sun and party image, Marbella has a dark side and there are certain people you really don't want to get on the wrong side of. But, as well as feeling bad for myself, I also felt bad for Hayley. Not so bad that I wanted to turn back and comfort her, mind you, but I did look behind to check that she wasn't still crying.

Big mistake. As I looked back, I saw a group of large, suited men heading towards her and calling her name. I forced myself to keep walking, assuring myself that no one would hurt his best friend's wife. I, on the other hand, was a legitimate target. I threw another glance over my shoulder. This time they looked like an oversized pack of prairie dogs, all sniffing around ready looking for their target.

Me.

From behind me, I heard one of them yell out where I was, and signal to them all to start chasing me. The shouting and yells were getting closer.

'Oi, get back here, you cunt! You're gonna get a fucking good hiding!'

Stupid twat, I cursed myself. They'd never have recognised me from that distance if I'd just taken my jacket off, but it was too late for that now. I ran as fast as I could in my new shoes and felt the leather soles slipping as I descended into the underground car park. I sprinted to my car. Then, realising that they would catch me on the way out, I decided to hide in the back instead. I crouched down on the back seat, turning my jacket inside out and laying it over me.

How on earth had I got here? I asked myself, trying to muffle the torn breaths coming from my exhausted body. I wasn't a gangster; I was just a college boy from Essex. So how had I ended up hiding in the back of a parked car in southern

Spain while a group of thugs with criminal records longer than my street tried to track me down? And they weren't looking to invite me to a Tupperware party, either.

I could hear the sound of the heavy car park door being yanked open and then the shuffling feet of the men as they burst in. The door slammed behind them and my heart pounded as I heard faint footsteps approach the car. I was completely vulnerable – only my pepper spray to hand, but there were too many of them for that to be an effective weapon. I had nothing else. My only option was to stay in hiding and pray they didn't find me. Then I noticed something that made my guts freeze inside me. I'd forgotten to lock the car doors.

The central locking would have made too much noise and alerted the men to my whereabouts, so I just had to wait there, like the proverbial sitting duck. The footsteps got closer and closer, and then they stopped.

'He's definitely in 'ere...' whispered one man. 'We know you're in 'ere, boy! We'll wait all night if we 'ave to!'

I listened to them continue their search for the next ten minutes, but then, suddenly, there was complete silence. Not a footstep, no whispering, just my heart, which was gradually slowing down. I sat up and peered out of the windows, keeping low so I would not be seen if they still were there. Then I spotted one of the men, hiding behind a pillar with a gun in his hand. I lay back down and covered myself again, deciding to wait there indefinitely.

'Come on, son! We only wanna talk to ya!' shouted the man behind the pillar.

Call it male intuition but I guessed this was not any conversation I was going to enjoy, so I decided to stay put. I lay there for another ten minutes, heart and mind racing, until finally he must have got bored and left. By that time, I'd drifted off into my own little world, hoping to fall asleep and wake up to find it had all been a dream.

Andy had told me, 'You'll get addicted. The money's too good. It's every man's dream.' But the risks had already started to outweigh the pleasures. Sternly I told myself that this was my last job; that I would never do it again. But, in the back of my mind, I knew that the next time my phone rang and there was a well-paying client on the other end, I'd find it very hard to say 'no'.

What seemed like hours later, I started the car and made my way home, still convinced that there was a suited gorilla waiting for me on every dark street corner. Locking my front door behind me, I felt as if I'd had the luckiest escape. For the first time in months, I longed to be coming home to someone special, who'd make me a cup of tea and give me a cuddle and tell me everything was OK. I knew that would soon pass and the next day I'd resolve once again to remain a lifelong bachelor, but just for that night I craved the companionship I'd shared with Chloe. I wanted to know there was someone who worried when I was late, and who was glad to see me home safe. Big tough guy, me.

The episode with Hayley taught me two valuable lessons: 1) trust your gut; if a woman's acting like she has something to hide, she probably has; 2) go for a car with tinted windows.

When, a few weeks later, I met a guy called Brian who

offered to rent me one of his Mercs at a not-too-extortionate cost, I jumped at the chance, ignoring the warning voice in my head that told me my new best friend Brian wasn't exactly legitimate, and wouldn't take kindly to his car being returned in anything but pristine condition. Funny how little time it had taken for that promise I'd made myself in the car park, about giving up the escorting, to completely recede in my mind. I was young; I was fit; I could handle myself. And now I drove a big, black Merc with leather seats. Things were on the up.

'Looking good, Deano boy,' I told myself, admiring my reflection in one of the black tinted windows. Of course, deep down, I realised that, when you play with the big boys, you usually wind up with big-boy bruises to show for it. But right then and there I wasn't going to let it bother me.

To my 22-year-old mind, I'd really made it.

CHAPTER SIX

Carly

*'Everyone is a potential client. A woman might look
like she has it all but, believe me, there'll be
something missing. And it's up to you to find
what that is and offer it to her.'* ANDY

The hotel porter led me along the hall to her room, shot
me a knowing smile and left. I rapped my knuckles on
the wooden door and waited for a reply. From inside, I could
hear the muffled sound of *Sky News* on the room's television
and a woman's voice. I knocked again, hoping she would
hear me this time.

'Who is it?' came the eventual reply.

'I'm from the agency.'

I saw the spy hole darken and knew I was being inspected,
so I turned slightly to the right to expose my good side,
pretending to be looking down the hall. My right side was not
pretty at all. My symmetry was ruined by a couple of moles
and a slightly bigger nostril. People never tended to notice
this while looking at my whole animated face, but close-up

photos revealed all of my imperfections. My saving grace? My eyes. Every girl or woman I've ever been out with has said something about them. If they were to be believed and the eyes truly are the windows to the soul, my soul was anything between passionate and driven (and occasionally bloodshot).

But to me, they were just blue.

The door opened and the first glimpse of my client was of her back as she marched back into the room, her flip-flops clapping. She continued to chat on her mobile, leaving a trail of smoke behind her. Her white bikini top and thong were clearly visible through her white linen top and trousers, as she walked away from me.

'Well, tell her she shouldn't have said anything! Why can't she just keep out!'

I edged into the room and watched as she sat on the edge of the bed, yelling at whoever was on the other end of the line.

Unsure of what to do with myself, I walked straight through the room and out to the balcony. On my way through, I noticed the coke-covered make-up mirror and the rolled-up 50-pound note. Been a while since I've seen one of them, I thought to myself, obviously not referring to the mound of coke. Not that I was a fan of the white stuff, but here in Marbella it was hard to avoid it.

I stood out on the balcony and waited patiently for her to finish her conversation/shouting match. I knew already that I didn't want to be on the wrong side of this woman. There was sudden silence, and then she appeared.

'Sorry about that, love. So you're Deano?' she asked, with a big chemically aided smile.

She should have checked herself in the mirror one last time before making her first impression, as her right nostril looked like a Christmas window display, snowflakes everywhere. I decided not to say anything until the money side of things had been taken care of and she had had a chance to look in the mirror one last time before we left the room.

'Here you go. This is for the day, and we'll work out the rest as we go, OK?' She smiled her big cheesy smile again.

'Am I going to call you Miss Mead all day or are you gonna tell me your first name?' After all, it wasn't as if I was being paid just to chauffeur her about. I was her escort, not her butler – and I reckoned that should at least earn me the right to be on first-name terms.

She looked shocked that I'd asked. 'You don't know who I am?' she exclaimed, raising an eyebrow.

'Should I?' I replied, holding my hands up in apology.

'I s'pose you don't get English channels here,' she shrugged off my ignorance.

'I don't watch telly.'

'Well, there you go then. It's Carly. Carly Mead,' she announced airily, grabbing her purse from the bed and opening the door. The name meant nothing to me, but something about her demeanour and air of authority made me think it probably should have.

'Shall we?' I squeezed past her and felt suddenly short of breath, intoxicated by her perfume. I hadn't been close enough to smell it before, but as she closed the door I leaned in towards her and inhaled the deep, heady scent.

'You like? My own blend.' She winked, and sauntered towards the lift.

Just before the lift doors opened on the ground floor, she grabbed my arm. We strolled through reception side by side, with Carly plonking her room key down on the desk as we went past and through the revolving door. Once outside, I opened the car door for her and strode round to my side.

'Rental?' she asked, admiring the Mercedes and evidently not believing for a moment that I was the owner.

'Friend's. OK, Plaza Beach, right?'

'Uh-huh. Music?'

For a second, until I registered that the radio was still there, my stomach turned over as I remembered whose car I was renting and what would happen to me if anything got broken or stolen. Brian, the car's owner, wasn't the sort of guy you wanted to go to with any bad news.

On the drive to Plaza Beach, I noticed Carly squinting and thought it strange that she had a pair of sunglasses hooked to her blouse and yet didn't wear them. I only wore mine for driving, as I've always felt that glasses and hats suit only certain people, and I'm not one of them. In an attempt to establish some common ground between us, I asked her about it. 'How come you don't wear your glasses?' I felt it safest to refrain from mentioning that her squinting into the sun added ten years to her looks.

'Well, they're prescription... just not my prescription,' she laughed, and unhooked the glasses to look at them. 'They look so much like mine. I don't know where I picked them up. They give me a headache if I wear them too long! But I can't go to the beach party without some sunnies, can I!'

Image is everything, right? I reckon that's why some women suffer for fashion – because beauty equals pain.

The underground car park was right beside the beach party, so on Sundays you were lucky if you could get a space at all. I stopped the car at the entrance and suggested that she should get out and start partying while I parked the car.

She sighed, rolling her head back on the rest. 'Why would I hire an escort, to arrive at a party alone?'

She had a point. Once again, I'd made the mistake of confusing the rules of dating and escorting – I'd think twice before suggesting anything similar to future clients. I was just about to pull away when a photographer I knew walked past and I instinctively called out to him. 'Johnny!'

He didn't hear me, so I was just about to shout again a when I heard 'SLAM'! I thought someone had driven into Brian's Mercedes and my heart stopped. But, as I turned around and saw the empty passenger seat, I realised that the noise had been the door slamming and now Carly was power-walking towards the taxi rank behind me. I yanked out the keys and jogged after her.

'Carly! Where you going? What's wrong?' I stopped in front of her and held up my hands, aware she had a temper and not wanting to risk grabbing her arm.

'You were gonna get your mate to take photos of us,' she yelled accusingly.

That's when I recognised her! I must have seen her standing just like this on the television years ago and all sorts of things about her character came flooding back to me. I did fleetingly consider saying something about my sudden epiphany, but realised it might not have been quite the ideal time.

'I was just saying hello, he didn't even hear me.'

'But he's a photographer,' she spat the word out with the same disgust as if she was calling him a child pornographer.

I shrugged and my brow furrowed in confusion. 'So? There'll be loads of photographers in there. You must be used to it?'

'I'd just rather not right now. And not with you. Don't take it personally.' Her arms were wrapped around her stomach and she was looking away, until she remembered she had cigarettes in her purse.

'I won't. OK, then. Where else do you wanna go?'

Are all these stars such high maintenance? I wondered. I didn't have a clue what was going on in her private life, and there was obviously something in the background that was complicating things for her, but, hey, I was just the escort. Why was it my job to chase her down the street and plead with her to come and get back in the car? Maybe that was how she got her kicks. Maybe having me chase her made her feel wanted. Maybe I just needed to get a move on...

'What about Nikki Beach?' she asked.

This was the obvious second choice. In fact, I was confused as to why she hadn't wanted to go there first – it was the best known of the beach parties – although the paparazzi presence would be just as pronounced there as it was here.

'That'll be crawling with cameras as well. You didn't really think this holiday through, did you!' I held in my urge to laugh, as I didn't want Carly to think I was patronising her.

Her head was down and she was pouting now, which was preferable to her earlier cockiness, and far more attractive. All of a sudden, I felt an urge to kiss her and give her a big cuddle, but again felt that would probably have seemed patronising – just a short-term remedy to greater problems. Issues I might never even scratch the surface of. And so I decided against rushing it. Carly seemed like she was definitely a woman of passion, but right at this moment she seemed more likely to want to hit me than have sex with me.

'I did think it through,' she protested. 'That's why I went to Nerja first.' Nerja is a lesser-known town east of Malaga, popular with geriatric British holidaymakers. 'I was bored shitless so I came here instead. I just want to get away from it all, but I don't wanna sit indoors, bored.'

Carly massaged her forehead with her fingers while holding the cigarette as far away from her as possible and taking a deep breath to calm herself down. I took the cigarette from her hand and took a drag before flicking it to the kerb. She gasped and pointed at the cigarette with both hands, looking at me for an explanation for what I had just done.

'Bad for you. Come on.' I nodded back towards the car and smiled, holding out my hand. The truth was that driving in Spain was stressful enough without having to worry about her burning a hole in one of Brian's seats with her cigarette. She took my hand and we got back in the car, coming up with some ideas as we drove.

'Why don't we go to Marbella?' I suggested. 'The Old

Town is buzzing at night. It's all Spanish; no one would know who you are.' I pointed up towards the Old Town as we drove along the Ricardo Soriano on our way back to her hotel.

'I don't speak Spanish.'

I didn't tell her that she didn't need to speak Spanish because there, just like anywhere else on this stretch of coast, everyone could muster up a fair smattering of English. It suited me for her to be impressed by my mastery of Spanish (well, it seems masterful to someone who can't speak a word). Languages earn you brownie points in any job, right? 'Don't worry about that. What about we go to the beach for a few hours and relax, have a few drinks, then tonight I'll show you round the Old Town.' I kept glancing over to see how she had reacted to my suggestions.

'Good sales pitch. I only wanted you for the afternoon!' she scowled, and continued rubbing her forehead with her hand.

'Well, then, I'll stay for the afternoon and you can make your own entertainment tonight.' I shrugged and turned to her with a cheeky grin.

She looked at me out of the corner of her narrowing eyes. Her lips were pressed tightly together and I was so sure that she was going to start screaming, I had to swallow. But then she convulsed, trying to keep in her laughter. In the end she burst. First breakthrough. I'd made her laugh. From here, things should be easier.

'You've gone straight past the hotel,' she said, sitting up and looking back at the hotel disappearing as the road curved with the coastline.

'I know a better beach. Trust me,' I told her. Now I know

that 'better' is all about perception, a matter of opinion, and that in fact all that exist are differences. The beach bar, or *chiringuito*, I was taking her to lacked the pretentiousness of Nikki or Plaza Beach, and maybe the service was not going to be what Carly was used to, but it had character. It stood out like a handmade toy would at Toys R Us, and like that toy it was overlooked and unappreciated by the majority, which made it special. But I was a tad concerned that it might have been too different to Carly's tastes.

We sat on the wooden veranda as the fat Spanish waiter made his way through the obstacle course of tables and chairs, pen and pad in his hand and a smile on his chubby face. Carly was watching a young couple on the beach chasing each other into the sea, but then suddenly she threw me a disapproving look as she heard me order water. 'You don't drink?' She leaned forward and looked me square in the eyes.

'Yeah, I drink. But it's still sunny, and it'd knock me out for tonight. Anyway, I'm driving.' I looked away at the same young couple, who were now kissing, before Carly's intense gaze could make me blush.

We both took in the view and Carly exhaled some of the tension that had evidently been building up over the last few weeks. She said nothing as the waiter placed our drinks down, then she leaned in again and I could feel that same stare burning into me.

'Do you feel comfortable doing what you do sober?' she probed, attempting to analyse me, as many clients had tried before. From the start, I'd decided that, if I had to lie about my life or my background, I would just leave things out or exaggerate about something, rather than creating people or stories to impress my clients.

First, this made it easier to remember the 'white lies' I had told and, second, I didn't want to get into the habit of lying to others all of the time. To be a good liar, you have to convince yourself that the lie is true and, once you start doing that, you start lying to yourself about all sorts of other things as well.

'What? Spending time with beautiful women... it's hard, but you get used to it.'

She kicked me softly under the table and mock-laughed. 'You know what I mean! Don't you need a drink to relax yourself?'

I was getting the impression that drinking was her relaxing mechanism as an actress. What she seemed effectively to be saying was: 'Well, if I need a drink to do what I do, you MUST need a drink!'

'Sometimes. But if I have to drive...' I shrugged and gave a wry smile, able to look at her again now.

'What about tonight? Will you drink tonight, if we go out?'

I began to smile but then her 'if' sank in and my head tilted like a puppy's does where it hears something unfamiliar. 'If? Well, OK, that depends.' I leaned forward and put both my forearms on the table.

'On what?' She copied me, leaning in, our arms meeting in the middle of the table.

I was amused, but unsure as to whether I was making progress or just being mocked. I had to appear confident whatever. Smile and keep eye contact. If it goes wrong, it'll give me something to laugh about in the future, I thought.

'On if you want me to dance or not.'

Her warm breath on my face as she laughed excited me. I could smell the Malibu and coke and my mouth watered as our heads moved closer to each other's, her eyes closing as she whispered, 'Yeah, I wanna dance.'

Our lips met and our tongues stroked one another's gently. Her hand moved to my forearm and our first kiss slowly, begrudgingly, ended. She sighed and looked at her watch, with her other hand still holding my arm.

'So what happens when the time's up? Do you turn into a pumpkin or disappear in a puff of smoke?' She tilted her head down and looked up at me with big wide eyes, Princess Diana style.

'You choose. I'm yours.' Either way I'd won. If she ended our encounter here, I had still been paid to kiss a 'celebrity'. If not, I was going to get paid for doing what I would have been doing anyway – partying in Marbella. But this time with a celebrity in tow.

'I like the sound of that. I should put a stop to it now before it becomes another expensive habit.' She bit her lower lip and looked at her watch again. 'I say let's make the most of the time we have left and then we'll see about tonight.'

We sat for a while in the little beach bar, watching the young couple and hearing their barely audible screams over the crashing waves. Now I knew the questions would come and, as I told her about my life, edited version or not, she reciprocated by sharing her stories with me. We went for a long the shore, shoes in hand, and she told me about her producer boyfriend and what an arsehole he was. In fact, what an arsehole every man was. I could empathise with her to a certain extent as even some of us men get infatuated with a 'player' at some point. The trick is not to kid yourself that you love them or, more importantly, that they could ever love anyone other than themselves. Carly already knew this, of course, but she was another shining example of someone who had all the knowledge and yet failed to use it. No one likes to be told that, though, so I held my tongue.

'You're young, so this probably sounds silly to you. But it gets tougher as you get older,' she informed me.

She was right; I was young. But age is no barrier to pain. I'd bet that a five-year-old feels no less distress at being denied an ice cream as Carly did at not being able to keep her man. It's all relative. As we get older, though, we don't seem to be able to stay in the present; that's why we drag out our painful times, unable to act either because we're stuck in our past or worried about our future. But what did age have to do with it really?

'You're right. I guess I won't know until I get there,' I said, shrugging.

Carly smiled at me and then looked back down at the tide rushing up to meet our sunken feet. She started jumping and screaming and for a moment I thought a body had washed up on the beach just as I had seen on the Spanish news so many times. But, no, it was in fact a jellyfish that had caused her to launch into an impromptu rendition of *River Dance*. We stopped as the sea went back out and the jellyfish was left stranded on the sand, its transparent body casting a shadow of colours as the sun passed through it.

'You ever been stung?' she asked me as we turned and began our walk back.

'By a jellyfish or a girl?' I said, referring to our previous conversation.

'Either.'

'Yeah. It doesn't matter how old you are. It hurts,' I said, and she grabbed my hand, holding it and rubbing the back with her thumb, 'but vinegar helps. Takes the sting right out of it.'

I laughed and she threw my hand away again, pushing me towards the sea.

'I forgot, you're a man. You're incapable of talking about your feelings,' she taunted me.

'Not incapable, just wary. I mean, you don't seem too happy with your life, so it'd be silly of me to go on about how wonderful my life is.'

She nodded in agreement. Fifteen–Love, Deano.

'But I've also got this phobia about tempting fate,' I continued. 'You know? Like, if I talk about how good things are, it'll all go tits-up.'

She laughed at the colloquialism and, realising that I didn't usually talk that way in front of clients, I laughed too.

'I understand. I think we're a lot alike, really. Or, at least, I used to be like you.' She sounded distant as she said it, as if she was replaying a time in her mind when she had said similar things, or had thought like I did.

'So if you were my age again, what'd you do differently?' I

was interested, but more in terms of what insight I could gain for my own life from her regrets. A habit I had picked up from working in bars was to ask older people what they would do if they were my age. Normally, I'd ask the men and the unanimous answer would be 'Don't get married!' with the occasional 'Buy land!' thrown in for good measure. Now I had a woman's perspective – another angle to the same question.

'If you're happy and you know you're not hurting anyone, including yourself,' she turned and pointed at me as she said that, 'then keep doing what you're doing.'

'I asked what *you* would do.'

'I know what you said. And that was my answer. I would do whatever I wanted to do. Whoever loved me would stand by me, whatever I decided.' She sounded distant again.

I felt quite grateful, then, that any betrayals I had experienced were in the distant past, too long ago for me to remember, no matter how painful they were at the time. The friends I had in my life were the good ones, the all-weather, loyal-till-the-end people who I considered as good as family. But I was no star and I was sure that her profession and all of the baggage that came with it would turn out to be the cause of many of her relationship challenges.

I drove her back to the hotel, got out to open her door for her and kissed her gently before she went back into the hotel. She said she would make her own way into Marbella later to save me driving, which I thought was her way of letting me down easily. So, as she walked back into the hotel, I couldn't help feeling sad. I thought it would be the last time I saw her – that she was one more 'one-off' client.

A few hours later, I was walking around the apartment in my boxer shorts, trying to sing 'Always' with an electric toothbrush buzzing in my mouth and toothpaste threatening to dribble out on to my clothes as I ironed them. (Yes, I can iron! Not always very skilfully, but my shirts normally look respectable enough. My never-fail trick is to put them on a hanger as soon as they come out of the washing machine and then just hook them on to the line.) I was gradually improving at multi-tasking – ironing, brushing my teeth, dancing and singing at the same time – but then the phone rang. I grabbed my mobile and ran to the bathroom to spit out the paste, so I could find out the identity of the 'unknown caller'.

'Hello!' I said with cool, minty fresh breath, examining my teeth in the large bathroom mirror as I waited for a reply.

The line went dead. I hated those callers. It had happened a lot since my number appeared in the local newspaper. I imagined they were calls from lonely women, sitting there daring themselves to call me and experience what it would be like, then losing their bottle and hanging up. What they don't think about is that phoning up late at night and then hanging up like that does nothing for an imaginative person's nerves. This particular evening, it didn't bother me too much as I was going to be leaving the apartment in a few minutes. But, on those odd nights when I decided to stay in, a phone call like that would invariably be followed by mysterious noises, which, because of overwhelming curiosity, I would scare myself silly going to investigate. I would keep imagining film titles like *Gigolo Stalker*, and take my pepper spray with me as I moved between rooms. In fact, I almost had a nasty accident with it in the bathroom when I mistook it for my deodorant after one of these searches.

The mystery phone call cut the singing session short and I dressed quickly, slipping on my shoes and leaving my shirt buttons to do in the lift. Once I was out of the building, my apprehensions gradually left me and by the time the phone rang again I was calm.

'Hello? Who's that?' I asked, trying to sound genuinely intrigued, knowing that, if the caller hung up a second time, my third greeting would not be so pleasant as the game was getting boring.

'It's me, Carly. I've 200 euros.'

Cheeky cow. She was negotiating with me. I knew she had bundles of dough; she was just saving it for her other addictions and trying to get me at a bargain price. She wasn't the first, nor would she be the last, and as long as she didn't become a regular and make a habit of doing it I didn't mind. So, I decided I'd do it, but out of principle I would leave her hotel the moment we'd finished having sex. It wasn't tit for tat, trying to make her feel cheap in return for her doing the same to me. It was just a question of me valuing my time more than she was willing to pay.

'OK. But you're buying the drinks, remember. Get the taxi to the pharmacy opposite the cafeteria.'

'And promise me we're not gonna bump into your photographer friend,' she pleaded. 'No photos. No friends.'

The line went dead and I thought to myself, I'm sure she'd be all right with it if they were die-hard fans who wanted her

autograph. But then, after seeing how she had reacted the last time, I thought it would just be safer to turn my phone off and avoid my friends altogether.

I passed car after car, checking my reflection in their windows – the ones that had windows, that is. I lived at the rough end of Marbella, the bit you never see on the travel programmes, next to Las Albarizas. I would say that it was the Spanish quarter, but it would be an insult to the Spanish if I gave the local mutants that label. The graffiti-covered housing development was originally built for the Gypsies but, as well as its intended inhabitants, it housed Marbella's heroin addicts and beggars, and was well known as a trouble spot by the townspeople.

Around the corner from the pharmacy where I was going to meet Carly, there was a square with an English bar, Jimmy Tramps. When I'd first arrived in Marbella, Frank's parents had owned the bar and I had worked there until Wayne found me the job at the restaurant. Now it was run by a nice old man called John, who bore an undeniable resemblance to Roald Dahl's *Big Friendly Giant*. It was a nice, cosy little place where you could easily forget that you were in this millennium if it wasn't for the giant plasma screen on the wall.

I decided to pop in for a beer before 'work', as it was so close by. While I was sitting there, I saw a selection of tabloid newspapers laid out as usual on one of the tables. I wondered what the chances were of opening one of them up and seeing her in there. If there is a picture, I thought, it would be nice to have as a souvenir – something to show the grandkids, while I explain to them how their granddad used to be a gigolo. I decided to delay looking for as long as possible but, just as I was about to give in to curiosity, fate stepped in again.

The phone rang, so I downed my beer and, without answering it, I trotted down the stairs and through the alley to the pharmacy where I'd told her to wait. As I turned the corner, I saw her pacing, with one arm across her chest holding the other arm as she waited for me to answer the phone. She spotted me and started tapping her watch, before crossing her arms in front of her chest.

I clapped my hands and rubbed them together. 'Ready?' In the hope of my enthusiasm rubbing off on her somehow, I probably overdid the jolly chappy routine, but at least I got a grudging smile out of her.

'I'd better be impressed,' she sighed, and latched on to my arm.

Our first stop was a tiny Spanish bar just off of Orange Square, hidden in the maze of alleys that makes up the Old Town. Tonelito, the little barrel, did as much business in four hours as some of the English bars did in eight. The walls were smothered in photos of previous wild nights and promotional posters. We sat on our stools at an oversized wooden barrel, topped with an ashtray and a plastic *Cruzcampo* serviette holder, and I pointed up to the chalk tapas menu hung on the wall.

'I'm not really that hungry,' she told me.

'Well, that's OK, tapas won't fill you up anyway. You don't have to eat it.' I attempted a wink, unsure of whether I had managed it successfully or not, but she laughed anyway so it had served its purpose.

When the two small tortilla sandwiches arrived on a silver tray, Carly reached for hers the second her plate hit the barrel top, taking a bite before the waiter had even collected the empty glasses and left. Her eyes lit up as she chewed and she made the 'OK' sign with her fingers, then she pulled a serviette from the holder and dabbed her mouth.

'So, this might be a weird question for you, seeing as you're an actress. But, who do you admire? Who's your favourite?' I asked.

She took a deep breath and closed her eyes, whispering the name, 'Gary Oldman... mmm.' She still had her eyes closed as she purred.

'I meant for their talent.'

'So did I. But he's got it all. I nearly worked with him once.' She shifted in her chair, sitting up and looking down her nose at me before she broke into a smile.

'And you? Heroes? Or dare I ask?' She was playing with her straw, biting her lower lip.

'Not really. I mean, professional role models are a bit thin on the ground in my line of work, although I did have a mentor of sorts,' I admitted.

'He or she? Please tell me if it was a he you didn't work with him.' She grabbed my arm as she said it, still biting her bottom lip, but this time I sensed some genuine concern about my answer.

'No, nothing like that. But he did give me some pretty

invaluable advice.' I thought back to my first meeting with Andy, the real gigolo, at the casino. 'So what is it about old Gary? What about him turns you on?' I asked, deciding it wouldn't hurt to get her to talk about getting turned on.

Andy had taught me that the more vividly I could get someone to describe whatever turns them on, the more likely they'd feel turned on and associate those feelings with me. I had to pay particular attention to the words she used and to her voice, as they were the keys to turning her on again, even after she'd changed the subject.

The bar was filling with rowdy Spanish football fans and the plasma screen was showing a match. As everyone booed and cheered, we sat in the middle, knees touching, facing each other and not the screen, leaning right into each other's ear to speak so we could be heard.

'He's so versatile; he never looks the same on screen. I could never see myself getting bored with him. He could be anyone. Whenever I've seen him, he looks so rough and ready, but you know he'd scrub up well if he needed to.' She went to add something else as I went to speak into her ear and our heads collided; I came off worse. She put her hands on my thighs, laughing with watery eyes as I leaned back clutching the bony bit above my eye. Each move we made to speak from that point on was exaggerated to warn the other and avoid any more injuries.

As we stepped out into the alley after finishing our drinks, the home team must have scored and the bar roared with excitement.

'They used to cheer when I walked into bars,' Carly sighed,

deep in reminiscences. Then she turned to me and laughed, sliding her hand into my back pocket and squeezing my bum. 'This is fun, but when can we dance?' she said.

'It's early yet. Let's have another drink and then I'll take you to a place I know.'

'What's wrong? Why are you trying to delay it?'

'I'm still not quite drunk enough...' I confessed, and then regretted it, as she burst out laughing.

'You don't need a drink to do what you do, but you can't dance without one?' She looked at me incredulously.

'I could dance – it's not that I *can't* do it. It's just I don't enjoy doing it sober. Too self-conscious. Too aware of everyone watching and... laughing.' Which, of course, was exactly what Carly was doing by this point.

We arrived at a second bar hidden in another alley off Orange Square and she mentioned how impressed she was that I could remember where all of these places were.

'Well, sounds to me like your sudden need for alcohol is going to end up costing me a fortune... but, whatever. I feel like a boogie, so, if you need to get wasted to join me, we'd better get you wasted.' She winked at me and then turned away. 'Where's that barman?'

Within half an hour, we had drunk shots of sambuca, Jägermeister, tequila, B-52s – you name it. And then, when the clock struck midnight and the rhythm was working its way up through my feet, I decided I was ready to go to the other bar. 'OK, there should be people there now, let's go and dance!' I said.

'Hold on,' she said, paying the barman for one last round.

'There you go!' She passed me a pint and a shot, while she had a half of beer and a shot for herself.

'That's not fair!'

'You're bigger than me. Anyway, let's make it interesting.' She tilted her head and looked me up and down.

'Go on,' I said.

'If I beat you, I get you for the whole evening for free.'

I'd do it for free anyway at this point, I thought. It was what's called a win–win situation. 'And, *when* I beat you, what do I get?'

'Anything you want.'

I really couldn't lose. Either way, I thought, tonight is going to have a great ending.

After one sip each, our depth charges were dropped into our glasses and, after a three count, we raced to finish our foaming cocktails. Drinking games have never been my strong suit, but I was up for the challenge and kept on drinking as fast as I could, and it was my glass that touched the bar first, the shot glass clinking inside the pint. Full of gas, my eyes watering, I looked at Carly, who was running her finger around her still half-full glass. She took another delicate sip, pinkie extended, and then put the glass on the bar and dragged me out. 'OK, you win. Let's dance.'

The bar was wall-to-wall with sweaty, semi-naked bodies, moving to the rhythm that was vibrating through my body from the huge speaker. In my drunken state, the girls all looked like supermodels and the steroid-fuelled men all looked like they wanted to fight. The different perfumes and smoke disguised the smell of some of the sweatier male patrons – unless they were pressed right up against me when a hold-my-breath technique was my only option.

Carly was lapping up the attention she was getting as she strutted through the club to the bar, while I was gradually being overcome by the music. It was so loud and as we passed one of the giant speakers against the wall the sound waves of the bass passed straight through my body, encouraging me to dance.

Looking back, I was clearly wasted at this point. I know this by the way I remember believing that I was John Travolta and Patrick Swayze all rolled into one. As Carly was trying to order more drinks, I had my hands on her hips and we were both making figure eights, going lower and lower. At one point, my legs actually gave way and had it not been for the passing Neanderthal behind me I would have ended up on my arse. Instead, I just bounced off him, turned around and smiled in response to his snarl, before going back to my dirty dancing.

'Keep a hold of these. I've gotta use the loo!' She handed me the drinks and then squeezed through the crowded dance area to the toilets. About a minute after she had left, with my brain cells rapidly depleting and the little head I keep in my trousers taking over any thinking that needed to be done, I forgot all about Carly and started talking to the passing beauties. I was doing quite well with a little long-haired Argentinean girl, when she asked me if I had a friend. I replied no, remembering at least that I hadn't arrived with any of my mates. But it wasn't until she asked me who the Malibu and coke belonged to that I remembered Carly. I made my apologies and went to look over at the toilets to make sure she was all right.

I really didn't fancy my chances of making it through the dance floor and still having any drink left in the glass by the end of it, so I stood on tiptoe and tried to see over the crowd. Through bobbing silhouettes, I could see Carly standing outside the toilet trying to talk to some pony-tailed Spanish bloke. Oi, I thought, you've promised me anything I want tonight, which at no point included your Antonio Banderas wannabe. They nodded to each other and then she started following him through the club until she reached me.

'Look, I'm gonna go with this guy for a minute,' she said, as she saw me frowning.

'Hold on, we only just got here. I thought you wanted to dance?' My hands were occupied with glasses and Carly was being pulled as if by some magnetic force, away from me and towards this bloke.

'I'll be back in a while. You're not jealous, are you?'

No, I thought, but I don't want sloppy seconds. Charming, I know, especially from someone who just minutes before had forgotten she even existed. I took a swig of my beer and put the drinks on the bar. Andy had warned me always to stay in control – but then getting me to lose control had been Carly's main objective up until that point. That was fine, as I wanted her to have a good time, but now I realised it was time to start pulling myself together. It could take only a split second for things to go from heady to heavy and one of us needed to know what they were doing.

'Come on then. I'm not letting you go alone. I'm the last

English-speaking person you've been seen with. If anything happens to you, I'm fucked,' I said, pointing to my own chest.

'Ahh, so protective.'

I understood that Carly was just a fun-loving lady but, judging by tonight's behaviour, it was easy to imagine the sorts of predicaments she must have found herself in over the years. So driven by her emotions and blind to the dangers, no wonder she's a state, I thought, as I reluctantly followed the pair.

When we reached Puerto Deportivo, I warned Carly that the place was crawling with people who might a) recognise her, or b) mug her if she were down there alone.

'Well, I'm not alone. We won't be long. Then we can go back to the hotel.' She smiled reassuringly and yet I was anything but comfortable about being there with her, knowing roughly what she was up to with her new dealer friend.

So Mr Ponytail opened the door to the bar and let us both in, closing it behind him. It was dark, quiet and not as busy as the other bar. The clientele were all dressed in baggy or ripped clothes, with funky hair or dreadlocks, all grungers and Rastafarians. And there I was in my Versace shirt and jeans and my Gucci shoes. Stick out much?

Carly disappeared out the back with the bloke so I sat at the bar and ordered a beer. It was then that I noticed the band setting up in the corner and saw why the bar looked so empty. Everyone was sitting at the far end on sofas, ready for the performance. Two guys got up and introduced themselves and the group. Flip Top Box? I thought. What sort of name is that? I was so drunk I may have even shouted words to that effect, but everyone continued to smile and to listen. The long-haired guitarist strummed his acoustic guitar and the shaven-headed singer took to the microphone. Forgetting about Carly was no surprise, but time actually seemed to stand still as those boys played. I got goose bumps and the hairs on my arms stood on end. I closed my eyes to appreciate the music more; a habit Jeana had left me with. But, just as I was really getting into it, I felt my arm being pulled.

'Come on, I wanna go home.'

'Just wait till the end of this song,' I pleaded.

'I'm horny. I wanna fuck... are you coming or not?' Her hands were on her hips and, where her mouth was open, I could see her tongue running across her upper teeth. Cocaine. It's an instant aphrodisiac for some people.

Undeterred by the knowledge that my sudden animal magnetism was more to do with a wrap of white powder than any particular magnetism, I stood up and followed her out without a protest. My appreciation of the simple pleasures, like food and music, may have increased since meeting Jeana, but sex still ranked number one for me.

Throughout the taxi ride home, I fluctuated between feeling incredibly aroused and feeling terrible for the taxi driver. Here he was doing the nightshift, and there we were on the back seat getting down and dirty. Carly's tongue was deep in my mouth and she had pulled out my dick and started to masturbate me. I put my hand up her skirt and reciprocated, pulling her knickers to the side and inserting two fingers, while massaging her clitoris with my thumb. I had to readjust myself as I got out of the taxi, pushing my rock-hard todger back into my trousers, and hoping my belt would keep it flat to my waist as we walked through reception.

The moment the hotel-room door closed, she pushed me up against the wall and dropped to her knees, tearing at my belt and jeans like a savage. As she took me deeper into her mouth each time, I was in ecstasy, and hoped she'd continue till the end. I knew this was going to be one of those occasions where Viagra or my visualisation skills were not going to be necessary. She paused and used her hand while the other took a condom from my pocket. She bit at the wrapper and spat out the foil while still keeping me hard. She put the condom between her lips and then with her teeth she rolled it on as far as she could before choking and having to use her fingers. I wished she had used one of the flavoured condoms instead of the extra-lubricated one as bitter experience had taught me that at some point we would both end up sampling that awful taste.

She got up and leaned over the hotel-room desk, opening her eyes occasionally to look in the mirror as I took her from behind. My hands on her hips, going harder and faster, louder and louder. The television looked as if it was going to fall off the desk at any moment, but neither of us cared. She took my hand from her hip and pulled it towards her mouth. While my chest was to her back, my other hand reaching round to grab her breast, she sucked and licked my little finger, covering it in saliva. Then she pushed my hand round to her arse and said, 'Gently.'

So, with my little finger, I gently probed until my whole

finger was in and I could feel my dick moving in and out through the thin wall. Eventually, I was using my thumb to stimulate her back door as I took her from behind. Her moans, a mixture of pain and pleasure, broke into a relieved sigh as I came and held on to her. Finally, as I removed my thumb, she gasped.

Despite my earlier resolution to leave as soon as my work was done, I felt too comfortable once I was in the hotel bed and too tired from drinking and shagging to make my way home. She was cuddling up behind me and playing with my hair; something that always relaxes me and makes me forget everything else. It's my nirvana, that place where I'm most relaxed but most alert, having my head massaged. And then she stopped, I felt her kiss my back and, shortly after, darkness.

The sound of snivelling and high-pitched whining woke me from my drunken slumber. I hate seeing people cry – it affects me more than blood or sick or anything. I just want to make them stop, whether that's by making them laugh or by showing them a little tough love. Crying doesn't solve anything and, although I admit to shedding enough tears of my own, simply taking a pen and writing about what I'm feeling can usually make me feel better.

Luckily, Carly was out on the balcony, so, by sandwiching my head between two pillows, I could more or less muffle the sound of her sniffles. I tried to sleep, but now it wasn't the noise that was the problem. It was the thought that she was out there, upset, while I was all comfy in bed, not a care in the world. As I sat up to go out and see her, she came in and walked straight past me to the bathroom. We were both silent and she wouldn't look at me. She was still snivelling in the bathroom, then there were two longer sniffs and suddenly I felt less sympathetic again. Whatever your troubles, the solution's rarely to be found up your nose. But then, not everyone can cope with facing his or her problems. For many, it's easier to escape by whatever means. I shouldn't judge, I told myself. When she came back to bed, I turned off the light and cuddled up to her.

'You OK?' I asked, kissing her shoulder and rubbing her arm as she lay on her side.

'He's with someone else! He doesn't want to see me-ee-ee...' and she burst into tears again.

Once more, her distress made her seem more familiar to me – obviously, her screen character must have spent a lot of time embroiled in emotional traumas. What else could I do, but hold her and say, 'It's gonna be all right, you'll see. Don't worry.' So, I fought the urge to fall asleep until her sniffs had stopped and her breathing was steady and shallow. Then, I lowered my head gently back on to the pillow and slowly gave in to my fatigue.

It's a horrible feeling, I thought, unrequited love. Better not to love anyone and expect not to be loved in return, like Andy. But then life starts to feel a bit like eating when you've got a cold, or when you don't stop to enjoy the food. Flavourless. Something I had only really started to appreciate recently.

In the morning, Carly snuggled up to me and proclaimed that the previous night's tears were just down to the coke. She was better now. Things were back in perspective. We made love one last time before I drove her to the airport. Watching her walk into Departures, head up, sunnies on, I felt privileged to have met her and spent time with her. Not because she was a star, but because she was so human, no matter how much she tried to hide it. She's an actress and only the strongest in that profession don't get confused about who they really are. What can you expect if you spend your life being someone else? And anyone who doesn't know who they really are can't really love themselves. And if they don't love themselves, how can they know or love anyone else? I understood precisely. I too spent my life being someone I wasn't. Carly was a glimpse at my future.

Before I drove off, she kissed me passionately and studied my face. 'You've got true eyes,' she told me. 'If you weren't who you are, I'd believe everything you said.'

So now my eyes were either honest or manipulative, depending on which way I wanted to look at it.

But to me, they were just blue.

CHAPTER SEVEN

Veronica

'For some clients, you'll just be another fashion accessory. Make them look good, or they'll drop you like yesterday's trend.' ANDY

'So, you just have to pretend you're my boyfriend. We'll stick to the same story until my parents leave me alone and that's it,' said Veronica, puffing on her joint anxiously, as if the dinner her parents had arranged were that same day. She threw her long straight hair back and looked to the heavens, shaking her head as she exhaled a cloud of smoke.

'You know how much I charge?' I asked.

She had found out about me through a friend of a friend, whom I knew for a fact had told her my price. Judging by the red Mini she had pulled up in and her upper-class British accent, money was not going to be an issue. And, from what my friend had told me, this girl would not be requiring my full range of services, anyway.

'Obviously, I'd normally ask a male friend. But most of

the men I know are gay and the others are just pigs, so...' she extended her bracelet-covered arm towards me, '...you are my last option.' She smiled briefly and, as she searched through her bag for her purse, I examined her more closely.

She could have been Spanish with her olive skin and long dark hair. Her face was pretty with delicate features, except for a slight underbite. Her body was like a swimmer's – firm and toned, and with shoulders a bit bigger than a girl should have in my opinion. Of course, a part of me admitted that I might just have been jealous of girls with big shoulders – or facial hair for that matter – due to the fact that I possessed neither and wanted both. The fact that she was a lesbian also went in her favour, maybe because I knew I couldn't have her. But more likely because the thought of her with another girl would be enough to keep any man awake at night.

'Money's no problem. Keeping the folks happy is my priority here. They're already... well, you'll see.' Veronica shook her head as she handed me 200 euros for the following night's job. Another princess whose diamond shoes are too tight, I thought.

As usual, when I find myself judging someone, I try to look at the situation from another angle. I thought, if I could see past her man-hating nature, which was an instant block to us forming any sort of relationship, working or otherwise, it would help the job go a bit smoother. I decided that Veronica was just a devoted daughter. She didn't want to make her parents unhappy by revealing that she was a lesbian and so she had hired me. If you can find some common ground with someone, or something to like about him or her, it makes it easier to laugh off any shit he or she throws at you. We both loved our parents – that was clear. She hid who she really was for the same reasons I did. For the fear of hurting them. Looking back, I realise that it would have been a hell of a lot easier for me to change my occupation to please my parents than for Veronica to change her sexuality to please hers.

During our first meeting the previous afternoon in Marbella's Puerto Deportivo, Veronica had laid down some ground rules. For instance, I was to be affectionate, but not overly so and under no circumstances was kissing necessary. Other rules included not getting chummy with her father and doing my best not to appear working class. I knew what I was and I knew that people like Veronica and possibly her parents would look down on me. But here I was being given the green light to lie through my teeth and be someone else. Someone Veronica's parents would approve of, someone to ease their concerns for a little while longer while Veronica built up the courage to tell them the truth.

As usual, Veronica had a joint on the go when she picked me up and took me to her parents' villa. She inspected me as I squeezed into the shopping bag-filled mini, squinting and then shrugging as she blew the smoke away. I was happy to have passed her first test, but en route there followed a pop quiz on our 'relationship', which was hard to take seriously as I became increasingly stoned from the fumes in the car. The new smell of the car was fighting a losing battle against her friend's homegrown wacky baccy.

'Where did we meet?' she asked, checking her rear-view mirror.

'Gay bar? You decided you couldn't live without...' I joked, finding myself ever so funny under the effects of the weed.

'Try again!' she sighed, smoke leaving her nostrils like some angry dragon, quickly growing impatient with me.

I cleared my throat and decided to save the jokes for the drive home. 'Art exhibition, Malaga. You were with your uni friends; I was there to give my artist friend some support.'

She nodded enthusiastically. Then her phone rang and she passed me her joint so she could grab her mobile from her bag. Her driving was beginning to worry me as she paid less and less attention to the road. I was on the point of suggesting that I took over when we stopped at the traffic lights. So there's Veronica chatting to her friend on the phone about some party and here's me, holding a sweet-smelling joint and drooling at the thought of taking a puff, when what should pull up to our right but a police jeep. My heart stopped as the Ray Ban-wearing copper reached out and tapped on the passenger window.

I turned to Veronica and her mouth fell open as she saw the white and blue jeep beside us. My right hand clenched around the joint, causing me to tense as it extinguished in the palm of my hand. Nothing could prevent that last puff of smoke from escaping from my fist and as I wound down the window I was sure that my Angel aftershave would be the last scent he would detect.

As the policeman reached into the car, I saw my life flash before my eyes. So is this how it would end up? Festering in some Spanish prison cell for something I didn't even do? It took me a while to register that I wasn't the object of the copper's vexation. It was Veronica. He was waving his finger at her and shouting. Finally, it clicked. She was being told off for using the phone while driving.

'*Perdon, lo siento*,' she hollered back as the policeman drove off at seeing the green light. My heart was pounding hard enough to distract me from the burn on my palm until I brushed off the tobacco and Rizla and saw the red mark. I looked over in astonishment as she drove off – phone once again glued to her ear.

By the time we arrived at the villa's security gates, my head had cleared and I was ready to play the part of Veronica's boyfriend. As I climbed out of the Mini, I could feel the pebble floor through the worn leather soles of my Hermes shoes. There was an oval pond in the centre of the forecourt, filled with lily pads and small spotted carp. Small fir trees encircled the grounds, hiding the fences protecting the property from the organised Eastern European gangs operating in the area. Veronica had asked me not to mention anything of a criminal nature. Not that she thought that I was that way inclined, but because her mother had been traumatised by their neighbour's burglary a few weeks earlier. Apparently, a gang had cut all the wires to their security system, shot the guard dogs with tranquilliser darts and then sprayed the owners with some paralysing gas. They had lain awake but unable to move for an hour while the robbers cleared out the whole villa.

As we approached the front door, it was opened by the Bolivian housemaid, Ana. Despite Ana's warm welcome, which I reciprocated with pleasure, Veronica was cold and stalked straight past her in search of her parents. They spoke in Spanish. Once again, Ana replied politely and warmly to Veronica's abrupt questioning about her parents' whereabouts.

'Would you like something for drink?'

I smiled at Ana and was about to reply when Veronica called to me.

'Come on. We'll wait in the lounge.'

She continued to ignore the maid and I excused myself with a shrug. Ana chortled and I realised that I was probably exactly how she imagined all Englishmen to be – lacking the passion and backbone to stand up to my bullying female companion. Too gentlemanly for my own good. Of course, had this not been a job, I would have spoken to Veronica about what I perceived to be plain bad manners. But this was work and I was in no position to tell Veronica anything, or my chances of a repeat performance as her boyfriend would be minimal.

I perched myself on one of the living-room sofas as Veronica snooped around. She opened drawers and cabinet doors, pulling out books to look behind them and then replacing them as she had found them.

'What are you doing?' I asked, believing that she was looking for a secret stash of money her parents may have hidden.

'Looking for Mummy's pills.'

Highly confused and slightly unconvinced as to why she would be searching in such unusual places, I raised an eyebrow and waited for a proper explanation. None was forthcoming.

It was none of my business and I knew it, but I also knew that she wasn't about to throw me out before dinner, so I chanced it and spoke my mind. 'Isn't all the puff you smoke enough? If she's been prescribed pills, you should leave them for her.'

'They weren't prescribed, and I wouldn't take them if you paid me. I just want to make sure *she* doesn't.'

Once again, she had surprised me. Her obvious affection for her mother seemed so at odds with the cold way she talked about everyone else, and I was looking forward to seeing how she acted around her.

As Veronica's father entered the room, I stood up instinctively and extended my hand. He looked incredibly smart with his tank top over his shirt and beige chinos, but I lost all respect for his sense of style when I saw the white socks pocking through his Timberland sandals. He smiled and I could see that it was an effort for him to be spending time away from whatever he had been doing, even if it was to meet his darling daughter's boyfriend.

'Daddy, this is Dean. Where's Mummy?' With the same coldness she extended to everyone else, Veronica walked straight past her father who was courteously shaking my hand, and called out for her mother, like a little girl lost. I understood now that her father's opinion was of no importance here. It was solely her mother I was here to impress.

'Call me Rupert,' said Daddy, forcing a smile. Then he turned to Veronica. 'Your mother is pottering about upstairs somewhere. Drink?' As he offered, he sat down and looked over to Ana, who had appeared at the door.

I had expected to see the same bad manners and indifference towards the maid, so I chose not to pay too much attention. Veronica, on the other hand, was staring fiercely at her father as he asked for the drinks and waffled on about some of the other household duties. Suddenly intrigued, I looked back at Veronica's father and then at Ana the maid. Her warm, friendly smile was now a cheeky grin and he had replaced his holier-than-thou air with a flirtatious smile and bedroom eyes. Veronica, however, was shaking her head and marching to the other end of the room, as far as she could get from her father and the woman it was now clear was his lover.

'I know it's early for dinner,' Rupert was saying, 'but I'm leaving for London early tomorrow morning. We thought it wiser to eat now. I'm sure Veronica has explained...'

I glanced towards her, but she was still facing the window, reluctant to turn around until Ana had served the drinks and left.

'I don't recall her mentioning it, Rupert.' I was on my own for the time being, so I didn't think I could do much damage by attempting to bond with her father. I knew he had several businesses and that he had to go back to London occasionally for meetings with investors and the people in charge. Rupert's talent, according to Veronica, was the ability to convince people that his point of view was right. This was how he had kept important investors during even the worst business ventures. This was also one of the reasons his daughter spent as little time at home as possible. Another reason could of course have been her secret sexuality. But it was the third reason that interested me most. In just the short time I'd been here, I'd already observed that inherent in everything Rupert said to Veronica was a subtle but nevertheless noticeable message: 'You should have been a boy.'

As Rupert was explaining to me about a crisis with one of his latest enterprises, which had necessitated this trip to London, Veronica's mother appeared. The same height as Veronica, but with much lighter skin and shoulder-length hair, she looked young and yet strangely lethargic. I stood again, but not half as quickly as Veronica, who seemed to skip up to her mother. Her movements were softer and fluid like a dancer and the hug warm and loving. The older woman welcomed her daughter with open arms but, abruptly, Veronica broke away.

'Couldn't you wait for dinner, Mummy?' she snapped in a disappointed tone, pulling back from her mother to look her in the eyes.

Her mother sighed and then straightened her dress, readjusting the huge seashell that hung from her neck. I felt like a fly on the wall. As if I shouldn't have been there. These were scenes that Veronica herself had escaped from and revisited as infrequently as possible. She had not brought me there to see that. I was there to be her boyfriend.

'It's just wine, pumpkin,' her mother smiled and then looked over to where I stood. She looked back at her daughter with raised eyebrows and they both smiled.

'This is Dean.'

Veronica's mother tried to glide towards me, but the wine had made her a little unsteady.

'*Soy* Sophie,' she said, as she held out her hand, which made me unsure where to kiss her until she offered me her cheek.

I took her hand gently and gave her a kiss on both cheeks; all that was missing was a bow.

'Do you speak Spanish? I'm trying. I've a wonderful tutor; I just wish I understood him!'

Veronica rolled her eyes and laughed with her mother.

Sophie hooked one arm around Veronica and one around me and led us to the kitchen, as if we were about to plot something against Rupert. I found myself stooping to be on the same level as the girls, met by Sophie's warm Rioja-scented breath. The kitchen led through to a grand dining room, lit by several chandeliers. The large dining-room table had been set for four people and Sophie guided us both to our seats.

'I suppose we should wait for your father. I hope you're hungry, Dean.'

Ana reappeared carrying in each hand a serving dish containing various types of meat and vegetables. She made several trips to the kitchen, each time returning with more food and pouring more wine for Sophie's bottomless glass. Giggling could be heard from the kitchen on one of her many trips, and then finally Rupert appeared and joined us at the dinner table.

'Oh, don't wait for me. Eat it while it's hot!' As usual, he was distracted from the food, his family and his guest by his maid-cum-mistress. He drank and ate sparingly as he questioned me about my background.

I lied, fluently and without remorse. This was what I was being paid to do. The whole thing was a lie and I had already been paid so it no longer mattered if I got found out. They all seemed so lost in their own little worlds that I fancied my chances of pulling off this con.

'Web design, hey? Too old for computers now. Scare me senseless. Much prefer pen and paper, they won't crash on you.'

That was a relief. Now I could really go to town. I knew nearly as little about computers as I did about football, but, now I knew Rupert was a technophobe, I was confident I could blag it. I knew about marketing and advertising – combine the three and I had a convincing career. Rupert seemed impressed, briefly. Then his attentions were drawn once again to the maid, who refused to let a glass stay empty and who had already used over a bottle on Sophie alone.

As far as I was concerned, Veronica had achieved what she set out to do. Her father seemed satisfied, although she could have brought Vinnie Jones home with her and I doubt he would really have noticed. Her mother, although in a world of her own for the most part, sighed wistfully and kept repeating, 'I'm so happy. You look so good together.'

Throughout the evening, I pretended to be the perfect boyfriend and, despite knowing that Veronica wasn't interested, I couldn't help but feel attracted to her. She was so much softer in front of her mother and – despite the fact that I knew she was faking it – she'd played the part of the loving girlfriend as best she could and I felt almost close to her. I entertained a fleeting fantasy of kissing her at the end of the night, but I was brought back to reality when she received a call from one of her girlfriends and had to leave the room.

'She's very special, my Veronica,' commented her mother.

I smiled and nodded, feeling a parental warning coming.

'Be patient with her. She'll thaw out.'

Thaw out? How could these people be so blind? Sophie had the excuse that she was blind drunk, I suppose, and Rupert was blinded by lust. But it made me wonder if one more bombshell like Veronica coming out as gay was really going to make a difference. Admittedly, Veronica herself obviously thought so, or I wouldn't have been there in the first place.

After a drawn-out absence, Veronica marched back into the room clenching her mobile. She avoided making eye contact with any of us and then just signalled to me that we were going.

'Is everything all right, dear?' Sophie was obviously concerned but her voice sounded tired and whiny.

Veronica just nodded and gave her mother one last hug as I stood up to join her. Her father came back into the room seemingly by mistake, as he was startled when he saw us all there.

'Do you need any money?' he asked, almost apologetically, and Veronica shook her head. He went to hug her, but she kissed him on each cheek and then gently pushed him away.

'I'll be away for the week, remember?' he warned her, but she had already grabbed my arm and we were walking out of the villa, waving goodbye.

Pebbles flew in all directions as we made our way to the

car. I looked back at the front door, where Sophie stood to wave us goodbye. There was a tense silence in the car and I wasn't entirely sure why. Had she received some bad news during the phone call? Was she embarrassed that someone had met her family? I didn't know and she didn't seem to want to talk, but I was a bit tipsy from the wine and so I tried to make conversation anyway.

'So, how was I?' My main priority was supposed to be my client's satisfaction so it seemed like an appropriate question.

'You were fine. I think we fooled them.'

I was relieved, but once again I doubted that it would have taken a genius to deceive her parents. 'Your parents are interesting.'

I felt her gaze burn into the side of my head and I turned to her with as innocent a look as possible. We both burst out laughing, and for a moment I thought that we were going to get on and was even looking forward to our next job together. But then she went back to her cool self and reached over to the glove box for another pre-rolled joint.

She dropped me off at the taxi rank beside Cafeteria Marbella, yelling to me as I got out, 'I'll call you in a few weeks.'

'Give me some warning. I might not be free.'

'You'll be free. I've got money. You're a whore.' And with that she drove away, smug in the knowledge that she could pick me up whenever she needed me.

But by this stage of the game I was no longer doing the escorting purely for the money. I was single and I had a fair bit of cash stashed away. It was the thrill that kept me answering the phone, the chance to meet interesting new people and the thought that there were few limits to what might happen between us. I was hooked on the job, just as Andy had said I would be. And loving every minute of it.

My days off were often spent at the beach, topping up my tan and watching the near-naked female bodies. You'd think I'd get enough of that at work, but it's a drive, an appetite, just like hunger or thirst. You can quench it for a while, but it will always come back, you'll always need more. The more clients I saw, the more my confidence and bank balance grew and it made me relax. I could take it or leave it. It's amazing how much more attractive you become when you lose that desperation and neediness. Jobs poured in, but I just diverted the clients to other escorts when I didn't feel like it and that seemed to just increase my popularity.

Nearly a month had passed since the dinner at Veronica's parents' house, and I was surprised to receive her call, especially as she sounded so urgent.

'Please, I need you here in Malaga.'

'Just get one of your friends to pose as your boyfriend.'

'I can't, I've already told them that we're still together. I wasn't thinking. You've been such a convenient alibi for the last month.'

'Well, tell them I'm working.'

'As far as they're concerned, you've been working for the last month – seeing clients, rushing to meet deadlines – they're going to suspect something soon.'

I didn't actually have anything planned and I was sure that the job was going to be straightforward, but something else was niggling at me. Her last words to me, 'You'll be free... You're a whore,' had stung more than I liked to admit. She clearly thought that there were no depths to which I wouldn't willingly stoop to earn money, and that rankled.

'Well?' She sounded genuinely worried, and I knew I'd probably end up taking the job. But it bothered me that I was just living up to her low opinion of me. She thought she just had to snap her fingers, and the clasp on her purse, and I'd come running – and here I was, doing just that.

'Say you're sorry for the "whore" thing,' I sulked.

I could hear her sighing and trying to compose herself, and then she said through gritted teeth, 'I'm sorry I called you a whore. Now, will you please come to Malaga?'

'Well...'

'Deano!'

'OK, I'm on my way. Give me a couple of hours.'

'But they're going to be here... OK, OK. I'll see you then.'

I ran back from the beach and quickly showered and changed. I wanted to look my best – but not just for Veronica's parents. This time we were going to be at a student housewarming party and I had high hopes for the night. I'd missed out on student social life while I was at uni because of being with Chloe, so I was looking forward to this chance to make up for my abstinence. That was of course if Veronica didn't throw me out ten minutes after her parents left. My only concern was that one of her friends would grass us up as not a 'real' couple or that Veronica would crumble under the pressure of carrying on the pretence.

I arrived in Malaga town centre earlier than I'd expected,

but spent another half an hour looking for somewhere to park. I'm not a big fan of big cities. To me, they're all alike. They just remind me of London.

I had the address, but Veronica had not given me any directions, so all I knew was that the apartment was close to the university. I went into the first shop I could find where two old men were chatting across the counter. The owner gave me a look that said, 'What do you want?', so I handed him the address and asked if he knew where it was. The two men proceeded to argue whether it was the fourth or fifth street along the same road. I thanked them and walked off with the address, confident I could find my way from there.

When I arrived at the apartment, I was disappointed at how grown-up the party was. There were no orgies or food fights, like I'd always imagined I was missing out on at uni. There wasn't even any loud music, or beer, from what I could see. Everyone was dressed smartly and appeared impeccably well bred. All these foreign toffs – and there was I, waiting for someone to ask me which part of London I came from so I could tell them, 'No, actually, I'm an Essex boy.'

Some of the other boys there were a little too friendly, but only with suggestive glances and comments, nothing physical.

Veronica was straight-faced as she walked up to me at the door. 'They're upstairs on the terrace. Come on.' She dragged me through the people and up the stairs to the terrace.

Rupert and Sophie looked strange together this time. Sophie seemed more in control and Rupert had lost some of that confidence he had shown in his own home. He looked a bit like a child hiding behind his mother on the first day of school. I looked around for Veronica, but she had disappeared.

'Dean, finally!' Rupert smiled and seemed surprisingly glad to see me. He shook my hand vigorously as he said, 'We keep missing you. How are things?'

'Nightmares at work, Rupert. You know how it is. I do apologise. I've hardly seen Veronica, so please don't feel I've been avoiding you both!'

We both chortled politely and I went to kiss Sophie. It seemed strange that, after only one brief meeting, I had been accepted so readily. But, in hindsight, being the first boy Veronica had brought home, I suppose they were keen to keep me around and make me feel welcome.

'Nonsense, Dean, we're not offended. We'd just like to see more of you. Get to know you a bit better.'

I nodded in agreement and was relieved when Veronica reappeared, holding a frosty glass of beer. My mouth watered as she extended the beer to me. I could almost taste it, but then Rupert's hand reached out and grabbed the glass and he took a sip. In her other hand, Veronica had a glass of water which had my name on it. I didn't hide the fact that I was put out.

'Well, you're driving – you can't drink.'

'Oh, poor Dean. Surely one won't hurt, dear.'

'Aren't you staying, Dean? Too much work, I suppose?'

'What sort of a boyfriend are you,' Sophie asked, in what she intended to be a jokey tone, 'letting her spend her first night here alone?'

Her knowing smile told me the game was up. We had been

rumbled. Someone at the party had let on about Veronica, even if they had no idea who I really was yet. Veronica stared at her mother and I could tell the remark had shocked her as her grip on my arm loosened momentarily.

'I didn't get the chance to ask, how was London?' I changed the subject quickly, ignoring the comment.

Rupert squinted and then laughed again. 'Gosh, that feels like a lifetime ago now. Splendid. Luckily for us, things were even worse for our competitors, so our investors decided we were the best out of a bad bunch.'

As soon as we started talking about work and Spanish classes, I thought we were out of dangerous waters, until another problem swam up to our little group.

Veronica had told me about one of her friends, Patricia, and she had not exaggerated. She did seem like the sort of girl you could have a good time with, but you wouldn't want to take home to meet your mum. Darker than Veronica, she was Spanish by birth but Colombian by heritage. She and Veronica had an on–off romance, which normally had plenty of 'off' periods due to Patricia's indifference about whom she slept with. Boys, girls; it didn't matter to her. Tonight, however, it wasn't her sexual appetite that was the problem; it was more her equally insatiable appetite for shit-stirring.

'Dean, folks – this is Patricia.'

Veronica's grip on my arm had tightened again as soon as Patricia kissed her father and then turned to me. 'So you're Veronica's... boyfriend?'

'Yeah, how long has it been now, two months?' I said, turning to Veronica.

'Well, let me introduce you two to some people,' Veronica said, grabbing Patricia's arm as well as mine to lead us both downstairs. She was livid and the charming Patricia did nothing to lighten her mood.

'Boyfriend? Come on! Where's *his* boyfriend?'

'You what?' I protested, my true voice returning as it often did in times of anger or excitement.

Patricia pretended to lose patience. 'Run along,' she drawled at me. 'My girlfriend and I have something to discuss.'

I was really angry and I wasn't sure why. Was it that she had insinuated I was gay? I could handle that. Was it just that here was someone else trying to control me? I took a deep breath and looked at Veronica, whose eyes were beginning to water, and I could sense how worried she was about her parents.

'Not while her parents are here,' I told Patricia. 'Stay away from them and she'll speak to you later.'

Patricia looked as if she had been slapped across the face, then, recovering, she looked at Veronica for confirmation.

'I'll talk to you once they've gone,' Veronica agreed, and Patricia replied by spitting out something in Spanish about taking my side over hers. Veronica simply repeated, 'Once they've gone.'

Patricia appeared deflated by this. She looked me up and down one last time and then stormed off into another room. As I watched her walk away, I felt a twinge of remorse that we had met under these circumstances. She was incredible and I saw exactly what Veronica saw in her, but I wasn't about to compete with my lesbian client for her girlfriend.

'She looks like trouble, that one. Keep your eye on her,' Rupert's voice came from behind us, making us jump.

Veronica went back upstairs to her mother and Rupert and I were left gawping at Veronica's university companions.

'I need a drink,' he sighed, and walked off, probably lusting after his past as much as after any of the intelligent, energetic and supple girls in the room.

I needed more than a drink, but that would have to do while I was working here. The four of us regrouped on the roof and, as expected, ten minutes after Veronica's parents left, I was asked to go as well. Patricia, it seemed, was a girl who always got her way.

Fast-forward a week or so. I still had Brian's Mercedes on hire so, thankfully, I could arrive at the garden party in style. I'd explained to Veronica that I had another client to see later that evening, but she said she needed me only for the afternoon. It was Veronica's birthday and her father was laying on a no-expense-spared barbecue party in the huge garden of their home. Along with the waiters and caterers scattered around the pool, there was a gazebo with a band playing. Rupert came straight over to me with a beer and put his arm around me. I decided that he was far too jolly to be sober and that, if he was in this state, Sophie would probably be worse.

'My nephew's here somewhere. He's a computer whiz like you. I'll have to find him,' he said jovially.

Damn. After two successful performances as Veronica's boyfriend, was I about to be outed by my lack of computer expertise?

'Oh dear. He's talking to that ghastly girl from the house-warming party.'

I looked around and then I saw her. The nephew was smiling and looking at the ground as Patricia whispered in his ear and looked towards me with a crafty grin. She was causing trouble. Probably asking him to quiz me on my job in front of Rupert, knowing it would blow my cover. She whispered some more and he continued to laugh. Then they both looked over at me and then at each other. Shit, I thought, here it comes.

'Here he comes now,' Rupert said happily. 'Ollie, over here!'

Oliver, or Ollie as everyone called him, was not just a computer boffin. He was built like a brick shithouse and, I later learned, had had trials for professional rugby teams. Now I was going to look doubly stupid. He had more brains, more brawn and, if Veronica had been my girlfriend and not my lesbian client, I would have feared losing her to him. But they were cousins by marriage and for some reason Veronica hated him. Well, of course she would; he screamed 'male' and 'masculinity'. He looked like a cross between Desperate Dan and a very well-built boy-band member.

'Ollie, this is Dean, Veronica's boyfriend. He's into computers as well.'

I was quite chuffed with the pride in his voice as Rupert made the introductions.

Oliver reached for my hand and I could feel the bones in my hands crossing over each other like tectonic plates as he shook it. There was no earthquake, just a wince and grit of my teeth. He had a permanent smile, which didn't seem to fit his Action Man look. I could see he was a little too interested in what I had to say and that probably meant he was waiting for me to slip up.

'Well, I'll leave you two to chat then,' said Rupert, as he hurried after the maid, Ana, who was disappearing inside.

Now all I had to do was steer the conversation away from computers and I could continue my role undiscovered. Ollie's vice of a hand landed on my shoulder and he leaned in towards me. I could guess what was coming. A warning growl to leave his cousin and her money alone, and let her deal with her problems another way.

'Veronica's friend says you know Torremolinos well?'

Dumbstruck, I turned to see him smiling, waiting for some sort of reply from me. In this part of the world, Torremolinos is famous as a gay hot spot. But surely he couldn't mean...

'Veronica would never have to know,' he confided.

I laughed and looked at him, expecting him to break into a smile as well and for the whole thing to be a joke. But his expression remained deadly serious.

'Excuse me,' I made my excuses and bolted for the toilet, passing a near-hysterical Patricia on the way. I knew she'd had something to do with that little encounter, but it wasn't until Veronica joined her that I had the proof. Veronica was drunk and so touchy-feely with Patricia; it was obvious she no longer cared what her mother thought.

'Is Ollie not your type, then?'

They both laughed. I felt betrayed. Veronica had been so worried about keeping her sexuality from her mother that I'd agreed to help her out of a misguided sense of sympathy. I'd even offered her other alternatives to hiring me, but it had been her choice to go down this route. Now she didn't seem to care and I felt redundant. Paid to stand there like an idiot, not making any difference either way any more.

In fact, everyone seemed to be having fun and enjoying the party except me. Two giggling, snorting friends of Veronica's occupied the downstairs toilet and I was forced to go upstairs. It was nice to escape the barbecue and listen to it all from a distance. What a release. I just wanted to be back in Marbella now with my friends. The money didn't matter any more, but I had to see it through. That was one thing my father had drummed into me.

'We finish what we start, and we don't let people down,' I remember him saying on several occasions. I had only another hour and then I was due to go to Puerto Banus to meet another client. I had to stick it out.

Cautiously, I opened the toilet door. Outside, waiting for me, was Veronica's mother Sophie. Before I knew what was happening, she'd pushed me back into the bathroom and wrapped her arms around my neck, kissing me drunkenly. I could taste the vodka and wondered for a split second if kissing her would get me arrested should I be breathalysed on the way home.

I pulled away and tried to reason with her. 'What about Veronica?' I whispered.

She laughed and stared at me incredulously. 'If she really is your girlfriend, you have some serious competition by the name of Patricia,' she snorted, before kissing me again.

This time I felt more comfortable kissing her back. I hadn't been having much fun up until that point and, although I knew I was getting paid and my enjoyment wasn't the issue, I thought I'd take advantage of this little bonus.

'And Rupert?'

'He has his fun, I want mine.' And with that, her hands were reaching for my belt.

As she slipped my trousers down, I kissed her neck and cleavage, and with my thumbs I hooked her knickers. Standing there with my trousers round my ankles and my rock-hard dick in her hand, I panicked for a moment that it might have been the second joke of the evening. But she was taking this all too far, too fast for it to be a prank.

Seconds later, I was re-enacting the Sonny Corleone scene from *The Godfather*, with Sophie pinned to the door. Her thighs were wrapped around me, her feet crossed across my lower back. I prayed that one of us would come, or someone would come knocking before my arms and legs gave way. I could feel them burning already and my legs were beginning to shake. I thrust so fast and furiously that at one point I worried the door might fall through and we'd end up on the lying on the floor in the hall. Finally, I climaxed and used the last of my strength to let her down gently. She pecked me on the forehead as I was pulling up my trousers and then she disappeared across to her bedroom.

I locked the door and once again felt the need to phone someone to tell them what had just happened. I looked around and saw that there was no bidet, so I washed myself in the sink after double-checking the door was locked. The last thing I wanted was for someone to barge in and see me with my privates dangling in the sink.

When I arrived back downstairs grinning, Veronica didn't say anything, but I was sure Patricia could smell the sex radiating from me. I ignored them both and worked my way through the crowd into the kitchen to get some juice. Looking across the crowd, I caught a glimpse of Sophie as she made her way to the garden. She winked at me and I turned to see Veronica's shocked face, not believing for a second that we had got away with our little encounter. I could justify it to myself though. She had hired me to keep her mother happy. I knew it wasn't what Veronica had had in mind, but it seemed to have done the trick.

The flaming cake came out and we all stood around singing a mixture of 'Happy Birthday' and '*Cumpleaños Feliz*' to Veronica. There was a chorus of 'For She's a Jolly Good Fellow' followed by Rupert shouting, 'Give the girl a kiss, Dean! It's her birthday, for God's sake!'

There were cheers and applause and lots of worried looks between Veronica, Patricia, Sophie and myself. But then I decided, Sod it. I mean, what was the worst thing she could do, apart from slap me in front of everyone?

Veronica looked petrified as I put my hands on her waist in front of everyone. I had no intention of shoving my tongue down her throat, but I had dreamed of kissing her from the moment we'd met. I planted a soft, lingering kiss on her lips and for the first few seconds she didn't react. Then her fingers clawed into my side and her lips tightened up.

While everyone cheered, except Patricia, I leaned in to whisper to her, 'Your mum knows.'

For the second time that evening, I had managed to shock her. When I left, soon after, I was surprised but pleased to see that Veronica and her mother were hugging. Whatever Sophie had known or suspected before, it seemed that a weight had been lifted from both of them now that the 'secret' was out in the open. I was even happier when I noticed Patricia glaring over at the two of them, looking like she was about to burst a blood vessel. Seeing her discomfort at being relegated to the sidelines after being so used to acting as the main player gave me more job satisfaction than some of the more obvious perks of my profession.

I can't say Veronica and I ever really hit it off, and I never got close to her parents (well, apart from those few moments in the bathroom). We're from different worlds, and there is no real crossover. But, nevertheless, it felt good to have been part of their lives even briefly, and to have helped bring about something positive in their relationship. This place is too small and the world too full of coincidences to say we'll never meet again, but I know that, if and when we do, I won't be getting paid for it, and that means I'll be able to be me.

Now wouldn't *that* be a novelty?

CHAPTER EIGHT

Wendy, Jason and Maggie

*'Women will go to great lengths for romance
and adventure. Men who can deliver both
are valued highest.'* ANDY

Divorce rates are high on the Costa del Sol and happy couples as rare as Spanish-speaking Brits, so Wendy's story was depressingly familiar. Listening to her talk about her situation, as we sat in Orange Square in Marbella's Old Town, reinforced my own fear of commitment and my conviction that escorting was the way to go.

The 23-year-old blonde from Devon was new to Marbella, having arrived only three months before, and in that time she'd tried several jobs. She had sold dodgy shares over the telephone, had her ample boobs felt up while PR-ing in Puerto Banus, and had more than one indecent proposal while working as a waitress. But one of these proposals had appealed to her more than the others, and she had quickly found herself embroiled in a difficult love triangle.

'God, I feel like I'm hiring a hit man or something!' she told me, after outlining what she wanted from me.

She was showing all the signs of being very nervous. The way her hand shook as she drank her coffee, the way she preferred to look at the table rather than look me in the eyes. The give-away came when she put her cigarette in the wrong way round and tried to light the filter. We laughed and she admitted what a 'scatty cow' she was, before taking a deep breath and explaining more.

'It's the kiddies. He can't leave them – they're just starting to settle in.'

I nodded in agreement, but behind my understanding eyes I had already determined that she was either in denial or just so unworldly she really did believe her lover's lies. She looked around, and kept attempting to lower her voice in case someone hiding behind one of the many orange trees heard her and accused her of being a 'home wrecker'; something I imagined was still frowned upon in her hometown.

'We love each other.'

Hearing her say that made me feel sorry for her, but then I reasoned that surely the guy must feel *something* for her. It was his money she was paying with and for 200 euros he could have had a girl just as pretty.

'This was his idea,' she told me.

Well, you don't say!

'It took him ages to convince his wife, but now she's finally agreed to go to the club.'

The club in question was a swingers club. It was located in nearby San Pedro and, even by my ever-falling standards, it sounded a bit sleazy. A dark bar, with a single pole at the end for dancers and a set of stairs that led up to some poorly lit rooms, where couples exchanged partners and had their way with each other. The end rooms were rumoured to have peepholes with cabins behind them, from where voyeurs could watch the wife-swapping couples.

'I need a partner. I can't go in alone. So...' She took a long drag of her cigarette and waited for my reply.

'So, I go with you, we meet them, he takes you away and I sleep with the wife.' I summed up the scenario just to make sure I had understood. It was a good job I had, because she winced and raised her hand.

'That's the other thing. He doesn't want you to sleep with her. Just seduce her, flirt, take her home, but... say you can't perform or something.'

I nodded and fought the urge to smile. This guy had it all worked out. He got his end away without feeling guilty, but was spared the jealousy of thinking of his wife screwing someone else. I was looking forward to meeting the man who had masterminded this whole sexual game. It's a sign of how far my morals had plummeted that I was already glad to be part of this job, just so I could see how it all turned out. It was interesting and sounded like fun, although admittedly I would have rather had Wendy herself as a client.

She paid me the money and told me to pick her up at the Guadalpin Hotel on the Golden Mile. Loverboy had even hired himself and Wendy a hotel for the evening. Genius, I thought.

Music always helped get me in the mood for going out in

general, but for 'work', as I had come to call it, only ballads would do. It had to be Bon Jovi, Aerosmith, Meatloaf and the like, from the moment I stepped into the shower to the final look at my hair before I left the apartment. Usher and Barry White were make-out artists – music to be played during the final stages of seduction or making love – but first I needed that energy, to light the fire behind my eyes.

I would sing along and visualise myself as the hero, the charmer, the knight in shining armour, the bad boy they'll never quite tame – every role I'd ever need to play. Like a fighter visualises every move he may ever need, I needed to practise these roles, or I'd run the risk of losing my clients' interest. I might have been the greatest sex god on the planet, but if there were someone else better at whichever role the client had in mind, I'd end up losing out. I had to believe in myself, that I could give them what they wanted or needed.

'The key is to judge which particular element is missing from their lives. If you can see what's missing, you can become that missing piece, even if what they want is for you to be as passive as possible and let them make all the moves. Play dumb if that's their thing, then they'll want you often, and pay you highly.' Andy's advice played through my head like a mantra each time I did up my shirt in the mirror.

I am doing something worthwhile, I'd tell myself. After all, I was bringing pleasure and happiness to women who had none, or wanted more. And what nobler cause is there than making other people happy?

Driving to pick up Wendy, I couldn't contain the smile on my face. Damn, I felt good. Sure, I knew that underneath everything I was Mr Average from Essex, but cruising along the Golden Mile in Brian's Mercedes, with my Porsche sunglasses and dressed from head to toe in Hugo Boss, I thought I'd really made it. I stopped at the traffic lights opposite Cafeteria Marbella and was well aware of catching more than one passing female's attention. I didn't care if it was just the car or the clothes – the appearance of success. All I cared about was that for once I felt as if I had found my niche. Here in Marbella I was a babe magnet, sex on legs (or on wheels) – something I'd never have been had I stayed in Essex. Yes, it could have been that here in Marbella I was just the best of a bad bunch, with the majority of the successful men being either twice my age or into other much more dodgy ventures. Women seemed to gravitate towards anyone who had the balls to just go for what they wanted. Which was great because, just then, just there, I did have the balls. I was doing it and that was my reality. That was my life.

As I pulled up outside the five-star hotel one of the porters, with his Madonna headset, approached the car. '*Hola senor. Puedo ayudarte?*'

'Just waiting for someone, thanks.'

And with that he nodded and walked back to his post on the revolving front doors.

I saw this hotel every day on my way to the restaurant and a friend of mine actually worked there in the kitchen. I'd often thought about taking a girl there to impress her. If I'm honest, the thought of the dirty things we could get up to in the glass elevator on the way up to our room was also a big draw. Mind you, knowing my luck, we'd get a room on the first floor. I laughed as I thought back to a year ago and how just going from the ground floor to the first would probably have given me all the time I needed. Andy's 'gigolo' flexes had really helped on that score.

Wendy woke me from my fantasy, as she appeared from the revolving doors wearing a black mini-dress, slashed at the front and back. She'd looked very prim and proper the first time we'd met and I had imagined that she would be wearing an evening variation on that theme. I'd forgotten what sort of club we were going to. Unsurprisingly, she looked uncomfortable, with her hands crossed over her chest and a jacket folded over her arm like a security blanket. We both knew what the porter was thinking as he opened the door for her. Prostitute. He was almost right.

'You look amazing,' I told her.

She smiled and shifted in her seat, pulling down the bottom of her satin Lycra dress. I openly admit that it was a struggle to keep my eyes on the road and ignore her legs and cleavage. Already, I was a little jealous of this guy. Not only was he as crafty as a fox; he would also get to take Wendy back to a flashy hotel that night and have his way with her. Git!

I was worried about parking in San Pedro, especially as it wasn't my own car. All of the stories I had heard about cars being nicked had taken place in San Pedro, although most of the Spanish kids brought the cars back within 24 hours. Someone had told me that, under Spanish law, the thieves could not be prosecuted if they returned the car to the same place from which they had taken it within 24 hours. I didn't know if that was true but I took no chances and checked three times that the car was locked before we left for the club. Wendy was ignorant of my paranoia, lost in her fantasy of finally being able to be with the man she had dreamed about for the last month. A neon sign flickered outside the door to the bar. We pressed the telecom system and were buzzed in through the security door. Steep stairs led down into the club and it was just as it had been described to me. Dark and dingy.

The lighting was low, presumably to set the mood. But I suspected it was more likely a way of helping the less attractive couples have a chance of swapping their partners for someone better looking. An oily, naked blonde occupied the pole and a burly waistcoated Spaniard manned the bar.

Wendy and I made straight for the bar and ordered our drinks, feeling like rabbits who had just stumbled into a fox's den. All eyes were on us. In my imagination, every couple there seemed to be planning to make their move to come and speak to us. I scanned the room, trying to pick out our couple based on the description I'd been given of Jason, the mastermind behind the whole evening. I was still glancing around, pretending to be looking for the gents but really trying to make out the couples standing in the dark corners, when a woman approached me. She smiled at me shyly, toying with her wineglass as she introduced herself.

'Hi, I'm Maggie.'

I kissed her on each cheek and introduced myself as 'Deano'. I never introduced myself as Dean any more, and only my parents and people who had known me from before Spain called me Dean, or Saunders.

'Tino? Short for Valentino?'

I smiled and nodded. What's in a name anyway? I decided that for this evening I'd be known as Valentino. In fact, come to think of it, Valentino was a pretty good name for an escort anyway. Perhaps I should consider a more permanent change.

I turned to Wendy to introduce her to Maggie and to inform her of my new name, but she was already talking to a man at the bar. Could it be Jason? I didn't want any mix-ups, so, in order to make sure the job went smoothly, I asked Maggie with a smile, 'What's your husband's name?'

Immediately, the woman's smile faded and her mouth set into a hard line. 'He's not into that sort of thing. We're just looking for another couple, to swap.'

I laughed and kicked myself for how my question must have sounded. 'No, sorry, I didn't mean it like that.' But I knew I had to come up with a legitimate reason for asking his name. 'I was just making sure that was your husband. It's happened before. We both get talking to separate couples and end up with neither one.'

I couldn't believe how quickly I came up with that one and mentally patted myself on the back. Beads of sweat had started to form on my forehead!

She laughed and again looked quite coy as she confessed, 'This is our first time here. I don't really know what to expect.'

I tried to act pleasantly surprised, as if I was welcoming her to our little group. I knew not to say too much or pretend to be too experienced. 'My girlfriend dragged me here the first time, and now it's working out well,' I reassured her, and she

looked relieved that she'd not been the only one who had needed coaxing. I knew that Jason had convinced her to come and she obviously still had her reservations about the whole thing. My first task was to make her feel some connection – let her know that we had, or at some point had had, something in common. Then I could make her feel comfortable.

Maggie was not what I considered beautiful, but she had attractiveness about her. She asked me a lot of questions about Wendy. It was my job to make Maggie believe that I loved Wendy, and that we felt so secure in our relationship we were willing to let each other sleep with other people. I told her that, even though it wasn't our first time, I was still nervous and a bit paranoid that she would decide she liked someone else better. The last part was not to scare Maggie, but just to make her think that I had similar concerns and therefore establish some common bond.

'But Wendy would never do that. It's not in her nature,' I added quickly, sensing her alarm.

Maggie seemed to relax a lot more after that, and invited me to go and sit with her at one of the tables at the far end of the bar. Wendy was laughing and flirting with Jason, so I left them to it. As Maggie made her way to the table, I got the chance to take a better look at her. She was dressed in a long black velvet gown with spaghetti straps. Her greying hair was bobbed and brittle. She was tanned and when the dim lights hit her face, her bleached facial hair gave her skin the appearance of a peach left too long in the sun. Not exactly my type. Normally, I'd have had a few drinks to summon up a bit of Dutch courage but, as I was driving (and driving

Brian's car, at that), this wasn't an option. Instead, it was time to put my visualisation skills to the test.

First, I had to try to imagine what she would have looked like at 18. Usually, this helped but, in Maggie's case, she was still not the sort of girl I would have walked up to in a bar with the intention of taking her home.

Next, I tried to defocus my eyes, blurring her features to see if I could summon up a resemblance to someone I did find attractive, like an ex-girlfriend or a celebrity, but still she was more Angela Lansbury than Angelina Jolie. I knew it wouldn't matter so much once my eyes were closed, but I needed to be able to find some seed of attraction to build on, no matter how small.

The last open-eyed technique Andy had taught me was simply to concentrate on her best facial features and body parts, exaggerating how attractive they were and actively ignoring the less attractive bits. Her mouth and cheeks, for example, were cute, like a rabbit's, so that was something to work with. Also, she had an enormous pair of tits, which I tried to imagine as full and firm, just to get me aroused. So, my eyes drifted from her eyes to her mouth, then to her eyes again, then from her eyes to her chest every fourth or fifth time until, to my relief, I could feel the blood heading south. As for the elements that turned me off – well, I just had to put them out of my mind and, if they did try to creep back in, I had to dismiss them as trivial and insignificant. Is a trim, toned stomach that important? No way; it's much better having something to wrap my arms around, and who wants to feel all those sharp, bony ribs?

Maggie asked me more questions about my relationship with Wendy, and I could see that she was feeling pangs of jealousy as she looked over and saw her husband laughing and joking with her.

'He hasn't laughed like that with me for years,' she admitted sadly, her eyes glazing over in reminiscence of some far-off time.

I wanted to make her feel better. 'He's probably laughing at her, you know. She's lovely, but my girlfriend's not the sharpest tool in the box.'

Poor Wendy. But then she didn't have to know what I was saying about her – and it had a magical effect on Maggie.

'Well, they're a good match then. He'll feel less threatened by her.'

I sensed Maggie was getting her claws out now and decided to change the subject. I needed to get her worked up and into the mood before making any suggestions about leaving.

'So, who's your type then?' I asked.

'Jason was ten years ago. But things change, people change, I suppose, and... well, here we are.'

Despite my best efforts, I could tell Maggie still wasn't enthusiastic about finding herself there. 'You've thought about no one else, in ten years?' I asked with a cheeky smile and a raised eyebrow.

'Well, everyone has their daydreams, but I've never acted on them.'

'Well, now's your chance. Just think of this as a dream.'

She looked straight at me and I could see she had

stopped worrying about what they were doing and was listening attentively.

'When you wake up, your husband will be there and it will be as if none of this had ever happened. No consequences. Just like a dream. And you both carry on, a happier married couple.'

'It's just so risky,' she said, shaking her head.

'Not really. If you really love each other, like Wendy and I do, then you'll want the other one to be happy, not keep them from having what they really want.'

'And if I don't want you?'

'I doubt that,' I replied, my confident smile disguising a momentary jolt of self-doubt. Luckily, Maggie laughed, so I continued, 'You just keep telling yourself that, because you're scared of what might happen.'

She looked up from her wineglass and smiled at me. This time there was open encouragement in her expression.

'Now, I'm not sure what they've arranged over there, but I'd like to take you back to your place,' I told her, mentally reading from the script I'd previously agreed with Wendy.

Maggie laughed again, shaking her head and looking at me disbelievingly. 'Are you saying I should grab my coat?' she asked, leaning closer, making it harder for me to ignore her impressive cleavage.

'That's what I'm saying.'

We stood up and walked over to the other two to get Maggie's coat. As she pulled Jason away for a final talking-to, I took the chance to speak to Wendy.

'How's it going?' I asked, already having judged by the

sound of their laughter that it was all going fine. But, to my surprise, Wendy scowled.

'He's been such an arrogant prick all night.'

I turned to watch him reassuring his wife, rubbing her arms with his hands and tilting his head to meet hers.

'He's never seemed that way to you before?' I asked, unable to understand how she hadn't detected his arrogance until then.

'Well, no. He was always lovely at the restaurant. It's just not how I imagined it was gonna be.'

'Do you want to call this off? I'll drive you home.' My fingers were crossed in my pocket as I prayed she'd let me drive her back to the hotel. In her disillusioned state, it wouldn't have been too hard to cheer her up and make the best of the situation. And I knew I wouldn't be requiring any visualisation techniques with Wendy.

But she shook her head and knocked back the rest of her wine. 'No. The hotel's paid for now.' She shrugged and got off her bar stool, using me to balance as she adjusted her shoe strap. 'I feel a bit bad for his wife now,' she said grimacing. 'How much would you need, to...?'

'Spend more time with her?' I interjected, sensing where she was going.

She smiled and pulled out a 50-euro note. 'It's all I brought out from the hotel,' she said, but I pushed her hand gently away, frowned and shook my head. 'No please, take it. It'll ease my guilt a little. God, what would my mother say about all this?' Wendy rolled her eyes and sighed, as she stuffed the money into my jacket pocket.

This was a change to the original plan that Jason had devised, whereby I went through the motions but pulled back at the last minute. But, hell, I had been paid whether I did it or not, and as I'd already overcome my reservations about the whole thing and talked myself into a state of aroused anticipation, why not? My whole rationale for being an escort was to make women happy. This way I got to please two birds with one stone, as it were.

Maggie signalled for me to go back with her to the table, so I kissed Wendy goodbye and wished her good luck. Maggie had ordered another round of drinks and seemed eager to pick up where we left off.

'Let's have another drink, then we'll go back to mine, OK?' she said, shifting on her seat and glancing over at the other two.

I could tell she still wasn't sure, otherwise we'd already have been in the car heading to her apartment. But I also knew that, as soon as Jason walked out with Wendy, her mind would be a fertile ground to plant some seeds. Seeds of jealousy, seeds of lust, whatever would speed things up and get me out of that subterranean shit hole.

'I couldn't wait to get out of there,' Maggie said, as if reading my mind, taking a deep breath of fresh air as we emerged from the smoky club.

'I know what you mean. I'm not exactly a regular there,' I replied without thinking, looking around to get my bearings.

'How else do you meet up with other couples then?' she wanted to know, linking her arm through mine.

'Internet mostly,' I mumbled, looking down at her beside

me and wondering why she had shrunk until I saw the heeled shoes in her hand. 'People are more relaxed about the whole swinging scene here, but they're less willing to try it for themselves,' I waffled, praying we were heading in the right direction for the car.

'You're right. People here are a little too relaxed for my liking. And it's contagious,' she joked coyly, keeping her head bent to avoid stepping in dog shit and glass. You wouldn't see that in Marbella, I thought.

'How so?' I asked, paying as much attention to where I was treading as she was – she may have had bare feet, but I was wearing my most expensive shoes.

'Jason used to work like a dog back home, but now he seems to be on a permanent lunch break,' she said, shrugging and shaking her head.

'Business is done differently here. It's a lot more sociable, that's all,' I told her, imagining all too vividly his extended lunch-break sessions with Wendy. While his wife was at home looking after the kids, and waiting for him to return, he was playing about.

But, when we arrived at the apartment, I had to do a quick readjustment to my mental picture. Stepping through the front door, I thought for a second that Maggie had been burgled. Clothes and toys were scattered everywhere and the windows were wide open.

'I told her to close the windows before she left,' Maggie muttered. 'Useless!'

If the open windows were all she felt the need to comment on, the mess had to have been the norm.

'Where are the kids?' I asked, removing a hand-held games console from the sofa so I could sit down.

'A friend of mine is looking after them,' she replied, and then she saw my face. 'I know what you're thinking. It's a bloody mess. We've been living out of boxes and suitcases since we got here.'

Did one of those boxes explode then? I thought, trying to give the impression that the squalor didn't bother me in the slightest.

'Our new place was supposed to be finished before we arrived, but there were delays. It should be ready by the end of the month.'

So that makes it against the law to do any cleaning at all, does it? As she came back into the room, I cleared a space on the sofa next to me, throwing the dolls across to the other shirt-covered sofa.

'So...' she said expectantly, putting her wineglass to one side.

I leaned in to kiss her, and closed my eyes so I could think of someone else, in this case Wendy. She didn't want to open her mouth, her tight lips preventing my tongue from entering her mouth. Some women, I had discovered, didn't like to open their mouths. Kissing was a lips-only experience, although this usually changed when they discovered how nice my tongue felt on other parts of their body. I was well aware that some of my clients would be doing the same as me – imagining I was someone else. But that didn't bother me. In fact, that made me feel better – I liked the idea that I was assisting them with their fantasies.

Maggie pulled away and delicately unhooked her dress

straps, rolling the top half of her dress down and exposing her giant breasts. Each one had to have been twice the size of her head and, despite the two children, they were still buoyant enough to hold my attention and help me visualise someone else. She took my hands and encouraged me to massage them, while she brought her hands up to her head and ran her hands through her hair. Then, abruptly, she stood up and grabbed my hand, leading me across to the bedroom. I unbuttoned my shirt as she pulled the dress over her curves and to the floor. I kissed the back of her neck and then her shoulders, one of my hands reaching round and massaging an enormous boob, the other slipping inside her knickers and feeling my way through the thick pubic hair. I was already hard and ready to have sex but, as turned on as Maggie was, she was still very dry.

I turned her around and kissed her on the lips, then, as her hands massaged my head, I kissed my way down her body. Pulling down her knickers, I knelt as they fell to the floor and kissed her scarred navel. Then I kissed her thighs, starting from the centre and working my way in. I felt her contract more than once as I approached her erogenous zones and nuzzled her with my nose. Gently, I pulled on her hands, until she sat down on the edge of the bed.

I started licking and sucking her clit and lips and eventually it wasn't my tongue that cramped up, but my neck from being at such an awkward angle. So I gently urged her to lie back on the bed, massaging her breasts as I continued to lick and suck, not swallowing at all, letting it get as wet as possible. I had been ready for a long time and I felt like I was going to burst, but I knew that this was going to take a while yet. Maggie's thighs locked around my head, blocking out all external sounds. I could hear myself breathing, my heart beating and my tongue and lips working and making her wetter. I found it much easier to think about being somewhere else and with someone else without the sound of her breathing bringing me back to the present. Once my eyes were closed, they could have been anyone's thighs my head was between. Any star, any girl. An eternity passed, and in my mind I had been between Wendy's thighs, on her hotel bed, the whole time.

Maggie's moans had ceased and her breathing was steady again. She remained on her back and watched as I put on the condom and slowly lowered myself down to enter her. She was anything but dry now. Oral sex always worked well, in most cases the saliva and juices were sufficient not to need lubricant.

Unfortunately, this time the combination of lubricated condom and natural moistness meant I could hardly feel a thing. It was all so wet and loose down there. I'd never been accused of being small, so I knew the problem had to lie elsewhere. However, it was fast becoming my problem, as, without a certain amount of tightness, 'Little Deano' loses interest even if 'Big Deano' is determined to please. Add to that how tight the condom was and I had a recipe for sexual disaster.

I could feel less and less, no matter how hard I thrusted, until, after a few minutes, I wasn't even sure whether I was still in properly. I stopped and kept on kissing her, fearing the worst, as my penis flopped into the 'at ease' position. Trying to hide my panic, I went back to sucking on her nipples and kissing her body and thankfully I felt some life and enthusiasm returning. As soon as I was hard enough again, I manoeuvred her on to her side so I could enter from behind. Once I was inside her, I got her to cross her legs as I pounded against her fleshy backside. Her moans began again and after a while we looked set to come together, but as she groaned 'Tino' I felt myself about to explode. I came hard, but kept on bringing her hips towards me and pumping in the hope that one more push would bring her to climax.

When I could push no more, my head slumped on to the pillow and I cuddled up to the first-time swinger, holding her hand and kissing her back.

'It feels weird. I should feel guilty, but I don't,' she declared, her tone of voice making it sound more like a question. As if she was asking me whether that was normal or not, as if I was some kind of expert on the matter.

'There's no need to feel guilty. We're not hurting anyone,' I said, stroking her curves and kissing her back and shoulders.

She chuckled to herself and then turned around to face me. 'So do we get to see each other again?' She bit her lip and raised her eyebrows expectantly.

'That depends on Wendy and your fella. If they liked each other, they'll wanna see each other again and so can we. If not...'

She looked sad at that thought and turned to look at the ceiling. 'He liked her, without a doubt. I hope she liked him.' She didn't sound very hopeful.

'I hope so, too,' I said.

I took my stuff to the bathroom, which was in no better state than the living room, and got ready to leave. Flannels and bath towels lay everywhere, along with dirty clothes, which had not quite made it to the linen basket in the corner. I thought to myself how I'd never been the tidiest person in the world. I'd let things get almost to the state they were in this apartment and then one day I'd have a mad clear-up. That must be what they're doing, I told myself. Don't judge.

Maggie was under the sheets when I came back out, her clothes still on the floor with all the other heaps of discarded washing. I walked over and leaned down to kiss her.

'I'll see myself out.'

'Bye then.'

'Bye.'

And that was that. At least I'd given her something to think about while she was tidying the house the next day (or, in her case, thinking about tidying the house) other than the waitress her husband was still probably banging at the flashy hotel. But, then, as the lift reached the ground floor of the apartment block, who should be waiting to get in but Jason, looking very fed up. Lost in his own little world, he didn't even look at me; he just got in the lift straight after I stepped out. You're back early, I thought. Things couldn't have gone as smoothly as he'd planned and I'd bet money that Wendy had decided to throw him out and enjoy the hotel by herself. I think he caught a glimpse of me as the doors began to close, but, by the time he'd realised who I was, I was long gone.

Driving home from La Cala, I had the crazy idea of going

to the hotel to see if Wendy needed some company. After all, there's something extra lonely about waking up in a hotel bed alone. Being in a strange place is always a bit easier to handle if there's something familiar there beside you when you open your eyes. I'd be doing the poor girl a favour, I told myself, pressing my foot down harder on the accelerator in order to reach Wendy that little bit sooner.

Pulling up outside the hotel, the same porter approached me with a knowing smirk.

Now, what was her last name again?

CHAPTER NINE

Cassie and Des

'Some women will pay for company and some couples want "the crowd", so you'd better get used to performing for an audience.' ANDY

The first text message I received from a couple looking for an escort sent my pulse racing. No amount of positive spin was going to convince me that it was excitement I was feeling. I was nervous. Even after all of Andy's advice and obtaining a canister of pepper spray, I could just see the worst thing happening.

What if I failed to get it up? I would have two frustrated people waiting on me instead of one. How embarrassing would that be? But I had Viagra, I told myself, so if all the visualising failed at least I had that to fall back on. But what if the bloke wanted to get involved? Well, I knew I had to set down some ground rules at the beginning and to make sure they were understood – no man-on-man action happening here. What if he changed his mind and tried to join in anyway? I always had the pepper spray if words failed to do the trick. And if that didn't stop him? Well, then I had Chris.

Chris was another Essex boy who Frank and I had known since we were kids, although he had chosen to stay in Essex and face the crap we had escaped. He was in Marbella on an extended holiday and bored of sitting around doing nothing but eat all day, so he agreed to be my bodyguard for the job. I could not have got a better minder for the price of a vodka and Red Bull, although we both knew that the chances of me actually needing him were slim.

Terraced houses lined the quiet street, lit by lamp posts and empty in comparison to Marbella. This was the type of suburb where you would want to bring up children, where you wouldn't think twice about leaving them to play outside or walk to school on their own. It was also where 'my' couple lived and, after passing their house a few times to have a look and plan where Chris could wait, we stopped outside.

'I bet you're nervous, ain't ya?' he said.

I just nodded and smiled, feeling too sick with nerves to answer. But, then, as I got out of the car and took a deep breath, I started to regain my composure. I was Deano, sex god, right? The door opened as I walked through their small front garden and I knew that there was no turning back now.

'Something to drink? Coffee? Whisky?' The skinny blond Geordie chuckled as he led me through to the living room where his wife stood waiting. We exchanged introductions and kisses, and then I sat opposite the couple, preparing to lay down my ground rules while at the same time sneaking a good look at the wife, Cassie. Her long brown hair was tied back exposing an incredibly thin neck. She had narrow eyes and a pointed nose, but her smile saved what was otherwise an unattractive face. She had on a skirt and a low-cut top, which was unflattering due to her flat chest. But her legs! She was only about five foot five, but her legs seemed to take up five foot of that and unlike the rest of her they looked more toned than malnourished.

'You're a lot younger than we thought you were gonna be,' she said, glancing uneasily at Des, her husband.

'So are you two!' I said smoothly. 'The couples I've worked with before have been much older,' I lied, both to make them feel more comfortable and to make myself appear more experienced. It also served as a compliment to Cassie, whose plain face lit up. And telling myself that I'd done something before, even if I hadn't, made me feel better about having to do it again.

'Here's the money,' said Des, passing me the 200 euros.

'Now you understand that's for my time,' I said, for the benefit of the Dictaphone in my pocket, still wary of any legal entanglements. 'I'll stay for two hours and whatever happens is between us consenting adults.'

They smiled and nodded, and then Des leaned forward, perching on the edge of the sofa with his hands clasped and his elbows on his knees. It suddenly felt more like a counselling appointment than the prelude to a sex session, and he seemed to think long and hard about what he was about to say.

'I don't wanna join in, like, just watch yous.' He looked round to Cassie who smiled in approval before lighting the joint she had left on the coffee table.

193

'That's fine, as long as that's clear. I'm not into that either.'

'No, no worries. You won't even notice I'm 'ere,' he said, and then he walked off up the stairs, leaving me with Cassie.

She held in the smoke and her eyes followed Des as he climbed the stairs, only exhaling once he had disappeared. Then she turned to look at me with her narrow eyes, and offered me the joint. I took a single drag and handed it back to her, not wanting to lose my concentration for the job at hand.

'D'you do this full-time then, or what?'

'No. What do you do?' I refrained from adding, 'When you're not paying other men to shag you in front of your husband.'

'Teaching. Bet you've seen it all though, ain't ya?'

'Pretty much.'

'We had a girl in last week. Lithuanian. Stunning. He loved it.'

'Does he always just watch?'

'No, he joined in with us that time. He probably just doesn't fancy ya!'

We both giggled and then she came over and sat beside me.

'We'll go up in a minute. Give him chance to hide.'

I nodded and suddenly started to feel the effects of the joint, so I was relieved when she reached over to the ashtray and put it out. Then she looked at me and smiled again, before leaning in and kissing me. Her mouth seemed so big, like she had half of my face between her lips as she kissed me. There was no tenderness; she just stuck as much of her tongue into my mouth as she could, leaving me with a strong desire to wipe my face as she pulled away. Creeping up the stairs, Cassie appeared to be listening out for Des.

We hovered on the landing, and then she turned to me as if she had something urgent to say. 'When you eat me, me stud might come outta me clit, so be careful.'

Classy. There I was thinking my biggest concern would be her husband and now I had to worry about choking on her piercing as well. I waited outside the door as Cassie fannied about in the bedroom – doing what, I have no idea – but then finally she called me in, using a different *sotto* voice.

'Come on, Des'll be out for ages.'

It was my turn to enter the charade. 'We'd better make the most of it then,' I replied woodenly.

As we kissed and stripped each other naked, I was concerned by the fact that Des was nowhere to be seen. There was the bedroom door and another door, which led to the en suite bathroom, but he was not standing at either of those. As I kissed my way down Cassie's body, on my way to her wobbly piercing, I glanced to my side and saw that the cupboard door was slightly ajar. It seemed too small to hold someone Des's size, but as the cupboard was shaking I was in no doubt as to his hiding place.

'Ooh, that's so nice. Suck it hard.' She moaned as I went down on her, reaching up to squeeze one of her breasts while simultaneously keeping my eye on the trembling wardrobe.

Being in a stranger's house and having sex with them a few minutes after meeting, knowing all the time someone was watching, was strange but exciting. But the shaking wardrobe was really starting to put me off. So, I closed my eyes and hoped Des was having far too good a time to come out of the wardrobe and try to join in.

Once Des was out of my mind, I started to really enjoy it again. I loved tattoos and piercings, and I'd only ever been with one girl with a pierced clit before. Cassie's pussy was also extremely well groomed. Not shaven bald, just neatly trimmed, short enough to see the dragon tattoo climbing up her belly.

I could feel her thighs on either side of my face becoming increasingly tense until, after a silent but powerful shudder, they relaxed again and I knew it was time to move my tongue anywhere other than her piercing. I kissed my way back up to her breasts and I felt her reach across to her chest of drawers beside the bed. As she pulled the drawer open, besides underwear I noticed a pink vibrator, handcuffs and several boxes of condoms. I reached down to my trousers and pulled my own condoms out.

'I've got... oh, OK,' she said, a little bewildered.

I didn't want to make a scene, but I had to use my own condoms. It may have been a psychological throwback to the days when I was sure some girl was going to get pregnant by me before I was ready, but I just didn't function well with other people's johnnies. I'd stay hard until the thing was on but then my cock would go down before I got it in, which was frustrating for everyone involved. So, armed with this little piece of self-knowledge and determined not to disappoint my clients, on every job I would take three condoms from my 18-pack, and there were never any problems.

I was on my knees as I slid myself in, she was on her back, her legs either side of my head. God, they were fantastic legs. One of my arms held her leg to my chest, while the fingers of my other hand rested on her stomach and my thumb rubbed her stud.

'More, har... ar... der,' she screamed as I pulled her towards me, pushing myself further into her.

After about half an hour of that, her legs were practically behind her head.

'Come, I want you to come!' she groaned.

I quickened up the thrusting and brought my mind back from the poem I'd been reciting in my head. Her legs came down and we were back in missionary position, my head buried in the pillow as I shot my load, her hand squeezing my arse and the wardrobe still rocking like a deranged Dalek. Moments after we'd finished, while I was still inside her, a text came through on Cassie's mobile phone. I rolled out and lay beside her as she read the message, watching her smile and then put the phone down.

'Des is gonna be a while yet, he's working late,' she told me, still playing the role of the adulterous wife.

I stifled a laugh, glancing over at the now motionless wardrobe.

'You wanna shower?' she asked, getting up and making her way into the bathroom. She looked back to make sure I was still coming.

SNAP! Right, get rid of that, I thought, and into the steaming hot shower we got. She squeezed some gel into her palm and started to lather me, leaving no limb unstroked and no crevice unlathered. I did the same to her until, completely covered in foam, we held each other and kissed.

Her sloppy kissing didn't matter so much in the shower as we were wet anyway and any saliva got washed away. I had adapted to her huge tongue and was now finding her overly wet kisses quite erotic. She kissed my chest and stomach, finally kneeling at my rock-hard cock and sucking on the end. The water still hitting my face and body, her wet hair in my hands and knocking against my pubic bone, I was in ecstasy. That was until I saw the man's silhouette through the steamed-up shower screen. If he had come any closer, I would have jumped out and ran, but he kept his distance and just observed as she worked me with her mouth and her hands.

She must have seen him leave, because the blow job stopped very suddenly. After all, it had only been for his benefit. We got out of the shower and she passed me a towel, wrapping hers around her and peering back into the bedroom. She went to my trousers and I was about to yell, 'What are you doing?' when she came back with another condom.

She leaned over the sink and I thought back to the exercises Andy had shown me to do every day. It was much better performing them with a girl between the sink and me, and I was pleased with my repetitions. But after a while Cassie decided she'd had enough of that and wanted to kneel on the bathroom rug. Less effort, I suppose.

When we finished, she went straight into the bedroom and leaped on to the bed, while I had another quick shower.

I don't have Obsessive Compulsive Disorder or anything, but keeping your tools clean is the mark of any good tradesman. When I got out of the shower, I strolled back into the room, drying myself with the towel, when, suddenly, the door slammed.

'Cassie! Where are ya?' yelled a man's voice from downstairs.

It was Des, but I was confused as to why he was asking where his wife was, especially as he had been perving over the two of us just a short time before.

I heard doors slam and once again he shouted, 'Cassie!'

I looked at Cassie, shrugging in confusion only to see that her narrow eyes had become wide with terror.

'You'd better hide!' she whispered urgently, shoving me towards the wardrobe. I was about to grab my things and run out, shouting for Chris, but, when I heard Des stomping angrily up the stairs yelling his wife's name, my nerve failed and I just got in and hid.

I was stark-bollock naked, except for the watch Chloe's parents had given me for my 21st birthday. I saw that their time was nearly up and hoped that, if I didn't emerge bang on the hour, Chris would decide to storm the place and help me get out.

But then the arguing stopped and was replaced by kissing and, the next thing I knew, I was the voyeur and they were going at it on the bed! I had no choice but to watch – I was stuck in their wardrobe, naked. I wasn't going anywhere. It wasn't like watching porn, of which I had been an avid fan throughout my teens. It was more like watching a nature programme, where you sit there and wish you could intervene at certain points, but accept you just have to watch and let nature run its course.

I thought about one time Chloe and I had been in Soho and went to a peep show. We paid a pound to stand in a tiny cubicle together while a letterbox flap opened up to reveal a busty topless dancer. I remember being more turned on that time, but probably just because Chloe and I were in such a small space together.

There was another time when I had a party at my house and, while people were hanging around for the toilet, we slipped into my bedroom for a quickie. She said she was really turned on knowing that there were people outside who could walk in at any minute.

Then I thought about how different Des and I were. I mean, he had sat in the wardrobe for three-quarters of an hour while I banged his wife. Then, he stood there and watched as she gave me head in the shower. I bet it wasn't the sort of thing that he went to a bar and bragged about with his mates (although the threesome the week before probably got dropped into the conversation at some point).

I still went crazy at the thought of Chloe with another man, and sometimes I woke up from nightmares of that very thing, crying. The awful truth was that Chloe probably had been with another man, ouch, if not several other men, ouch ouch, and I was going to have to get used to that. It had been nearly a year, but the wounds were still open.

After five minutes scrunched up in the wardrobe, I decided that nature was running its course far too slowly and, as Chris had not shown up, I was going to have to make a run for it. I already had my clothes in there with me, but there was no room to change. So I slowly opened the door and got out naked, covering myself with my screwed-up clothes. Then I backed out of the room and ran down the stairs, putting just my trousers on and then running out of the house to the car.

I saw Chris's eyes widen as I approached the car running and semi-naked. I jumped in and assumed that he would just start the motor and speed off, like in the movies. Instead, he looked at me and asked, 'You all right?' before pulling away as calmly as if he was taking a driving test.

On the drive home, I got dressed as I recounted what had happened.

Chris shook his head in disgust. 'Can you imagine...' he began.

'I know!' I said emphatically.

'With your wife!' He shook his head again. 'He ain't right, is he?'

At least I knew I was not alone on that one. I knew that there would probably be some people out there who would see something noble and strong in being able to sit back and watch someone else pleasure his wife, but Chris and I were in firm agreement that for us personally it was a little 'fucked up'!

And yet, when it came to the lovely Lithuanian Cassie had bonded with the week before, our Mary Whitehouse moral stance suddenly deserted us. Husband watching while other man screws wife: sick. Husband watching while other woman screws wife: perfectly understandable. I'll admit our moral framework lacked a bit of consistency. But the fact that we were in agreement with each other convinced us that we were in the right.

Of course, the one thing I didn't mention as we passed judgement on poor old Des was what it said about a man who was willing to screw a woman he'd just met for money, while her husband crouched in a cupboard and watched. Where did a man like that come in the overall moral scheme of things?

Best not to ask.

CHAPTER TEN

Keely

*'It's not a movie. Things won't always go smoothly.
But, as long as you can both laugh about it,
nothing is too bad.'* ANDY

When I wasn't working at the restaurant or escorting, most of the time I just wanted to stay in, watch a film and veg out. But Frank would ring me constantly, trying to tempt me out. And if that didn't work, he'd use the guilt trip. 'What sort of a mate are you? 'Ere I am, all alone... tell a lie, there's a couple of stunning birds just walked in, Oi Oi! Savaloy!' And half an hour later I would be there, pint in hand, singing karaoke, playing pool or talking to whichever girls Frank had been flirting with.

There was never a dull moment with Frank around, which was great most of the time, but, with the rest of my life being so crazy, I could actually have done with a few more dull moments. I liked my evenings in because they gave me a chance to recharge my batteries, to just be myself and be comfortable. But trying to explain that to Frank was like talking a foreign language. He would just frown and shake his head in confusion.

On one of these occasions, I was just getting up to leave Stars in Marbella, after having been talked into playing in a pool competition, when four women on a hen night walked in. All of them were dressed up as schoolgirls and the bride-to-be had her 'Learner' sign around her neck. They were all in their early to mid-forties and their combined cackling nearly drowned out Frank's booming voice, which takes some doing. They were all pretty curvy, and looked great in their uniforms.

Of course 'eagle-eye Frank' spotted them immediately, but he also noticed me trying to leave, so I sat back down quickly, knowing what he'd do if I didn't. Frank was introducing the karaoke so he had the microphone – his favourite weapon – in his hand. His playful verbal attacks were the sort that could have the whole bar laughing while his victim just prayed for the ground to open up. He'd done the same thing even when we were kids, without the microphone, so you'd think I'd be immune to it. No chance.

With the microphone in hand, he approached the women's table, striking a pose as he arrived. 'Hello, ladies. Can I interest you in a beverage?'

Frank put on one of his many comical accents and steamed right in as always, and nine times out of ten it paid off. So, he put their first round of drinks on his tab, then he got them up dancing and singing karaoke, downing shots with him and generally having a great time. As Frank was fully occupied with the ladies and someone else had the microphone, I saw my opportunity to sneak out unnoticed.

'Woah, woah, woah! Where d'you think you're going! Sally, come 'ere!' Frank called out to me and then back to one of the women, before putting his arm around her and coming over to introduce me. 'Sally, Dean, Dean, Sally. This is one of my oldest pals from Essex. I've known him since I was one!'

Here we go again, I thought.

'And he's a gigolo, and he's loaded, so he's buying the next round. Come on!' Frank laughed and signalled towards the bar, whereas his new friend, Sally, stood there open-mouthed.

'You're a gigolo?'

'An escort,' I said shrugging, as if there was a huge difference between the two.

Normally, being an escort wasn't something I bragged about. You never knew how a woman would take it. I reasoned that, one day, I would meet someone I really liked and, if I told her I was an escort, I'd blow my chances before I'd even got a foot in the door.

'Would you sleep with her over there?' Sally wanted to know, pointing to one of her companions, the bride-to-be no less.

''Course he will darling. How much?' Euro signs had appeared in Frank's eyes as he saw the chance to make some easy money.

I turned to him and slapped his arm with the back of my hand. 'Are you pimping me out?'

'Damn right, 50–50 sounds fair to me son.'

'No, seriously. If we pay you, will you take her home?' Sally was completely sincere, her eyes wide.

'She's wasted,' I said, a feeble excuse as the woman in question was quite clearly the soberest one of the four.

'When's that stopped you? Come on, d'you need a Viagra?'

'No, I don't need a Viagra!' I protested. I need my fucking head checked for always letting you talk me into these things, was what was going through my mind.

'Come on. Don't let the side down,' Frank laughed as he said it.

'Go on. Her fella's a right bastard, cheats on her all the time. She's too good for him. Go on. She's really nice. It'll be a laugh.'

I took a good look at the three women dancing at the far end of the bar. The bride-to-be was the best looking out of the four friends, with her long dark frizzy hair in pigtails and her freckles painted on her prominent cheeks.

'Come on, we'll all go somewhere a bit quieter so you can talk to her,' Sally urged.

What she failed to realise was that, wherever we went, we would be taking Frank with us so the chances of it being any quieter were minimal. Still, introductions were made and then the six of us left for another bar.

'You concentrate on the bird, I'll handle the money side...' Frank laughed again, both of us knowing full well that the money would be spent long before I'd finished with the girl. 'She's got a ton, that'll do won't it? Fifty each. Just take her back to yours and send her off in a taxi in the morning.'

I shrugged; by that point, I had decided to just enjoy it, get drunk and have a laugh. The bride-to-be – Keeley, I found out – was as adventurous as they come.

'Sky-diving, bungee jumping, mountain climbing...' She

counted the list on her fingers as she tried to remember. But then, after a stroll along the beach, my suggestion of skinny-dipping was met with a very definite refusal.

'You said you were adventurous! Come on.'

'Not in water. I can't go in the water, not at night,' she said, pulling on her pigtails.

'Why not?'

'Der-dum, der-dum, der-dum-DUM-DUM!' she giggled, as she sang the *Jaws* theme tune with her hand on her head as the dorsal fin.

'Come on. There are no big sharks in the Med. You'll be all right.'

'Don't swim off – stay close to me, all right?' she said, undoing her school tie.

We both stripped off, leaving our clothes on the beach before running into the freezing sea. I kept wading further and further out, against the waves. I wanted to make sure the water was at least at waist level to cover certain bits that were shrivelling unflatteringly against the cold. First impressions and all that!

Keeley had her hands clasped together and her arms were covering her boobs. She kept walking towards me, still concerned about sharks, while I backed away making her follow me further out.

'It's fr-ee-ee-ee-z-z-zing!' she shivered.

'Dunk your whole body in. Seriously, you'll warm up,' I said, kneeling so the water came up to my chin.

She dunked her head backwards and ran her hands though her long frizzy hair, exposing her glistening chest. I edged a little closer and then, as she looked around her, scared of what might be swimming around us, I extended my leg and with my toe and touched her foot.

'AGGGHHHH! Oh God!' she screamed, and jumped straight to me for protection. It would have been erotic, or at least funny, if her grip hadn't been quite so tight.

'It was my foot!' I told her, trying to calm her down.

She was shivering from the cold and, embarrassed by her little outburst, she turned and put her head on my shoulder. I held her, running my fingertips along her back until she brought her head up to look at me. She was biting her lower lip and I was sure that she was going to tell me to let her go. But, instead, she closed her eyes, lifted her head and waited for me to kiss her.

As our lips met, I could feel her face trembling from the cold. We kissed and held each other, then I pulled her up and she wrapped her legs around my waist, the water making her weightless. We stayed like that, kissing, her fears and the cold water no longer a problem.

Without saying anything, she got off me, took my hand and started leading me to shore. I thought we were going to do it there on the beach, but as we got closer to the shore I saw two men running off in the opposite direction. While we'd been otherwise engaged, they'd obviously been having a good look through my stuff.

I searched through my scattered clothes to see what they had taken. The wallet had no money in it, but the worst part was that they had taken my mobile. The phone itself was worthless, but the numbers of all my clients were in it. I had only written some of those numbers down and now without my old number they had no way of contacting me. I knew I'd have to text the numbers I did have with my new number immediately and I'd also have to change the newspaper ad and the website.

As I watched them run off, I burst out laughing at the thought of chasing them, stark-bollock naked with my, now, semi-erection.

'I feel so bad, they didn't touch my stuff,' Keeley commiserated. 'Why are you laughing?'

'The thought of chasing them had crossed my mind,' I said.

She looked me up and down and chuckled too. 'I've got money. I'll pay for the taxi.'

And so her mind had already been made up. Still naked, I went and kissed her again, until we were heckled by some passing kids on the boardwalk. After we'd got dressed, we went back to my apartment. I made Keeley wait outside for a moment while I threw dirty clothes into the wardrobe and cleared all my books and magazines off the bed.

The next day, after sending her back to her hotel in a taxi, I went to see Frank, expecting to collect my 50 euros and then go and buy a phone.

'I tried to call, but your phone was switched off,' he said in a wheedling voice.

Immediately, I knew what had happened. 'She didn't pay, did she?' I asked, already seeing from the wry smile that she hadn't. It was not the first job where I'd walked away with less than I had expected, but this job had also cost me my phone and most of the numbers that were on it.

I'd been warned by Andy that these things were bound to happen from time to time, especially when your 'pimp' for the night is more interested in shagging your client's friends than collecting the money you're owed! So, I decided it was for the best for me to go back to being in charge of my own affairs, as I always had been.

'Did you have a good night?' Frank asked.

'I got robbed on the beach and she wouldn't give head. Does that answer your question?'

We had a laugh about the previous night's events and he agreed that he'd leave me to sort out my own clients in future.

'With one exception, right,' Frank said. 'If Robert Redford offered me a million euros, then I would definitely set you up with him for the night.'

You know what they say: every man has his price...

CHAPTER ELEVEN

Vivian

'You can bend the rules for regulars. It's like
a customer loyalty card. You keep them coming;
they'll keep on coming.' ANDY

Another day, sitting on the beach, reading, topping up my tan and looking up at the occasional piece of eye candy. I had a few days off work and was contemplating going fishing that evening, when I received a call.

'Hello, Deano speaking. How can I help you?'

'Hello, yes, I'd like a companion for the weekend.'

Jackpot, I thought to myself, as I heard the assertive posh voice over the phone. Although wealth and accent did not necessarily correlate 100 per cent of the time, in my mind the two were always linked. Anyway, I had nothing planned for the weekend other than seeing my friends, and the woman on the phone sounded friendly enough, so I decided not to pass on the job to one of the other escorts.

'The whole weekend? OK. Have you been on the website,

or have you used one of our escorts before?' I asked, ever the professional.

'Well, no, I just saw your number here and called. I need someone sporty, with lots of energy. Are you sporty?' She sounded very saucy and even if I wasn't 'sporty', as she put it, I wasn't about to let her know that.

My curiosity was well and truly aroused – and I hoped other parts would soon follow suit.

'Yes, I suppose I am. So where and when shall we meet?' I asked, slapping my oily, undefined belly as it browned in the sun.

After haggling a little over my weekend price, the woman gave me the address of a villa in Estepona, telling me to bring tennis gear and evening wear. Tennis gear? I had shorts and T-shirts, but none of these was specifically designed for tennis. Concerned that I was going to be taken to some country club, I rushed out to the local sports shop and bought some shorts, some trainers and a polo shirt. Now all that was missing was the faintest idea of how to play the game, but hopefully looking the part would be a good start.

The following day, I set out early to get to her villa for ten o'clock. It was going to be another scorcher so I had creamed up before I came out and, guessing that tennis would be our first activity, I had put on my smart new gear.

The road up to the villa was only just big enough for two cars and on several occasions it looked as if I was going to lose a wing mirror. By the time I parked up outside the house, I was a nervous wreck and needed to sit in the car for a moment before getting out to greet my client.

Too late! She'd seen me arrive and rushed out to greet me in her own tennis gear. She had the legs of a 21-year-old below her pleated white skirt and, despite being in her fifties, the way she carried herself meant she could have passed for a decade younger. Her green eyes were framed by thick lashes and there was a penetrating energy about them. The grey streaks at the front of her long dark hair seemed to give her an air of serene wisdom. Her body was toned and athletic and she moved with such grace I detected a theatrical or dancing background – something I would later be proved right about.

'Psyching yourself up?' she asked, walking up to the car and leaving me no time to calm down after my traumatic journey.

'Hi, I'm Deano,' I said, kissing each of her cheeks as she offered them and then turning to lock the car.

'Vivian,' she said, moving her hand to her chest, smiling confidently and as relaxed as if I had just come to clean the pool. 'I hope you've got energy,' she said as she unsheathed her racquet.

I had plenty of energy, but discipline and the ability to lose gracefully were not my strong suits. The more I struggled and concentrated on playing well, the worse I became. As she scored point after point and won game after game, I started to lose patience with myself, and cursed the fluffy yellow balls under my breath.

'Best out of seven?' I said, resenting the 3–0 whitewash and kidding myself that I had just been unlucky and that I was just getting warmed up.

'Then you have to win the next game. Are you sure you're

up to it?' she asked coolly, barely having broken sweat while I looked as if I had fallen in her pool with my clothes on.

'Yeah...' pant, pant, '...the next one's mine!' I said, gesturing for her to 'bring it on' and serve.

Miraculously, I did win the following three games, although the only workout Vivian appeared to be getting was from how much she was laughing at me. Perhaps it was her inability to stop laughing at my lack of athletic grace that cost her the three games, or maybe she was just being kind.

'Deciding match... now you'll see the real Deano...' I said, wiping the sweat from my brow with my forearm, steely determination written all over my face.

'God, no! That was funny enough! Why don't we leave it as a draw?' she said, almost sympathetically, walking up to the line and extending her hand.

My whole body was so sweaty there was nowhere I could wipe my hand to make it any drier for her to shake, but she laughed and shook it anyway.

'OK, well, that was entertaining. Do you play golf?'

My face froze in horror and I shook my head, still trying to get my breath back and praying that tennis had not just been a warm-up for a round of golf.

'We'll just have a dip in the pool today, then; we'll play golf tomorrow,' she said, watching the look of relief on my face as she announced the change of plans.

I limped back to the car to get my trunks, towel and other clothes from the boot. Looking back at the villa, I saw Vivian shedding her tennis gear by the pool. I had plenty of opportunity to admire her bottom as she unzipped her skirt and slipped it off to reveal her thong bikini. Now not every woman can pull off wearing such a bikini, regardless of her age. But, apart from being depressingly good at tennis, she was also one of the most physically stunning women I had ever met and I was in little doubt that she had been under the knife. What particular features had been artificially enhanced, however, I couldn't decide. Everything looked so natural, although age-defyingly firm.

As Vivian lounged by the pool and I trod water, I felt bad for having made her change her plans. She had taken one look at me after tennis and decided, quite correctly, that I was in no fit state to go and play golf. But that was a while ago and after the dip in the pool I felt fine again.

'If you want to play golf, I'll carry your clubs. It's just... I've only ever played crazy golf.' As I made my shameful confession, she sat up and laughed hysterically.

'OK, now we have to go tomorrow!' she said, getting up and making her way to the pool. She sat on the side, dangling her legs in before twisting to lower herself in and simultaneously give me a great view of her backside.

'You must spend your whole life at the gym to get your body like that,' I said, tempted to swim towards her and see if she felt as firm as she looked.

'God, no. I can't stand gyms or fitness clubs, yuck!' she said, pulling a face and somehow still managing to appear attractive.

'How do you stay so fit? I mean, apart from wearing out young men on your tennis court.'

'I wear young men out in a lot of other ways, too, you know,' she smiled and started to circle me. 'But mostly it's just tennis and golf. I used to be a dancer, so that has put me in good stead.'

So I was right about that, but I could still find no signs of surgery and was rapidly accepting the idea that she was just naturally beautiful, like Andie MacDowell or Helen Mirren.

'Do you hire escorts a lot?' I asked, turning as she circled me.

'Not always. My friend let me down this weekend so I thought I'd see what you had to offer.'

I chose not to ask what she had thought so far, as Vivian seemed like the type who would only share that with me if she felt it was worth saying. I was still feeling inadequate after my sporting failure, but she obviously detected that because, quite unprompted, she reassured me. 'You're still young. You've plenty of time to learn.'

Later, as I massaged her with coconut oil by the pool, I discovered that she told herself the same thing over and over again each morning and evening.

'It's not getting old I'm worried about. It's just what everyone makes "old" out to be. Wasting away, dwindling social life, shutting yourself away from the world...' She definitely did not appear to be doing any of those things, but it was clearly a preoccupation of hers. '...not enjoying yourself any more. I've had so many friends practically lock themselves away as soon as they turn 50!'

I loved giving massages, especially when the woman's voice betrayed how much she was enjoying it. I loved that breathiness as she fought to keep talking, while all the time giving into my strong hands kneading out her knots and relaxing her muscles. Vivian was too classy to fall asleep, mouth open, dribbling, but more than one woman I'd massaged had woken up attached to her towel by an unbecoming string of drool.

I'd often thought about qualifying as a masseur, mainly so I could prowl the beaches plying my trade to any girl I liked the look of. But, like so many of my other dreams, I'd procrastinated too long on that and it remained one more talent that I had no qualification for.

'I want to take you shopping for something to wear for tonight and tomorrow, OK?' Vivian said, as I finished her massage. It was phrased as a question, but it came out as a command.

I shrugged and nodded, then went for another dip in the pool. Perhaps she was not keen on the clothes I'd brought with me. Maybe that was another area in which I'd failed to come up to scratch. But then she'd definitely seen something she liked or she would have sent me home by now. Instead, she was obviously planning to mould me into her perfect weekend companion.

'Are you adventurous?' she asked, sitting up, putting on her sunglasses and sipping from her bottled water.

'I like a challenge. I don't gamble, though.' That was because I'd be sure to lose. I had a definite weakness for challenges – the stupider the better. Ruefully, I thought back to the numerous occasions I'd risked life, limb and liberty just to fulfil some ridiculous dare someone had set me.

On one drunken occasion, coming out of a nightclub in Romford, one friend had suggested car hopping, which – in case you don't know – is when you leap on to a car bonnet and continue to run on to the roof before jumping off. After some daring hops, one of my friends suggested car hopping the police car parked outside the taxi rank. The challenge had been set and I was foolish enough to take it. My swift run-up was cheered on, but as I leaped on to the bonnet there was silence, followed by uncontrollable laughter as my foot caught on the police lights. I slipped and splattered across the roof of the car, then collapsed into a drunken heap on the ground. The next thing I knew, I was being picked up by the coppers – who owned the car – and given a severe lecture about the dangers of drinking and diving over vehicles. Needless to say, I haven't car hopped since, but I'm still a sucker for an impossible challenge.

'OK, well, my challenge is a sort of bet,' Vivian murmured, flexing her toes as she played with her bottle of water.

'Go on, I'm intrigued.' I swam up to the end of the pool and rested there while I listened to her proposition.

'It'll have to wait till we get to the shops,' she said. 'Are you on?'

'What's the stake?' I asked, stalling for time.

'If you succeed, I'll pay for the lot. If not, I'll have to take it out of your fee.' One eyebrow arched up behind the sunglasses and she didn't bother to disguise her grin.

'Fine by me,' I said, and pushed off the side of the pool to continue treading water. I could end up with some new clothes and 800 euros here, I thought. But then, there was the risk of losing some of the money if I failed to meet the challenge. And then there was the challenge itself. What could it be that was so awful she couldn't prepare me in advance?

I rarely shopped for myself in Puerto Banus due to its largely overpriced shops and my variable income. But, after I had driven Vivian there in her blue Audi, she gave me strict instructions not to look at any price tags.

'Don't you like shopping? I thought young men were keen on fashion these days.'

'I would be, but I'm colour-blind. I always need to be with someone or I end up looking like a clown,' I told her.

For some reason she found this hilarious. 'Are you serious? Oh, God, how awful. What colour's this?'

I rolled my eyes as she asked me the same question everyone else did on hearing about my disability. Why don't people just believe you when you say you're colour-blind? They all feel the need to test you, as if you would make up something like that. They would believe me if they saw the colours I would wear were my clothes not numbered.

I was a bit sensitive about my colour-blindness when I first found out. After failing the ink-spots test, I was handed a list of jobs I was told I could forget about applying for. Among these was the police force, so that was my childhood dream out of the window – although, later, I was extremely thankful for that. The other option, which I felt robbed of, was the armed services, as my family had a naval history and in fact my brother went on to join the navy. I found it difficult to commit to any career decisions after that particular blow. Nothing else really appealed to me, which is why, even after university ended, I remained completely clueless about my future direction. Spain had been a convenient excuse for putting off that decision.

But there I was, a year out of university, still in Spain and working as a male escort. As Vivian picked out several shirts, I thought back to some of the other jobs I'd done. I'd worked in a gym, a scaffold yard, in the bar and on the door of the same nightclub, on the turnstiles at Arsenal's football stadium, in warehouses. But at no point had I envisaged that I would be in Puerto Banus with some sexy, mature woman, dressing me up to take me out on the town.

'OK, I like these. Try these on,' she said as she picked up a selection of classy shirts and hooked them on to my hand.

I looked around for the changing room, but as I headed in that direction she stopped me.

'Oh, no. You can change here. It's part of your challenge,' she said, leaning on the clothes rack, her eyes on my chest as I began to unbutton my shirt.

Feeling self-conscious, but relieved that this was all the challenge was, I tried on the two shirts and one polo shirt she'd picked out for me, keeping my eyes on hers and trying to ignore anyone else. One of the female shop assistants had started to fold pairs of jeans on a stand near by and I could feel her stare burning into me, but I kept on looking at Vivian who was now scouting for something else.

'My shorts are fine.'

'Yes, they are, but you'll need more shorts tomorrow for golf. Ah, these look perfect.'

She tossed a pair of shorts over to me and gave a cruel shake of her head, as I looked over to the changing rooms with 'PLEASE?' written all over my face. She was clearly enjoying this. The shop girl was still watching and for some reason seemed to be getting closer, which made me feel even worse about what I was about to do.

When I had taken my trunks off back at the villa, I had put my shorts back on, but no underwear. Vivian knew I was naked under my shorts, and this was part of the challenge. Would I be brave enough to get changed in public, in front of her? Despite the shop girl's presence, I ran the risk of losing a good portion of my fee if I failed to go through with it. I thought it through. What was the worst thing that could happen if I did it? That I'd get thrown out of the shop? Or maybe arrested? In a second, I made my decision and, to the backing track of the shop girl's gasps and Vivian's giggles, I stripped down and tried on the new shorts.

'Yeah, I like them,' Vivian said, trying to control her shaking voice. 'Take them off so the nice girl can scan them.' It was the first time she'd acknowledged the shocked salesgirl.

There were clothes racks everywhere and it looked as if only the girl and Vivian had seen that I was naked, but this was a huge glass-fronted store with people passing by and looking in constantly. The truth was that anyone could have seen me. To my surprise, I found that knowledge a bit of a turn-on. Like being naked in Jeana's Jacuzzi, it was liberating and at the same time naughty.

Vivian paid for the clothes and we left the shop before any security arrived to deal with their 'flasher'. She handed me the oversized bags and hooked on to my still trembling arm, saying, 'Well done. You're a good sport after all.'

Later that night, we went out, giving me a chance to wear one of the shirts I'd earned.

'If you have to wear black, at least make it shiny or frilly or something,' she said, giving me fashion pointers that sounded at best dubious to this particular Essex boy.

'Frilly?' I asked, one eyebrow raised.

'You know what I mean. Something you wouldn't wear to a funeral!' She stifled a laugh as the waiter arrived with our menus, dressed all in black.

As we ate at the Italian restaurant, I began to feel a real connection building. We talked about travelling, about work and she shared stories about her current dream of becoming an actress.

'Acting and dancing cross over all the time; it's all just performance,' she said, picking at the olives in the middle of the table.

'Why did you wait until now?'

'Other things on my mind; other obstacles in my way. But now I'm ready. Anyway, someone has to play the grandmother or the wicked old witch.'

'I don't think you'll get those parts,' I told her, complimenting her on how good she looked for her age.

'Maybe without the make-up?'

'Even then, your body would give you away.'

She sat up and smiled as I said that, and I could see I'd won myself a few brownie points. We talked about Stanislavski, and I tried to remember everything I had learned during Mr Horncastle's GCSE drama classes and A level theatre studies, which was apparently more than I had given myself credit for. Emotional recall, circle of solitude – you name it, I was up with the lingo and I even remembered some of the Chekhov, Ibsen and Shakespeare that I'd read.

I felt my phone vibrate in my pocket at one point and decided to excuse myself to go and check who had called or texted me. But, as I stood up and made my way to the toilet, a white-bearded man at one of the other tables beckoned me over.

'*Garçon!* OK, are you ready, son?' he said rudely. 'Right, what's everyone having?'

The man's wife cringed and looked at me apologetically as I stood there lost for words. Glancing round, I could see Vivian laughing behind her hand at our table and I felt my face burning.

'He's not a waiter, dear,' the old man's wife corrected him.

But, instead of apologising, he just turned his back on me and focused his attention on the real waiter who had finally arrived. At least this allowed me to continue my trip to the toilet, while wondering if the man would realise he was in an Italian – not a French – restaurant, and whether that would cause any confusion when he ordered his *moules frites*.

The text was from my dad, reminding me that my mum's birthday was coming up. I was quite impressed that, despite resisting technological advances such as computers and emails, he had finally worked out how to write and send text messages. I felt terrible as another one of their birthdays was about to pass without my being there. I felt even worse about the fact that they had funded all those years of study, and yet, when anyone asked them what their son was doing, they were never quite sure how to answer them.

I looked in the mirror while I was in the toilet and saw the same thing I always saw. A boy pretending to be a man; a barman pretending to be a male escort. I was never happy with just being myself, always trying to be someone else and yet never quite feeling right for the part. The old man had seen through my disguise and no doubt Vivian could, too, but she had preferred to keep the pretence going for its comedy value. But so what? My job was to please her and she had been smiling and laughing the whole time I had been with her. There's more than one way to achieve an outcome, I suppose.

When we arrived back at the villa, I was confident that if I hadn't redeemed myself already by passing her shopping challenge, I would regain the upper hand once we reached the bedroom. Without saying a word, she closed the front door behind us, took my hand and led me up the stairs. We came to the door of the master bedroom and she stopped to peck me softly and slowly on the lips. A surge of adrenaline shot through my system, making my heart pound and increasing my urge to hold her. I couldn't wait to get her clothes off and make love to her, and, even though I was duty-bound to make sure her pleasure came first, I had no doubt she wouldn't be the only one enjoying herself.

'The spare room is at the end there,' Vivian smiled and broke away from me. She turned and disappeared into her room before closing the door, leaving me speechless for the second time that evening.

What happened there?

I loitered on the landing for a few moments after she'd

224

gone, perplexed by the strange sequence of events. Then, sulking, I retired to the spare room. Lying in bed, I stared at the ceiling and wondered if my poor show at tennis was to blame for my being exiled to the spare room. At no point did I consider myself irresistible and I understood that some clients had no wish to have sex, but I'd never been asked to sleep in the spare room before. I felt like Vivian's pet, and like a new puppy I was tempted to whine all night until she gave in and let me sleep in the bed with her. But I resisted. This was work. My client's pleasure, however she derived that, was my priority. At times, my job could be bloody frustrating.

As expected, 'little Deano' was already awake when I woke up, and had been awake most of the night sending me messages like, 'Well? Are we going?' and 'You know you'll sleep better if you just give me a tug.' But I had resisted that urge, too, and, after what little sleep I had managed to get, I felt ready to tackle the 18 holes Vivian did want me to play with.

The moment we arrived at the golf club, the solemnity of the other male players was intimidating. I had friends who played golf and they'd always practised at a driving range before spending money out on a proper game. But, hey, it wasn't my money. I sliced the ball, I hooked the ball, I let go of the club a couple of times and almost bent one in half on the putting green. After 12 shots, I had still failed to get the ball in the hole.

'Having trouble getting it in?' Vivian's voice was mocking.

Saucy, I thought, but it helps if I'm sleeping in the same

room. She was having more fun from watching the expression on my face each time I missed than she was from playing golf, having to stop herself from laughing before taking her own shot a few times. By the third hole, I was frustrated; by the fifth hole, I threw the ball instead of teeing off, once again causing Vivian no end of amusement. By the next hole, however, I had just accepted how crap I was, so, instead of simply smashing the ball, I decided to watch Vivian and the other golfers, and see how much I could improve. My definition of improvement for my first-ever game of golf: I didn't lose a single ball after the tenth hole.

I desperately wanted a drink after the game – a beer to chill me out before driving back to the villa. But Vivian walked straight past the bar and waved me out with her. 'We can have a drink once we're home,' she said. 'Anyway, I feel like fucking.'

There's something about hearing a posh bird say something dirty that knocks me for six almost every time. I can't help going red and, if my mouth doesn't just fall open, I end up with a goofy smile on my face. I whizzed back to her villa in her Audi in super-quick time and, unlike the previous night, when we made it to her bedroom it was access all areas. We spent the rest of the day there, popping down to the kitchen for food and drink in between our lovemaking. At the end of the night, I was pleased not to have been asked to sleep in the spare room. In the morning, Vivian's head was still resting on my chest, her sweet-smelling hair catching on my unshaven chin. There were times I loved my work.

'Listen, I could really use you up here this weekend. Can you come?'

It had been a while since I'd heard Vivian's voice and it brought an immediate smile to my face.

'Madrid? OK!'

'Great. Just get your flights and I'll pay you back when you get here.' Then she was gone, rushing off to whichever meeting she was late for. And so began what would have been my jet-set lifestyle – if I'd had the sense, or the class, to take a plane. Instead, with my inbuilt Catholic guilt gene convincing me that God would know why I was taking the trip and strike me down in mid-air, I decided to take the bus.

The seven-hour coach journey left me more vagrant than fragrant. Some classy gigolo I was, in my crumpled clothes and unkempt hair. Taking the Metro into the city centre didn't help, either. By the time I arrived at the hotel, I was in very poor shape. At first, I'd been confused as to why we were staying at a hotel, as I knew her main home was in Madrid. But she explained that her ex-husband was staying temporarily at her house and she felt it inappropriate for us to stay there. I'll admit it sounded suspicious but, at the time, I was doing my best not to judge people or situations and to look for the positive. She was just being considerate towards her ex-husband's feelings, I told myself.

She had agreed to meet me outside, but after waiting ten minutes for her I walked up to the reception desk and asked if I could speak to Miss Whatever in room Whichever.

'*Si! Eres Senor Saunders* [sow-oon-dairs]*? Hay un mensaje para ti.*'

The message read: *I'm so sorry – this meeting has turned into a dinner. Put your stuff up in the room and go do what you like for a few hours. I'll be back by midnight!*

After showing the receptionist my passport, I was taken up to the room, where 200 euros had been left along with another note duplicating what the one downstairs had said. She must have written the first note without thinking how I was going to get into the hotel room, and then left one at reception to make sure I had no problems. I assumed the 200 euros was some play money to help keep me occupied until she returned. I put the money in my wallet and went out to explore Madrid. But, conscious of having to return at midnight, I knew that sampling its notorious nightlife wouldn't be such a good idea.

As I've said, I've never been a fan of big cities. Everyone is so anonymous and too busy to care who anyone is or to stop and ask how they are. In Marbella, people knew me and I knew them, and I liked that. People looked out for each other there, whether it was with finding jobs, or apartments, or whatever else. Strangers were welcomed and shown a good time, unless they did something to outstay that welcome. But, from the moment I entered big cities like London or Madrid, I felt as if I had already outstayed my welcome and I looked forward to getting home – whether that was Marbella or Rainham.

While I wandered about aimlessly, I noticed a poster on a bus top. At first, it just looked to me like a cigarette ad, but then I recognised the band members. It was Bon Jovi, and they were playing that evening on the outskirts of Madrid.

They had been my favourite band from the age of 13, and I had gone to see them twice with Chloe back in the UK. I was seriously tempted but, with no one to go with, I hesitated momentarily. Perhaps I should hire an escort to accompany me, I joked to myself. But then I decided to stop worrying and just go for it. There was always the chance of hooking up with someone there. After all, everyone had one thing in common from the start: we were all fans.

When I got to the stadium, I phoned all my friends to tell them where I was and bought a T-shirt for one of them as a souvenir. I was tired from the bus trip and I knew I needed to save some energy for later that night, so, instead of standing in the crowd, I sat at the top row of the stadium on my own. I sang along as the Spanish made up their own lyrics ('Leaving on a prayer'? No, I'm sure it's 'living'!). This was fine until Jon went off and then Richie came up front to do a ballad on his own. It wasn't even 'our' song, but all I could think about was how depressing it was to be sitting there without Chloe or even a temporary stand-in.

As I made my way out of the stadium at the end of the concert, I got trapped behind a queue of Spaniards. The Spanish don't queue for anything, so that was the first thing I noticed. And then I realised that everyone there was with someone else; arms around each other, hand in hand, hand in pockets – whatever – but with someone. I was alone – the only animal who would have been turned away from the ark by Noah: 'Your bird's not with ya, you're not coming in.'

For a while, I felt achingly sorry for myself, but then I comforted myself with the thought that I was not going to be spending the rest of the evening alone. Someone was waiting for me. I pulled out my mobile, expecting to find the usual lack of missed calls or text messages, except perhaps a *Telefónica* promotion. But when I saw the screen I was excited to see four missed calls from Vivian.

'Where are you? I've been calling!' she said anxiously as I returned the call.

It must have looked like I'd just taken the money and left, as I doubted she would have checked under the bed for my bag.

'I'm on my way back, sorry! You said midnight.'

'OK, well, don't be long.'

I sensed the relief in her voice. Once again, it might have been that she was simply relieved that I hadn't run off with her money, but I turned it into something positive. It showed I was in demand. She wanted me, or at least she wanted what I could give her. So much so that, when she thought she wouldn't get it, she'd phoned and let her guard down.

Once again, Andy's words popped into my mind: 'Remember, it's the size of your ego that matters more than the size of your equipment if you want to survive this trade. Hide it when you need to, but keep it strong.'

Not wanting to keep Vivian waiting any longer than necessary, I took advantage of a kissing couple's oblivion to a free taxi and climbed in, only to see them dumbstruck as the driver and I drove off laughing like two successful bank robbers.

I knocked on the hotel-room door and when Vivian opened it I was standing with my head bowed, my eyes looking up and my lips pouting. It was the face she usually pulled whenever she'd taken a joke too far. I thought it might go some way towards defusing the situation. She looked angry, and she pulled me in and pushed me up against the wall before kissing me passionately. I could hear water running and the news was on. She was still in her blue business suit, but her shoes had been kicked off at the door.

'You're going to scrub me down and then you're going to give me a nice massage,' she ordered.

'Please?' I joked, but she was not in the mood for niceties.

She kissed me again before dragging me to the bed in frenzy. We didn't even take our clothes off; we just unzipped and pulled down what we needed to; she put on the condom and then we went at it like rabbits. Suddenly, all thoughts of Chloe were banished from my mind and being single seemed once again a desirable lifestyle choice, rather than a sad indicator of failure. Remember, this isn't love, I told myself. But the passion was exhilarating, pure and natural – albeit the kind that would always die out, eventually. Andy was right, I reasoned with myself, it was unnatural to be a one-woman man. Better to remain a player, at least until I wanted children.

As we cuddled in the bath, I thought about love again and how, although this was not what I had felt with Chloe, it had all the makings of a love relationship. When I made love to Vivian, it was passionate, and, while we were away from each other, we genuinely missed spending time together. I cared about her like I cared about all my other friends, but no words of love had ever crossed either of our lips.

She knew I saw other women and I was fairly sure that no

one man would ever keep her amused for long, but neither of us seemed to mind. It was just never mentioned, and if one of us was busy we just left the other alone. Even the money part of our arrangement was different. She never tried to pay me less, but she made a point of preferring to buy me things rather than just hand me the money.

I would spend one weekend a month in Madrid and she would come down to Estepona as often as her schedule permitted. She was my favourite client and on a couple of occasions I even passed on or cancelled other jobs I had in order to be with her. When she came home from acting classes, I helped her go over what she had learned and, over the course of time, I picked up a trick or two myself. Vivian was impressed, and urged me to come with her to her class, but I chickened out and faked a headache.

One day, though, after hearing how excited she was at having got a part in a television ad, I was swayed and agreed to join a casting agency along the coast in Benalmadena. Within a few weeks, I was phoning Vivian to tell her about my extra part in a film called *Wish You Were Here*. We laughed at the fact that, out of more than 50 extras, I was the one they chose to play the waiter! Can you believe it? And so the nickname 'Garçon' stuck.

Our routine continued nicely and I was content until one particular outing in Marbella. We were out on a cruiser belonging to one of Vivian's friends. I was obviously the youngest person on deck but, as Vivian's guest, everyone made an effort to be polite to me. All except for one silver-haired old boy called Humphrey.

Vivian had warned me about their short-lived affair and admitted that she loved parading her young studs in front of him, to wind him up.

'He's not into fisticuffs, is he?' I asked, not worried but just wanting to be prepared.

'Humphrey? God, no! He's not a fighter. Actually, he's not much of a lover, either, but I'm sure he must have something going for him,' she giggled.

Being on the boat made it difficult for me to avoid Humphrey and I frequently caught him staring at me, with his piercing eyes and flared nostrils. Careful, I thought, this can't be good for your heart, getting all worked up like this. Vivian and I were one of three couples on board, and then there was Humphrey, another stray gooseberry, and the captain, Francis. He was a sturdy red-haired man with a permanent squint and a moustache that hid his mouth.

'You can tell he's smiling when his 'tache curls up at each end,' Vivian had joked as she quietly explained who everyone was.

Once we were a fair distance out to sea, Francis turned off the motor, jumped down from the wheel and joined everyone else for a drink and some tapas – specially made by his Spanish wife who had stayed home.

'So, Deano,' said Francis, looking like an interrogating police officer in a sailor's outfit, 'Viv says you're a psychology graduate.'

'Yes, that's right.' But please don't ask me what grade I got, I thought.

'Top stuff. I never went the distance. Read economics for

years. Dropped out in my final year. Oh, but the parties were worth it.' He leaned forward to slap my bare thigh in what he obviously considered a matey manner, his eyebrows momentarily lifting from their squint.

If he had been poor, Francis would have been labelled 'mad'. But, as he was stinking rich from some very shrewd investments he had made while working in the City, everyone commented on how 'eccentric' he was. I liked him, and not just because he made me feel better about my university failings. He simply had that ability to make you feel important, as if your happiness mattered to him. It was the same quality I had tried to cultivate with my clients, although in some cases I'd ended up feeling more like a social worker than an escort.

'Does he play tennis?' asked Humphrey, not acknowledging my presence and directing the question at Vivian.

'Ask Deano, Humphrey. He speaks several languages, so I'm sure he'll understand your waffle.'

I could tell Vivian was put out.

'Well? Do you?' he said, barely glancing in my direction.

'Understand? Yeah, just about,' I replied, making Vivian chuckle.

'No, do you play tennis?' he said, even more irate.

'I'm improving.'

I looked over at Vivian pointedly and she returned my smile, which aggravated Humphrey no end.

'What about golf?' He tilted his head to the side and raised his eyebrows.

The vein on the side of his head appeared to be pulsating

dangerously. I was past competing, unlike Humphrey, who obviously thought that, by exposing my lack of expertise in the sporting field, he could make me feel like an inferior person entirely.

'I'm not that good,' I admitted.

'Well. What's your handicap?' Humphrey's voice was strained, impatient, and everyone else was quietly observing the spectacle.

'Oh no, I'm not handicapped – I just need more practice.'

While everyone rolled about the boat laughing at my joke, Humphrey went bright red and decided to disappear, probably before his head exploded.

Vivian came and put her arm around me and kissed me on the cheek. 'That was priceless. If you can make him go that colour again, I'm yours for life.'

I knew she was only joking and maybe that was why her statement bothered me. I could talk my way through my feelings and understand the logic and the mechanics of why I felt like I did. It was a simple case of the whole 'wanting what you can't have' scenario, but knowing that failed to stop me feeling what I had begun to feel for Vivian. I was convinced that it was not love but, all the same, it made me sick with wanting her.

Francis tried to teach me something about sailing – to do with the different-coloured flags and buoys – and when I told him about my disability do you know what he said?

'Really? Colour-blind, hey? How many fingers am I holding up?'

As I was already prepared to tell him politely that 'I'm not sure what fucking colour it is!' his question completely threw me and we both ended up falling about laughing. I spoke with Francis about his cruiser and listened as he told me of his plans to sail to Majorca with his wife. I was anxious to do anything to keep out of Humphrey's way and help me think about something other than Vivian for five minutes.

But, then, as we docked in the port and everyone made their way off the boat, Humphrey grabbed my arm and pulled me back. From the look on his face I knew he wasn't about to congratulate me on my sea legs. 'You're just a whore. You should be ashamed of yourself.'

He had mustered up as much venom as he could manage at his age and, had Vivian not pre-warned me of his aversion to violence, I might have been worried by the sheer hatred in his voice. But I wasn't. The thing was, the bloke was right, about the whore part. But, for some reason, maybe it was just growing up in Essex, being called a whore was no longer the worst thing in the world. If he had called me a 'cunt', mind, he would have gone overboard tied to the anchor, but a 'whore'? Well, I decided to let him off with that one. I must have been mellowing.

Just after that boat trip, I stopped playing the field in my private life and fell for a Scottish girl called Jodie. I was still doing the escorting, but, off-duty, my emotions had been running high for a while with Vivian, so meeting Jodie – somebody I thought I could actually have – was like therapy.

Her hair was dyed black and her body was firm and curvy, and she had such an expressive face that, even had she been a mute, I would have understood her perfectly. But that accent... as I've said before, I'm a sucker for a Scottish accent. Being with Jodie was much safer than falling for a client such as Vivian. There could be no issues about power or past events, as there would have been in any relationship that had begun as a business transaction. The only problem with this otherwise stunning girl was that she wouldn't sleep with me until I had told her that I loved her.

But the truth was, although I cared about her deeply and fancied her more than anyone else at the time, I didn't love her. I didn't want to tell that lie because I knew how much damage it would do when I couldn't pretend any more. It wasn't as if she was a client; I couldn't simply use the 'sorry, other clients are monopolising my time' excuse if things became too intense. I tried everything else I had learned, but what it came down to was that either I say those three little words and make some sort of commitment, or I walk away.

I chose the latter.

The relationship ended and we didn't see each other after that, although I often missed her. One thing I had gained from it, though, apart from some wonderful memories, was the definite urge to be with one girl again. I felt as if I was ready to handle a commitment – as long as it was as perfect as the one I'd had with Chloe.

Not such a tall order then!

Apart from the sudden desire to be coupled up again, I also developed a sense of urgency about my need to work on some sort of career. Acting? Well, everyone wanted to do that and they weren't getting anywhere, so why would I?

Songwriting? Since I'd been in Spain, I'd used my guitar for only one thing – as a cash deposit box. At the time, I had several thousand euros taped to the inside. But that wasn't going to get me on to the bottom rung of any career ladder. Writing? Well, apparently, a writer is someone who writes. So that ruled me out then, as I hadn't written anything in years.

While surfing the net, I typed in a search for 'TEFL' – Teaching English as a Foreign Language. A long list of courses came up – too long for me to look at everything – so I narrowed my search to 'TEFL, Spain'. I found a course running in Madrid by a group called EBC, which cost 900 euros and took a month to complete. Feeling suddenly motivated, I rang the number and booked a place on the spot.

The next time I saw Vivian, she told me I could stay with her in Madrid until I'd found a place to stay for the duration of my course. So, I spent the month in Madrid, going to the school every day, studying every evening and, slowly but surely, running out of money. I had no time to find a job, and most of my clients were in Marbella, so escorting was out, which meant that I just had to make do for the rest of the month.

But at the end of that month I came out with a pass with distinction and I was a qualified TEFL teacher. That certificate meant more to me than my degree, because it showed that, when I dropped everything else and gave my all to something, I got the best result. I'd also discovered that I loved teaching and, even better, I was good at it.

I headed straight back to Marbella and, undeterred by failing to get a job in any of the language schools, I tried to

set myself up as a private tutor, starting an exchange night so the Spanish could come and learn English and vice versa. I also used the evening to recruit new students. Within a short while, I was teaching English to a psychiatrist, an architect and a lawyer, as well as other professionals and children.

But, satisfying as teaching was, I wasn't earning the financial rewards I'd been hoping for, and it certainly wasn't enough to keep me in the manner to which I'd become accustomed. I knew it was only a matter of time before escorting was back on the menu. When I told Vivian about the teaching, she was pleased for me, but wary as well. She knew enough about my boredom threshold by that stage to worry that teaching from a textbook wasn't going to hold my interest for ever. As I put the phone down to her, I realised two things: 1) a relationship that had begun as a business transaction had ended up being one of the most valuable friendships of my life, and 2) she was right.

CHAPTER TWELVE

Diana

'Women enjoy sex just as much as men do.
But a woman who wants it as much as a man usually
has something to prove. Be careful.' ANDY

Taking a break from escorting to do the TEFL training meant I lost quite a few clients, and the hole in my budget was painfully obvious. But, as I was trying to make a move away from escorting and into something more 'legitimate', I didn't want to start canvassing for new clients. When my regulars called, I went to them, but apart from that I wanted to leave my old life behind. Not that I'd suddenly realised the error of ways or anything, but I just felt it was time to move on to another phase in my life. Only trouble was, I missed the money, plus 'going legit' was harder work than I'd imagined.

Escorting gave me a few chances to network and offer my services as an English tutor, but obviously I had to be selective with whom I approached. At some of the parties I was invited to, many of the fabulously wealthy men were accompanied by South American or Eastern European prostitutes who wanted to improve their English. It should have been a perfect opportunity for yours truly. But, after their partners had seen me in my other role, they made sure that the ladies were suddenly unavailable for classes.

One night, while drinking in the port, a client introduced me to one of her male colleagues and his date, a stunning Swedish blonde called Diana. She looked young enough to be his daughter and yet much classier than most of the working girls in the port. I was curious but, of course, asking outright would have been out of the question.

When I noticed Diana sidling up in my direction, I rehearsed a suitably innocuous opening line – something bland about the boats or the company – but, before I could open my mouth, she was already speaking.

'What's your hourly rate?'

She said it quietly but, even so, I nearly choked on my beer and quickly looked up to see if anyone else had heard. Luckily, my client was busy talking to Diana's date but, as small talk goes, it was a humdinger.

'I don't know what you mean,' I smiled.

'You don't work much in the port. I've not seen you here before.'

'I've been away.'

'Me too. Ibiza. Live sex shows pay extremely well there in the summer.'

'Really?' I said, trying to give the impression I met women every day whose job was performing live sex in front of paying strangers. 'So, what brings you to Marbella?' I was trying to keep my tone even, but was finding it impossible not to conjure up images of her at work.

'Opportunity. I know some people looking for... erm, performers,' she said, looking me up and down.

Suddenly it dawned on me; she was eyeing me up as a potential partner. 'Same thing?' I asked, playing down the sudden enthusiasm I was feeling about this new career opportunity that had fallen into my lap.

'Yeah, interested?' The smile she gave me as she looked up through her clear blue eyes made it obvious that she knew exactly how interested I was in her little proposition.

'Maybe,' I replied airily, as though I'd simply add it to the list of all the other options I had to consider. 'But I've got tattoos and pierced nipples. Is that a problem?'

I thought I should forewarn her about the body decoration, but I was also looking for possible reasons not to do this job. I'd developed that habit after the whole colour-blindness discovery. I didn't want to set myself up for disappointment if I could help it. I remembered all too well what had happened when I'd gone to a porn audition I'd seen advertised. Having to sit around for hours with men twice my size and with four times as much experience had been chastening enough. But, then, to get through to the casting directors only to be turned away the second I began to strip was one humiliation too far. The reason: my tattoos. To be honest, I don't know what I'd been expecting. All I'd been thinking of is how porn seemed the perfect combination of my two main interests in life: having sex and making money.

Mind you, with the ball control I had at that time, they'd have had to loop the same three-minute clip 20 times to get one 60-minute feature! But I had kept that to myself.

'Tattoos? No problem for me,' Diana pouted and shook her head.

'Are you with him for the night?' I asked, nodding over to her date.

'Hey, I'm no whore. He just bought me dinner; I can go when I please,' she said, slapping my arm playfully with her handbag.

'Well, I have to stay until this little shindig is over,' I told her. 'But, if you like, I could meet you after.'

'You wanna go for a drink, and talk about the money side?'

'No, I was thinking more along the lines of rehearsals.'

She laughed and rolled her eyes before rejoining her date.

Across the bar, I could see my client greeting someone else and went over to her with a drink, fully expecting to be mistaken for a waiter as per usual. Thankfully, her swift introductions saved me from being ordered back to the bar for a round of martinis and a packet of cigars.

Later that evening, I collected Diana from the port and took her back to her apartment in Nueva Andalucia for a practice run. Once our first passionate 'rehearsal' was over with, she talked me through the whole thing from start to finish. Routines I would have to learn, changing from one position to another smoothly and performing to music. There was a lot more involved than I had realised, but it still beat stacking shelves in Sainsbury's.

On the surface, Diana was a cool girl who had the whole

package: brains, beauty, business sense. But her wild streak didn't end at performing sex shows. Each week she snorted hundreds of euros of earnings up her nose, relishing the energy and lack of inhibitions the cocaine gave her. Diana also loved to dance, and the first thing she did each morning when she woke up to the radio was dance her way to the bathroom and back. To her, having sex was just an extension of that – she saw her live sex shows as performance art, and couldn't see anything to be ashamed about.

A week after our first meeting, she had organised a show at a private villa in Sotogrande. Some rich architect was having a birthday party and thought he would outdo his friend's 'prize fighter' birthday with a sex show.

'Now, remember the audience is going to be pretty close, so you may hear them say stupid things.'

'Like?' I was curious as to what she'd heard before.

'About your body, about how you're doing it. They're going to judge you.'

'Great. Well, it's only half an hour, right?'

'Exactly, and remember...' she leaned over my crotch and undid my fly, '...whatever they say, it's you I'm fucking.'

And, with that, she proceeded to ease any tensions I had as best as she knew how. She said she always made sure her partners came a few times during the day before the performance to make sure it lasted, and she reckoned that they shot more come if they came regularly. This ran counter to my experience, but who was I to argue? She took out a Viagra from her purse and bit it, swallowing half herself and giving me the other.

Of all the villas I had been to, this was the most impressive. The high security gates rolled back once Diana had announced our arrival to the intercom system, and as we drove in we were both speechless. A pond with fountains and lights was surrounded by a selection of Bentleys, Daimlers and Porsches and the like. A man with a Doberman on a short leash was circling the perimeter, and I suspected there were several more just like him. Cameras were secured to the palm trees that surrounded the premises, and another security guard came to meet us at the door holding a walkie-talkie.

'Can I see some ID?'

'We don't have any, we're the performers.'

The man looked down sternly at both of us and then radioed to somebody inside the house for 'clearance' for two performers, one male, one female, both white, mid-twenties. Diana looked at me and shrugged, then, as the man stared down at the floor and nodded, I knew he had received permission through his earpiece for us to enter. He opened the door and we were met by a male servant, who asked us to follow him up the spiral staircase. The villa itself was large enough to be a school, with more rooms than I could ever imagine anyone needing. Works of art hung on the walls and expensive vases sat on antique tables. The servant stopped at a room at the end of the hall, which was long enough to need an intercom at each end just to speak to each other.

As we got changed and tested our music, I could hear a crowd not so far away. I opened the other door to see where it led, and there was the host, just about to knock on our door.

'Hi, there. Are we ready? The bed's set up as we discussed, Diana.'

'Great. We'll be five minutes, Tom. Oh, this is Deano,' she said, gesturing towards me.

Tom grabbed my fingers and his hand felt limp; it was like shaking a wet fish. He eyed me nervously and then minced back out to the other room where the guests were waiting.

'I don't think he'll be watching you,' I said.

'He'll be watching us both. He's an artist, so he appreciates this on a whole other level.'

Art. I knew this was another area where my lack of sophistication showed, and that I should learn to appreciate art just as I'd learned to appreciate food, but it simply did nothing for me. I could look at a picture and think, Cool, or Weird, but there was so much that escaped me and, as a result, I knew I was missing out. I wanted to open my mind and experience what we were doing as art, but with the moves I had to remember, and my performance anxiety being greater than ever before, it was all I could do just to concentrate on the job in hand: pleasing the audience.

Diana and I walked out and the lights went down as the crowd gathered, mumbling quietly around us. I'd been nervous beforehand about what would happen if I got the moves wrong, or couldn't 'perform'. But as soon as the music started I was right back in her apartment where we'd practised. For the whole of the performance, I had no recollection of anyone else being there. Instead, I concentrated on doing everything just the way she'd taught me.

To be honest, there wasn't a whole lot of plot to our little show. First, I was to convince her, the reluctant maiden, to let me kiss her. Then slowly I stripped her clothes from her before throwing her on the bed and going down on her, still fully clothed. I had to keep my head to one side and come in at an angle, to provide a good view for our audience.

Then, once she had pretended to come, she became the dominant one, jumping to her feet and stripping me, before throwing me on the bed and kneeling to give me a blow job. The different songs would be our cues to change, though on more than one occasion I was enjoying myself so much that I nearly forgot. After giving me the blow job, she produced a condom from the side of the bed and put it on with her mouth. Then she straddled me while facing the audience. She rode me while playing with herself, and the music got louder and more powerful along with her groans. This was my cue to start thinking the dirtiest thoughts possible as she removed the condom and started to give me another blow job. As the louder music came to an end there was a long fade-out to give us some 'ejaculation' time. As I came, she would rub my dick all over her face, making sure her chin was as wet with come and saliva as possible. Proper porno stuff and these people went wild for it. Cheering as I came and clapping as we got up and went off to get cleaned up.

Was it artistic? Maybe. But to me it was just very surreal.

We did a few of those shows together and we were both approached for threesomes and orgies, but we had set our price at 500 euros each and we promised we would only work together. I had warned Diana that some of my clients came first, which was hard for her to accept because we could make more money doing the shows.

But it came down to a loyalty thing for me. Some of these women, who had given me as much pleasure as I had given them, were like mentors to me as well as clients. They had helped fund my lifestyle and the life experiences they had made available to me were invaluable. I would have to leave them, too, eventually – I knew that – but, if something had to go, it would have to be the shows.

'Start looking for someone else now,' I told Diana. 'Then there's plenty of time for them to take over. I don't want to leave you in it.'

'I've been looking. It's harder this time of year.' Her voice had become whiny, and she helped herself to a huge heaped line of powder.

'Slow down, Diana. You're gonna fuck yourself up with that shit.'

'Fuck off! You're not my father, OK!' Her eyes were not her own as she said that, and for a moment she looked like a woman possessed.

A few other girls in the port had warned me about Diana. They had told me some horror stories about the nights she had been thrown kicking and screaming from cars, before getting up and carrying on her search for coke. She had a habit, and a temper, but she had always been all right around me until that point.

But she was right, I wasn't her father and I had no right to tell her anything. You can only help those who want to help themselves, so anything I would have said would have fallen on deaf ears. I just prayed she found someone else soon so that I could get out of the arrangement.

One night, on our way back from a show, she asked to see the money from that night's show. It was in an envelope inside my jacket pocket, so as I drove I took it out and passed it to her, not paying it any attention. She counted it over and over until, finally, after a lot of prolonged glances I said, 'What's wrong?'

She didn't say a word; she just dived at my jacket pocket and felt around, finding a 50-euro note.

'You fucking arsehole! You were going to screw me over!'

Over 50 euros, which had obviously just fallen out of the envelope! This was insane. I knew she had snorted a few lines that evening, but I had never seen her in this state before. She lashed out, beating my arms and even the side of my face as I drove. I had to pull over to the side of the motorway as she continued to punch and scratch at me, completely out of control. I didn't know what to do – I'd never hit a girl in my life but I came close to it that night, just to make her stop. Then I remembered my pepper spray. I took it out of my other jacket pocket and sprayed it into Diana's face, the cloud filling the whole car and causing us both to jump out. As she crawled around on the ground, coughing and sneezing, I pulled her by the hair to the side of the road and told her to stay there or she'd get run over. Then I went and opened her window and shut the door, before opening my window, too, and getting in the car. I drove off before she realised what was happening. After about five minutes, once I'd calmed down, I phoned a taxi to go and pick her up from the motorway.

The last I heard of her, Diana had gone to London and was looking to repeat the same sex shows she'd done all over the Med. I wished her well but knew that, unless she cut down on the drugs, her performance was going to become less about art and more about just making enough money for her next fix. It's always a shame when someone so young and vibrant and full of energy squanders his or her potential on the quest for a never-ending chemical high. But I was young and shallow enough not to consider the bigger picture at that point. Diana thought she was an artist and I was sharing in her creativity. As far as I was concerned, she was a nutter and I'd had a lucky escape.

Funny, isn't it, how two people can emerge from the same situation with such totally different points of view.

CHAPTER THIRTEEN

Chloe

'Escorting is like any other addiction. You think you control it, and it's only when you try to quit that you realise it's the other way round.' ANDY

When Christmas time came, my students all wanted to have a break and restart in January, after Three Kings day (this is the 'real' Christmas for most Spaniards, when the whole town turns out and gets pelted with nasty boiled sweets by costumed men on a giant float). This was great for me because I liked to go home for Christmas and see my family. Apart from my first year in Spain, when my parents had come out to me, I went back every year. I would spend Christmas Eve with my friends at the Ford and Firkin in Romford and then, depending on how drunk I had become, I would go to midnight mass at La Salette church, never failing to be surprised by how much bigger it always was in my mind's eye. I had given up on going to confession, as each year I seemed to spend longer and longer in that booth, but I always found the masses uplifting.

So, as per usual, it was Christmas Eve and I was standing in the Ford and Firkin with my friends, trying to resist the temptation to get wasted and miss the only church service I would attend that year, when I saw her.

From the entrance of the pub, bright-eyed and with the widest smile, Chloe came up to say hello. She was wearing a tight black top, black tights and black boots, with a tartan skirt. Her long brown hair was in pigtails and she looked exactly the same as she had when we first met at college. My heart skipped a beat as our eyes met and it pained me that, after having been so close for so many years, we were like strangers as we stood there with each other. She looked happy, and I was worried that a boyfriend might have had something to do with that. Our conversation was strained and brief, and we stayed at our separate corners of the pub for the rest of the evening. All the while, I tried not to look in her direction for fear of seeing her with someone else. I left the pub intent on going to church, but fell asleep on the bus home and woke up miles away from my house. I walked back in my drunken state, talking to myself about Chloe, rationalising why it was never going to work out and why I should just put those thoughts out of my head forever. Visions of her celebrating Christmas with some other bloke brought tears to my eyes and a couple of expletives from my mouth.

Christmas was pretty much ruined by the thought of being so close to Chloe and yet having no contact. Apart from seeing my family, I spent time with some friends in

London and hooked up with an old girlfriend who wanted some company while I was there.

But then, Chloe called. Apparently, she had been going through the same thing, only she had been the bigger one out of the two of us, and had phoned me.

'D'you wanna go out for a drink?' she asked.

'Yeah, all right. Pick me up at eight.' See how cool that was? Nothing about how I'd ruined my Christmas moping around after her. Just non-committal and to the point.

Of course, my cool melted the minute I clapped eyes on her, and before we'd been in the pub ten minutes we were having the same old argument that had split us up in the first place: she wanted me to settle down and commit; I wanted more adventure.

'When are you coming back from Spain?' Chloe asked for the hundredth time.

Much to her displeasure, my reply was still, 'I'm not coming back. I'm just here for Christmas.'

Then it was my turn to ask, 'When are you coming to live with me in Spain?' as I had done many times before.

But this time was different. This time she didn't say 'no' straight away, but sat looking at me in silence. Finally, she spoke. 'Do you love me?'

I didn't even need to think about my answer. She felt like part of me, like with my family. No matter how much we yelled and screamed at each other, in the end we always knew we loved each other.

'Of course I love you – you know that. That's never been an issue.'

'And you promise you'll take care of me?' she pleaded.

I nodded and smiled and then reached for her hands. For the first time, she had said 'yes' to the idea of moving to Spain, but she hastened to add that she needed more time to think about it and that it would take her a while to quit her job and get everything in order.

'That's fine. That'll give me time to get out of Wayne's and get us an apartment!' I was genuinely excited. For the first time in years, it looked as though Chloe and I had a future together again.

Chloe and I had only been reunited for two days when I got a call from Vivian. She was desperate for a date in Marbella for a private New Year's Eve party and she promised to pay me 600 euros for the one night. Not a large amount considering the occasion, but she was a special case and she had also offered to pay for my flights, so I agreed to the job.

I spent 29 December with Chloe and left the next afternoon, after a teary goodbye. Knowing that Chloe was coming to Spain really made me want to knuckle down and do things right, concentrate on teaching and make a nice life for us in Marbella.

I spent the whole plane journey thinking about the wonderful places I'd been to with my clients and how I could take Chloe to see them. I also came to one unwelcome, but unavoidable conclusion. Escorting was not compatible with having a serious relationship. I'd have to let my clients know that I was no longer available.

I was taking early retirement. I'd already planned to tell Vivian about my new 'taken' status at the end of the night, before any lovemaking could take place. I had no intention of cheating on Chloe and I knew that telling Vivian the truth was better than just suddenly cutting off all contact without an explanation.

In my tuxedo, I fetched her glass after glass of champagne as she called me 'Garçon' and slapped my bottom. Then, when midnight arrived, we ate one tiny grape at each of the 12 strokes of the clock, before washing them down with more champagne and kissing each other. Everyone kissed at midnight, so this didn't count as cheating. Anyway, she put *her* tongue in *my* mouth.

In the taxi, on the way back to her villa in Estepona, Vivian's hands were all over me, and when I failed to respond she knew something was wrong. My immediate impulse was to lie and say I had a headache. I know it wasn't original, but I didn't want to ruin her night. Better for her to think I was unwell than that I wasn't available or, even worse, didn't fancy her. But my acting let me down on that occasion and she saw straight through me, jumping to the most hurtful conclusion.

'You don't want me.' Her normally authoritative voice quivered and tears welled up in her eyes. Vivian was a strong woman and I'd never seen her this way before – well, only when she'd been rehearsing for a part. This new 'vulnerable' side was painful to see. I realised she must have upsetting memories that she'd buried deep. I didn't want to be another one of them.

She was wrong about me not wanting her – very wrong. As drunk as I was, my erection had been unavoidable and it had been a real struggle keeping my hands to myself. I told her that, and she grabbed the bulge in my trousers for confirmation and then laughed, relieved that I was still attracted to her.

'I got back with my girlfriend – the one from college. Chloe.'

'The one who never wants to leave England?' She sounded incredulous.

'She's coming here to live with me. I can't do this any more,' I explained.

Vivian sighed and there was a brief pause. 'When is she coming?'

'February, maybe March.'

'So you're just going to wait for her for two or three months?'

'Yeah.'

'When you could be earning money for you both? How selfish!'

'What?'

'You're sacrificing being able to make her life as comfortable as possible, just so you don't feel guilty?'

'Well, yeah.'

'Do you not feel guilty about all those girls you've slept with since you've been apart?'

'No, not at all. We weren't together. I was single, so was she...' I hated to think about that – Chloe going with other blokes just as I had done with the girls in Spain.

'So, what difference are a few more months going to make? She's there; you're here. Once she gets here, you can quit then.'

And I had been seduced, as easily as that. Blinded partially by alcohol, but mostly by her seemingly good logic, I went with her to her bed and we made love. But unlike before, where my mind had been on Vivian while we were together, from that point on I always thought of Chloe.

I'd been living in Spain for three years and had lost count of the amount of times I had been to Malaga airport. Apart from my own trips back and forth to England and a few other European destinations, I'd met family, friends, girlfriends and clients – at one point on an almost weekly basis.

I remember on one occasion I had a client from Newcastle who wanted to be dropped off at the airport just a few hours before I was supposed to be meeting an Austrian girlfriend there. Sipping a *cerveza* as I watched the people come and go, it amused me how I'd spent so much time and energy chasing girls in the past, and yet now I just had to sit in the Arrivals lounge and they came to me.

Chloe's arrival, however, was to mark the end of most of those trips. I was determined to stop escorting. The last three months without her I'd been busy earning money from escorting, teaching and other odd jobs, to make sure she was as comfortable as possible when she arrived. I'd moved out of Wayne's and a lovely lady called Jacqui had found me a two-bedroom apartment, with a huge terrace, in the Old Town. I got my old job back at the restaurant so that, even if my students cancelled their lessons, I knew I could still pay my half of the rent each month. Everything was ready. But was I?

I'd been single since Chloe had dumped me three years

before, and when I used the term 'girlfriend' now it was in a loose sense. I'd never lived with a girl or made any attempts to be monogamous, and I'd had everything my own way. I could go out when I wanted, with whoever I wanted and do whatever I wanted to do. Sex and love were two very different things and my appetites had dictated that no one girl was enough.

But I hoped it would be different with Chloe. She reminded me of my past, when some of my innocence was still intact and, although we had both grown up, we still had those childhood feelings for each other. Chloe and I had never lived with each other, or anyone other than our families for that matter. And, even though we had lived in each other's pockets for the four years we were together, and that had never caused any problems, I could see trouble ahead.

I had grown up in a household where males outnumbered females three to one. There was me, my brother, my dad and then just my mum. So, any polite requests (her words; 'nagging', my word) from her were met with a kind of pack mentality response: well, the other two aren't doing it, so why should I? Toilet seats left up? Why not? Clothes left where they fell? Easier to find in the morning. Iron? Unless you meant West Ham, we were clueless. But then my brother went to the navy and became surprisingly domesticated, so when I had arrived in Spain I'd made a half-hearted effort to do the same, without very much success.

Now, all my *huevos* were being piled into one basket and I wasn't sure that moving in would help my commitment phobia. But, then, I reasoned that, if it all went wrong, splitting up wouldn't feel as bad as last time because I'd been there before and this time I knew what to expect.

Watching Chloe walk through the Arrivals gate felt strange, as if, even though I knew it was going to be her, I expected it to be a client. Perhaps I had been wishing with all those clients and girls that one of them would actually be Chloe, and, now it was really happening, it felt bizarre. As soon as we got out of the terminal building, I gave her a big cuddle and she admitted how surreal the whole thing seemed to her as well. We kept looking at each other and laughing, for no reason other than how weird it felt to be where we were after having been apart for three years.

'Everyone at home reckons this'll be a big test for us, living with each other,' Chloe said, as we drove back from the airport.

'It's a big step. But, however you want me to do things, you know, like squeeze the toothpaste or whatever, I'll do it that way.'

And I meant it. I didn't care about any of that; I had no fixed way of doing anything really – it was all quite random. I'd leave the apartment in one state one day – another, the next. Some days, I'd leave the washing up until the end of the day; other days, I did it as I went along. But now, I decided I would just do it however Chloe wanted it done.

To my relief, she liked the apartment and settled into Marbella quickly, landing a job with a real estate company. She preferred the more low-key bars and restaurants in Marbella to the bling-bling ones of Puerto Banus, because she said the atmosphere there reminded her too much of

Romford. She cried occasionally as, being a home bird, she missed her family. It must have been hard enough moving in with a bloke for the first time, without the added pressures of being in another country without her parents to run to if anything went wrong.

Thankfully, apart from a couple of tiffs, nothing did go wrong at first. This was surprising, as, from the start, I had decided to be honest with her about some of the local girls I'd slept with, so it couldn't have been nice to keep seeing them in the bars we visited. Had the tables been turned and I had been forced to spend a single evening with one of Chloe's ex-boyfriends, I don't think I would have taken it so well.

One thing I hadn't been so honest about was escorting. She knew about Jeana paying me to spend a few nights with her and she'd seen a television programme in which I'd been interviewed talking about being a gigolo, and a bit about me in a book written by the same bloke who'd made the programme. He was a friend of a client and I'd treated both things as a bit of fun, a break from routine and something to tell the grandkids. But I'd been quick to laugh the whole thing off at the time and, like many people back home, Chloe had dismissed the whole thing as a bit of a joke.

In the end, I decided that maybe honesty wasn't always the best policy and what Chloe didn't know wouldn't hurt her. I didn't do that to be clever, and I didn't feel like I was lying; I just withheld information. Anyway, as far as I was concerned, it was in the past and this was a fresh start.

A few times while we were out, I saw clients walk by and saw how they looked at us. The expressions on these clients' faces varied, from ones that said, 'If only she knew!' to 'Bitch! How does she stay so thin!'

No client ever dared to walk up to me while I was with Chloe because, for all they knew, any woman on my arm was likely to be another client. On one occasion, while I was out on my own, a former client approached me. For the sake of an easy life, I whispered, 'I'm actually working,' and then I nodded to the closest female to cut our chance encounter short. 'Call me, OK?' I added.

Although I had stopped escorting, I was still receiving calls and passing these on to the other escorts. It was actually good for business that former clients were seeing me out and not being able to speak to me – it reminded these women that a good escort would pay them his undivided attention. By making my time scarce, they were willing to pay more for it. And my very unavailability had sparked a certain desire in these women, which guaranteed the other blokes work, so a lot of the other escorts earned well out of my retirement.

For three months, Chloe and I lived blissfully in Marbella, spending afternoons on the beach and taking strolls along the promenade at night. We weren't making bundles of money, as we would have been in England, or if I'd been escorting, but our money went further and we were never short.

I remember feeling quite disappointed with myself when I thought about all the money I'd made through escorting, and how quickly I'd spent it on fancy clothes and expensive nights out. I felt bad that I hadn't saved anything or invested in something sensible, my only consolation being that I had never asked my parents for anything either. I'd been independent for a long time but, now I had Chloe as well, I wanted bigger and better things for the both of us.

I thought things were going fine for us, until one day Chloe told me she was going back to the UK to see her family and friends. Nothing wrong with that – except that she seemed to be saying something more.

'I just don't feel like I'm fitting in here,' she said sadly.

She'd been in Spain for only three months and yet I think she'd expected to be as established as I was after my three years here. She had told me once or twice that she felt more like 'Deano's girlfriend' than 'Chloe', when she went out with anyone we knew.

'You've only just got here! Come on, how easy is life here?'

Chloe always listed an easy life as one of her number-one priorities. But obviously she'd changed her mind. 'That's the other thing. Life is *too* easy here. I feel guilty or something. I don't feel like I've worked for three months!'

The old men who'd advised me never to get married were right when they told me, 'You'll never win with a woman.' I had purposefully been trying to make life as easy as possible for Chloe, believing that was what she wanted, but, now she had an easy life, it turned out she craved a challenge. By this stage, I'd learned enough about people to realise that, a lot of the time, what they say isn't what they mean. They're just saying words and hoping they match what they're feeling emotionally, even if they don't really understand how they feel. It's human nature to look for meaning in things we don't understand, but sometimes we can assign the wrong meaning. Chloe was feeling down, but the last thing I wanted was for her to associate her negative feelings with me. So, I knew I would have to let her go. But I wasn't happy.

'What's wrong with life being easy? I thought that's what you wanted,' I told her.

The confusion in Chloe's eyes revealed that she knew I was making sense. 'I don't know. Just let me go back and think for a while. I'll still give you rent.'

The money wasn't the issue, although admittedly it would have been hard for me to rent the apartment alone with just my restaurant and teaching wages. But focusing on the money side helped distract me from the sadness I felt at the possibility of losing Chloe again. It was easier to channel my thoughts into the problem of raising the other half of the rent, or of moving back into Wayne's, than to think about the reality of being without Chloe again after the three glorious months we'd just spent together.

'I don't want you to pay if you're not here. But if you're not coming back I need to rent out the spare room or something,' I said.

'I'll give you the rent and we'll see what happens, OK?'

Obviously, she didn't want me to rush into renting out the room in case she did choose to come back, but I was still disappointed. I couldn't have done any more to please her, and yet what she needed I was unable to give. She needed her family, her friends, a challenging career, and all of that was back in the UK. Maybe it was just different because I'm a boy, but a phone call once a week and a visit at Christmas had been all I needed to keep homesickness at bay.

I went with her to the bus station and we said our goodbyes before she left for the airport. She looked more relieved to be going home than upset to be leaving me. Standing there waiting for the bus, I tried to hide how frustrated I was at having changed my life around for the sake of three short months. Maybe she'll come back, I thought. But I knew that the probability of her choosing me over everything else she wanted and needed in her life was pretty slim.

Chloe had been gone a week and called me every day to say that she still loved me, but was still unsure of what she planned to do. My future was in her hands. My whole life felt like it was on hold until she came back. I had lost control over what happened to me.

Then the phone rang. A new client.

Deano was back.

In order to overcome the guilt I felt about contemplating escorting again, I worked myself up into a state of outrage about how unfair it was for Chloe to have gone home. She'd made me drop and change everything for her and then had just run off, back to her family. Now, if she didn't come back, I was going to have to find someone to rent the spare room, or earn enough money to afford it myself. And there on the other end of the line was the solution to my financial problems and already mounting sexual frustration.

What's a bloke supposed to do?

I could justify my actions to myself, but I knew that no one else would see things my way and that, if and when Chloe returned, someone would be only too happy to tell her

what I had been up to. So, when I resumed my escorting career, I had to take even more precautions than before, steering clear of many of my regular haunts in Marbella and taking my clients to more obscure places that I hadn't had the opportunity to try and test. As an escort, this is always a risk, as your job is to make sure that these women have the time of their lives. If you suggest somewhere and you haven't been there yourself, there's a real danger it will be a complete dive and using the 'friend recommended it' excuse just won't cut it.

If a woman comes to a strange town and she hires an escort to show her a good time, he must know where to take her. Not to where he goes himself to have a good time but, based on her preferences, where he believes she would like to go. But, with the possibility of Chloe coming back to Marbella, my options were very limited.

The restaurant I took my new client to was mediocre but, luckily for me, she had chosen it. Even more luckily, food didn't seem to be at the forefront of her mind. As soon as she'd downed enough wine, the skinny, highly strung accountant blurted out what she'd clearly been dying to ask since the evening began. 'Can we go back to the hotel?'

As soon as she'd said it, she acted as if she hadn't, busying herself with folding and refolding her napkin, as if it were the most engrossing task in the world.

We went back to her hotel. But even this part of the job I could justify to myself and I felt surprisingly little guilt about it. I knew that it meant nothing to me and, although the money would come in handy, I would never think about this woman again sexually. In fact, I wasn't even thinking about her while we had sex. On that particular occasion, no sexual thoughts or visualisation were needed, as, after a week or so without sex, I was hard at the drop of a hat and fit to burst.

If it hadn't been for Andy's exercises, I think the sex would have been over quite quickly but, to ensure client satisfaction, I had also decided to bring some condoms with a desensitising gel. I felt in complete control, like I could have gone for hours, but she was pretty sensitive and after an hour and a half she couldn't take any more.

I saw myself out because, she told me, her legs were so wobbly she daren't walk to the hotel-room door. Another satisfied customer.

I kissed her once more before leaving, and then went to Puerto Deportivo to get shit-faced. I drank till the early hours knowing that, when I finally woke up, most of the previous night would be a blur and any embers of guilt I might have felt would have been doused.

Three weeks later, Chloe did return, happy to be back and rejuvenated after having spent some time with her friends and family. She had come to her senses while listening to everyone complain about their jobs or their boyfriends and decided that, as they were all only a short flight away, she could bear living here in Spain.

Great news! I thought, but at the same time I also felt justified in having gone back to escorting. Chloe was fantastic, but I'd decided she was also fickle, so it made no sense any more for me to organise my life solely around her.

I convinced myself that my escorting would benefit us both and that, at least, if she decided to leave again, perhaps indefinitely this time, I'd know I hadn't put my life on hold for her. I remembered the pain I had felt when we broke up three years earlier and, looking back, I could see that I was different now. I'd never stopped loving Chloe, but I had loved other girls in various ways; ways that had distracted me from my constant thoughts of her.

I'd also learned, now, that love and sex were two very separate things. I no longer felt rejected on the occasions when Chloe didn't want to have sex, but I also felt justified in getting sex elsewhere, with my clients. It didn't mean I loved her any less – I wasn't going to run off and leave her – but sex is an appetite, like hunger or thirst, so why should I starve? I told myself.

It was a bit unfair, as my appetite seemed unquenchable at times, but that's why escorting made so much sense. I had all this excess energy and I knew that it probably wouldn't last my whole life, so why not make the most of it while I was young and able to earn some money out of it? I knew Chloe wouldn't see it my way, and that I had double standards. Although she'd never have dreamed of prostituting herself the way I did, if she had suggested it, the very thought of it was enough to make me feel crazy. That was where my well-thought-out argument fell short and I began to feel the twinges of guilt again. If the situation had been reversed, I knew I wouldn't have been able to stand it. In the old days, that realisation would have been enough to make me quit but, like I said, I'd changed. I'd found ways to justify what I did to myself and hide it from anyone I thought I couldn't justify it to.

So, having decided to continue escorting, but also to keep it a secret, I needed to start planning ahead. I knew I couldn't take clients out in Marbella in case I bumped into Chloe. Although it was unlikely, this was such a devastating scenario that I had to avoid it at any cost. I needed an alibi, which of course would be Frank. My other options were Wayne, whose lips would have sunk ships had he been in the navy, or Chad, who would probably have brought Chloe straight to wherever I was with my client, thinking he was being helpful.

'Where are you two off to all dressed up?' Chloe asked, as I opened the door and Frank appeared in a similar dark suit to my own.

We looked like the Blues Brothers and, unfortunately, with Frank being so tall and skinny, that made me the fat one.

'Casino. It's a mate's birthday,' Frank said, faithfully following the script we'd rehearsed.

'Who? Do I know him?' Chloe said, pretending to be interested.

'No, I don't think so. Billy don't come down this way much.' So far so good, but Frank never could resist a bit of ad-libbing. 'Come on, get your gear on and come with us,' he said to Chloe, smirking as I turned pale.

'She's tired, Frank. Come on, let's go,' I pleaded with him, the subtext being: 'Stop fucking about and ruining a perfectly good alibi!'

'Come on, Chloe, you'll love it.' Frank was enjoying himself, dragging the joke out longer than was funny.

I could see Chloe toying with the idea in her head and I felt my heart sink as I saw what should have been a perfectly straightforward evening becoming ever more stressful. Thankfully, she decided to stay put. 'No, it's too smoky in there. I'd rather not.'

Frank pretended to be heartbroken. 'Your loss. See you later darling,' he said, before giving her a peck goodbye.

As we made our way down the stairs, I went to give Frank a slap around the back of the head, but he ducked and I missed.

'Oi! I just did you a favour. Now she thinks she's got the better deal for the evening.'

He was right, but I told him not to invite her along next time I asked him to be my alibi. Frank's inability to take anything seriously was something I admired, as long as it was from a distance. I knew the consequences of getting found out and I knew that losing Chloe, after having convinced her to live with me in Spain, would have been no laughing matter. The important thing was that Chloe's mind was always at rest. I knew to phone her just before I picked up a client and at any opportunity during the evening, just to keep her sweet. She'd be in bed by ten most nights anyway, so, while she was busy getting her nine hours of beauty sleep, I was out entertaining clients. Well, some of the time.

Some of the jobs were, as we call them in the trade, 'wham bam thank you mams', where a woman would call you up to her hotel room for an hour or three and then you were done. It made no sense to go straight home after a job like that, so I'd go and meet Frank or Wayne for a drink in Stars afterwards. When I arrived home, I'd give them a shout 'goodbye', whether they were there or not, just in case Chloe was still up, and then I'd go to bed. In the morning, I'd wake up guilt-free and a little richer for my escapade.

It worked perfectly for a while, except for having to turn down lucrative trips to Madrid, Seville and a weekend in Tarifa, which I had to pass on to other escorts. But then I started getting sloppy. I stopped bothering to get Frank to come round and meet me and forgot to say where I'd be when I called her. Leaving everything to the last minute made life exciting, but each time I thought Chloe had found out I kicked myself for taking such stupid risks.

One day, however, she found something. A book of matches from a restaurant in Elviria. I'd told Chloe the night before that Frank and I had gone to Puerto Banus, when in actual fact I had taken a client out and, after lighting her cigarette, I'd stupidly put the matches back in my pocket.

'Have you got something to tell me?' Chloe wanted to know, dangling the matches in front of me.

'One cigarette!' I shouted. 'In how long? You know I haven't smoked for ages, then Frank just left them pointing at me on the bar in Desvan's.'

'These matches aren't from Desvan's,' Chloe said triumphantly.

'I know, they're from some restaurant the barman was plugging. I've made us reservations to go tonight, so dig out something nice, OK?'

Sometimes I amazed myself at the ease with which I could think of a plausible lie on the spur of the moment. Chloe's eyes lit up and she came over and gave me a big hug, before running off to the bedroom to find something to wear. It had been a stupid mistake, but I wouldn't make the same one again.

In every challenge, there is an opportunity. Any time Chloe challenged me, about anything, I used it as an opportunity to show her what a good boyfriend I was. It was true. I was a good boyfriend... apart from being a gigolo on the side.

Then, one morning, she found something else. I walked into the living room and she was sitting there with my wallet, which had 'fallen' out of my jacket by her account. I knew there were no numbers or incriminating evidence of where I'd been so I just asked her why she looked so concerned.

'Where did all this money come from?'

She knew full well I'd only had 50 euros when I went out and now there were 250 euros in the wallet.

'I won it.'

'How? You don't gamble.'

'I know. They talked me into playing poker. I just kept winning. Beginner's luck. I won't play again.'

She seemed to be OK with that excuse, and this time I really thought I'd learned my lesson. From that point on, I never put my wages in my wallet, I would always put them in my trouser pocket or my sock until I got home and then I'd hide it.

But then one night a few weeks later I came home drunk, forgot about the money, stripped off and left my trousers on the floor. In the morning, when she picked them up and found 400 euros in the pocket, she broke down in tears.

'Where did this come from? What have you been doing?' she wailed.

'A mate owed me it. He's only just paid me back,' I said. It was the first thing that came into my head as a friend had come up to me the previous evening to apologise for not having paid me back some money he owed me.

'Don't lie! It's drug money, isn't it!' Chloe looked so disdainful that I burst out laughing with relief.

Putting my arms around her, I reassured her that I had nothing to do with drugs and she should know that. I didn't buy them, sell them or take them. Not that I'm anti-drugs; I can see the appeal, it's just that my mind and body can't handle them. I remember buying a tiny amount of puff when I was a kid and convinced myself that every car that drove by on my way back from the dealer's flat was a copper. The last time I'd had a line of coke I'd ended up in tears, after smashing my fist into a tree and accusing the mate I was with of something ridiculous.

So, no, drugs are not my cup of tea. But I knew the truth was not much better, really, in terms of the effect it would probably have on Chloe. I decided on a sort of half-truth.

'Now, listen to me before you start getting upset,' I said, warning her of what was about to come.

She sniffed, her eyes still teary and her lips quivering.

'I haven't cheated on you.' Which was true in my warped little mind, because I had been paid for it. 'But I've been escorting a few older women. That's where the money's come from.'

She looked bewildered. 'When... oh... what, really? I thought that was all a joke.'

'It was, but then women started calling for real. The

274

money's too good, Chloe, and I don't have to sleep with them or anything.'

'They pay you just to take them out?'

'Yeah, all right, don't sound so surprised.' I thought that turning the argument around and making her feel sorry for me might be a good idea at this point, before the shock wore off and she got angry. 'I just thought, while you're in bed and my mates are pissing their money up the wall, I could earn a few bob. Then we can get a place of our own out here.'

I suppose deep down I knew what I was doing when I threw that into the equation. Now she had the issue of whether or not she wanted to buy a place in Spain to deal with, instead of thinking too deeply about my escorting.

'Do you trust me?' I asked.

'I did. I don't know what to think about this.'

'Hasn't everything been great between us?'

'Yeah, but I don't wanna have to share you.'

'You're not sharing me. You're in bed, you don't need me – you're just lending me out for a couple of hours.' I laughed, but she just sighed and wiped her tears away before going into the bedroom and shutting the door behind her.

As arguments go, I thought I'd got away with that one pretty lightly. But Chloe had never been one to scream and shout – not in an argument, anyway.

I picked the money up off the floor and went into the living room to watch the news on the only English channel we had. I heard the bedroom door open again and expected Chloe to appear with suitcases in her hands. Instead, she came in and sat beside me on the sofa. We cuddled, and then kissed, and not another word was spoken about the money or escorting.

That whole summer passed harmoniously, with me escorting while she was in bed and then treating her with my earnings, after I had put some aside for a rainy day. I'd take her out clothes shopping, but drew the line at jewellery shops, dragging her away from more than one window. I still wasn't quite ready to put a ring on her finger, but she seemed content anyway. Our friends and family came to stay with us and we enjoyed barbecues on our terrace, during which I'd never have my phone on. I might not have been monogamous, but I still wanted to be respectful and keep Chloe as shielded from my escorting as possible.

More and more of the men I came across talked to me about wanting to be escorts, but I'd stopped the website by this stage and had no 'agency' to speak of. I worked around that by employing a bartering system with these men, whereby I'd send clients their way and they would reward me in kind by sending any clients they couldn't handle my way. By the end of the year, I knew masseurs in most of the top spas, porters and pool boys from the top hotels, country club waiters, diving and dance instructors, every one of them owing me favours, and every one of them wanting to step into my shoes and give escorting a go. And, yes, I encouraged them. Why not?

One estate agent took a client out partying, joining her in her coke binge line-for-line until they arrived back at her hotel and he realised he had a problem. It was three o'clock in the morning when I received his phone call.

'My dick's gone!' His voice was low and strained.

'What? Are you still with her?' I asked, getting out of bed and making my way up on to the terrace to get a better reception and not disturb Chloe.

'She's in the bedroom, waiting. I've shrivelled up to nothing.'

I didn't know what to tell him, other than that he should've known better. I wanted to hang up on him and get back to bed, but I realised that this bloke had never had an 'Andy' and it was my time to pass on some knowledge. 'Have you got any Viagra?'

'Yeah, but it's not working.'

'How long ago d'you take it?'

'About five minutes ago. I've been in here that long and nothing's happened!'

'OK, it'll take a while. Go in and go down on her for a while...'

'Fuck off, I'm not eating her out!' he said.

'You've got two options, Stew. You can go down on her till you're hard, or you can run out of there with your maggot and get laughed at.'

Sometimes you have to be cruel to be kind. Luckily for him, by the time she had climaxed, he was ready. Not so luckily, she decided she didn't want penetrative sex anyway and refused to do anything with his by now painful erection.

Life was good, and it looked as if it was just going to keep getting better. I had the best of both worlds: on the one hand, the stability of the bar job and a great girlfriend at home and, on the other, the money and excitement that came from escorting.

But then came Christmas time and Chloe was once again homesick. She wanted to go back to the UK and she wanted me to go with her.

'I can't just leave, Chloe. I've got commitments.' Instantly, I regretted using that word. The last thing any woman wants to hear is about your commitments to another woman or, in my case, women.

'Well, I'm going,' she said, sulking on the sofa. 'I can't believe you're going to make me spend Christmas on my own.'

'You're going back to your family. How are you going to be alone? If you feel alone there, don't go!'

'You know what I mean! Without you!'

'I can't just pick up and go like that. I've got too much to do here.'

And so it looked as if we were going to spend our first Christmas as a couple in four years in separate countries. But then December turned out to be not as busy as I'd expected it to be, what with my students wanting their break and a few of my regulars being away. I had a brainwave. Why not go back and surprise Chloe?

When she woke up, the day before Christmas Eve, I was sitting on the end of her bed looking at her and smiling. She nearly fell out of the bed when she saw me, she was so shocked, and for a brief moment I thought I wasn't welcome.

'My mum told me you'd come back,' she said, hugging me and putting my doubts to rest.

As usual, I stayed with my parents in Rainham for Christmas, but they were just a 20-minute walk from Chloe's parents, so I alternated between the two. Chloe seemed so much happier to be around her family and friends, and on more than one occasion suggested we came back to the UK and stayed for good. But, as I looked out at the grey skies and watched the rain stream down the window, all I could think about was being back in Marbella.

It rains in Marbella, too, of course, but, even when it rains there, it always seems colourful and brighter. Maybe I suffer from that seasonal affective disorder, I thought to myself. But then I realised that it wasn't just the weather that bound me to Spain. When I first arrived in Marbella, having been in education all my life and with a girlfriend for four years, my identity was incomplete. I still had so much to learn about who I was, what I wanted and what I was capable of. In a way, going to Marbella was like being born again; like I was having a fresh start, could be whoever I wanted to be and forget about my past. But now, being back in Essex, living with my family and going out with Chloe made me feel like I was back to square one. It was as if I hadn't grown at all, as if all of those painful lessons were worthless.

'I can't stay here, Chloe. Not yet,' I said, worried what her reaction would be.

'I know. It doesn't suit you here any more. I'm just being selfish.'

'No, you're not. It's just; I don't feel like I'm anyone here. I feel trapped, like I'll never get anywhere.'

'Where do you wanna get to?' she asked, looking at me and waiting for an answer.

But even after all that time I wasn't sure what my future could hold. I could see the problems we'd have financially if

I was 'just a teacher' or 'just a barman', but I was well aware of the consequences if I carried on escorting.

Chloe saw my indecision. 'I just want you to be happy. Whether that's here or in Spain. But I just want it to be you and me.'

I looked into her eyes and realised that this was my ultimatum. She was putting her foot down and telling me to put an end to my escorting, or risk losing her.

'I don't care about the money. I don't care if you're a teacher. But the nights out, they've got to stop.'

I knew what she meant. She would never have stopped me seeing my friends, but, even when I'd successfully hidden all evidence, she instinctively knew when I'd been out with a client instead of with mates. How could I tell? Because if I'd been out with friends, the next day she'd always ask me if I'd had a good time, whereas, after the nights I'd been out with a client, I got the silent treatment. I'd kidded myself that I could get away with working without hurting her feelings, but, even though I'd done all I could to hide it, I suppose there's only so much any woman can take.

If the roles had been reversed, I don't think I could have been as forgiving, but I had been given a final chance to prove myself. When she asked me where I wanted to get to, Chloe knew it wasn't ambition I lacked, but direction, and she needed to know we were both heading the same way. When I had first become an escort, I was single. Now that wasn't the case, I had to come up with a new plan for making my fortune.

Chloe was right that money wasn't everything. But in my

time I'd been reasonably well off and I had been flat broke, and I knew which one I preferred. Whatever happened, I was still going to work towards earning some proper money, but this time I wasn't going to put my health or my relationship at risk. And the only place where I could see myself being able to do that was Spain.

CHAPTER FOURTEEN

Gemma

'Some women are born faithful. Even while they're paying you to sleep with them, in their heads they're still faithful. It's in their genes.' ANDY

From 1 January 2006, I'd worked every minute my brain and body could handle. If I wasn't at the restaurant, I was teaching English. If I wasn't teaching, I was writing. I'd decided to try and get some of my gigolo experiences down on paper, as much so that I could make sense of them as anything else. Although we were living together, I hadn't seen Chloe for more than an hour at a time since her return from England a month earlier, so I'd promised to take her out. I had made reservations at Da Bruno's on the seafront and I was planning to surprise her by telling her about the trip to Granada and Sierra Nevada that I'd booked.

When we first got together, I had bought Chloe snowboarding lessons for her 18th birthday, and I went along with her to see if I would enjoy it as well. I thought it was quite a laugh but, after breaking my wrist on a dry ski-slope in Brentwood, I lost the urge to go again, despite knowing how much Chloe had enjoyed it. Neither of us had ever been on proper snow and I knew how much she had always wanted to go, so after dinner it would make a great surprise.

We were cuddling on the sofa, her watching *Sex in the City* and me trying to forget about work and money for a moment, when my mobile rang. I felt Chloe's attention shift to me as I slipped off and up to the terrace with my mobile. I had a legitimate excuse to do this as the apartment was made of stone and, as a result, we got a very bad signal while we were inside. Still, I seemed to get as much of a workout from constantly going up and down those stairs as I did at the gym. The most frequent phone calls I got now were from students rather than clients, as I was holding to the promise I'd made at Christmas to quit escorting. I had no desire to make Chloe cry any more than she had done. I wanted to be a good boyfriend and eventually a good husband and father, and so I knew I needed a proper career and to earn some real money. But that meant taking the time to develop the career, which meant suffering financially. That was where the decision to stop escorting had been difficult. We were OK financially, but not as comfortable as we were before. That skiing trip would mean I had to take on more students, work more shifts at the restaurant and that meant less time for writing. I seemed trapped in a vicious circle of poverty, doomed to work long hours for little benefit.

Which is why, when I heard the woman's voice on the phone, a little voice inside of me said 'why not?' She asked for the escort service she'd been told about by a friend. She requested me specifically and said she'd pay me 400 euros for the night.

Looking back on it, I could easily accuse myself of being motivated by lust or greed, but I know that at the time I felt justified in agreeing to the job. When I heard the amount she was willing to pay, all I felt was relief. Like the pressure was off me. I could finally relax and spend some time with Chloe without feeling guilty that I wasn't working and earning money. When I returned, phone in hand, Chloe had pressed pause and was looking at me expectantly. This was my opportunity to come clean to her, to tell her I'd just made a stupid mistake but would rectify it right away, that of course I wouldn't do anything to wreck the night out we had planned. But of course I didn't.

'Just a friend,' I told her.

I hadn't been out with my friends or Chloe for weeks. The only time I'd left the apartment was to work. When Chloe went to bed, I sat up at my laptop, and when she got up in the morning I was often still there. Having to cancel our evening together was bad enough, but going out and leaving her on her own, to think about whether I was just with friends or not, was worse.

Chloe could tell I had something on my mind. She sat up and turned the television off, already suspecting what I was about to say. She looked down and shook her head silently as I came and sat next to her again. I was unsure whether she was going to cry or beat me to death with the remote, so either way holding her was a sensible move.

'I love you, babe,' I said, pulling away from her but still holding her arms, just in case.

'You're going out, aren't you?' She tensed up and I had to say something before she started crying.

'I'm taking you to Granada. I've booked a hotel and we're going to go snowboarding...'

There was a silence and then suddenly Chloe's body relaxed. 'What? You said you were too busy!' The disapproving look vanished and her mouth was wide open in shock, while her eyes smiled. She threw her arms around me and sighed in relief.

'It's booked. Two weeks' time,' I said.

She groaned with delight as she squeezed me.

'But I have to go out tonight,' I added. I tried to pull away, but she held on to me so tightly, pleading for me not to go. I felt her tears wet my back as they rolled off her cheeks. 'It's just a few hours, Chloe. I'll be back later,' I said, pulling away and wiping the tears from her face.

Then she sniffed and nodded. 'You're just going out?'

I nodded and tried to smile. 'Yeah, just out, with some mates.'

'We're really going snowboarding?'

'Yeah, on snow. No more dry ski-slopes!'

'Do you have to?'

'Sorry, babe. I'll make it up to you, I promise.'

And I meant it. I hated seeing her upset and I knew that spending time with me was what she wanted – not skiing trips, clothes or other things. I felt terrible knowing that I was about to break my promise. Even if I chose not to sleep with this client, I was still lying to Chloe.

After getting ready, I gave her a long kiss goodbye and opened the door to leave.

'Be careful,' she said, smiling, but still with watery eyes.

'I love you, Chloe,' I said, watching her mouth the words back as I closed the door.

I really didn't feel in the mood for this job, knowing what I was risking with Chloe. I wanted to turn the car around and take her to the restaurant. So what if we've got no money? I thought.

But then, at a red traffic light, the voice in my head stopped as I looked at myself in the rear-view mirror. 'You're not doing this for you,' I told myself, looking sternly into my own eyes, hoping to override my guilt and my fear. I was in the car now, this was my last time and I was going to make it good. No nerves, no more hesitancy, my last escorting job ever.

As if I needed any more discouragement, before the exit for Puerto Banus the police were flagging drivers over to breathalyse them. I hadn't touched a drop so I knew I was OK on that count. My main problem was that I had no identity card or passport and the papers in the car were Brian's, not mine. I handed them to the copper anyway and pretended that I didn't speak Spanish, only to discover that his English was more or less fluent.

He walked back to one of the police cars and showed the others my papers. They called out over their CB and I stared at them trying to detect any change of expression on their faces. They nodded to each other and then took a final look at the papers, before heading back towards the car.

'Next time, take with you your passport. *Vale?*'

No problem, officer, thank you and good day.

In my stupidity, I took this as a good sign. Things were going to go right from here on. Now if I could just get to my escorting job, please. I hung on to the little plastic mouthpiece in case I needed to prove to my client why I was late.

As I pulled into the PYR hotel's forecourt, I saw a brown-haired middle-aged woman in a stylish black slip dress standing at reception, looking hopefully at me. Not knowing whether or not this was her, but wanting to give an appearance of confidence, I got out of the car and walked around to open the passenger door. The woman was hesitantly making her way towards the door, still staring at me, so I smiled and nodded towards the passenger seat. She smiled back and warily made her way towards the car.

'Are you Deano?'

'That's right. Gemma?' I said, kissing her on each cheek before taking her hand and helping her into the car. I closed the door and skipped round to the driver's seat. 'Sorry I'm a tad late. The police were stopping everyone,' I said, pointing at the small white plastic mouthpiece on the dashboard.

'So, where would you like to go?' I asked, revving the engine and then pulling out of the hotel.

'Ooh, I'm not sure. Where d'you think's nice?'

'There are plenty of nice places. Do you like seafood?'

'Not really. Gives me a funny tummy.'

'So you like meat?'

'Ooh, yeah. Meat and veg. Keep it simple.'

This was good news as there was an Argentinean carvery around the corner from her hotel. I parked in the underground car park, where I'd hidden once upon a time, and walked her to the restaurant. There were pictures of South American revolutionaries and flags over the walls, and wine racks were located at various spots. A young Moroccan waiter brought our drinks and explained that their 'all-you-can-eat' price didn't include the alcohol.

'That's fine. Ta,' said Gemma, eagerly watching the table opposite as another waiter carved a generous slice of meat from the skewer on to an old man's plate.

'So, how long are you in Marbella?' I asked, already wondering to whom I could pass on her second call.

'My last night tonight. I leave tomorrow afternoon.'

'Well, you're going back with a lovely tan,' I said, comparing my hand to hers. I hadn't seen much sun so far that year as I had been too busy working to sunbathe or go for my usual walks along the promenade with Chloe.

'Thanks. That's all I've done. Eat, drink and sit on the beach reading.'

'Sounds like a great holiday.' If it hadn't caught the light at that moment I'd have completely missed the ring on her finger, which showed how even a few months off had made me rusty.

She saw me spot the ring and she cleared her throat.

'Separated?' I asked, looking away to the bar as if the answer to that question was of no importance to me.

She smiled and gave a sad nod.

As the juicy meat fell to our plates from the skewer,

Gemma told me all about her life in Nottingham. It was a lovely place, she told me, apart from the gangs.

'I heard there's a fair bit a bother over here,' she said, eyes wide with anticipation.

Whenever I talked about Marbella or Puerto Banus, I would never lie, unless I wanted to impress someone about my 'knowledge' of the place. But I did have a tendency to miss certain things out. Like the hairdresser shooting. Or the Linekers shooting. Or the leg found in a bin in La CampaÒa.

For the residents, these things were rarely a surprise as we'd all grown accustomed to the downside of living in an area heavily populated by criminals of all nationalities. But, for the holidaymakers, I saw it as bad PR to inform them of something they could read about back in the UK once their holiday was over and which, nine times out of ten, would never affect them anyway. But, then, if someone had heard something and they asked you about it, it made for interesting conversation.

'...But they'd kidnapped the wrong guy!' I explained, recounting the second-hand tale of one of my students. He was a policeman and he'd worked on the 'mistaken-identity kidnapping' in Nueva Andalucia. He had arrived late for his lesson and told me what he could, and then later, when the man was released and told the newspapers his story, I'd found out the rest.

'Still, it's everywhere nowadays. There's no escape,' she sighed, shrugging her shoulders.

'So what do you do for fun back in Blighty?' I asked, trying to get back to a brighter topic.

'Don't laugh,' she said, touching my arm, 'but I go salsa dancing with me mate on Thursdays and bingo on Fridays.'

'Salsa dancing?'

'Yeah, we're not right good, but it's a laugh.'

'Well, you're gonna have to show me.'

'You what?' she said, looking around the restaurant as if I were asking her to dance there and then.

'I know a place on the Golden Mile that does salsa every Friday night. We'll go after this,' I said, taking the lead but watching for any real resistance.

She bit her bottom lip and gave a wide-eyed nod.

Now, unlike normal dancing, Salsa doesn't freak me out so much. There are set moves and so you can just copy what everyone else is doing without appearing to be taking the piss. If you look at another couple, they're usually flattered that you are using them to see how it's done. It's not like proper dancing where, in Romford at least, if I stood beside a bloke and started copying his moves he'd be more likely to deck me than smile at me. A few girls had actually shown me some salsa moves in the past, but I was usually drunk and, instead of watching where our feet were going, I would be looking down the girl's top. But I always blamed my terrible memory and lack of co-ordination for my slow learning.

So, after our meal, we got back in the Mercedes and headed towards Marbella on our way to The Loft on the Golden Mile. The fact that there were a few beginners on the floor getting instruction helped me to relax. Gemma, however, was clutching her bag and drink, and hugging the back wall of the club.

'Leave your drink there. You can't dance with it,' I said, but she shook her head.

'I'm not putting my drink down.'

She was quite firm about that, so I smiled and laughed and tried to get her to dance on the sidelines with me.

'Everyone's looking,' she said, scanning the club.

'No, they're not,' I replied, ignoring everyone but her. It was weird doing that again after so long. Pretending that we were the only ones there; forgetting about everyone else and concentrating exclusively on making her smile, laugh or feel wonderful.

'They probably think I'm your mum,' she said.

I was used to these self-deprecating comments, as so many of my clients had felt as if they didn't deserve the attention or the compliments they were getting.

'Why do you care what they think? You're going home tomorrow. Last night tonight, so you'd better enjoy it.'

And so, with her bag on her shoulder and her glass in her hand, we attempted to salsa. I acquitted myself rather well, I thought, considering the circumstances and the fact that every sudden move brought a cascade of wine down my back.

After her second drink, Gemma decided that she was salsa'd out and wanted to go back to the hotel. She started to talk very rapidly as we approached her room and the confidence she'd oozed on the dance floor was once again hidden. Perched on the edge of the bed, she wrung her hands in her lap, as if waiting for some terrible news. I sat beside her, putting one arm behind her and another on her thigh.

She looked up at me nervously and I smiled. This would have usually been where I comforted the anxious client and told her not to worry about anything – to relax. But not this time. Before I had even got halfway through my 'relax' routine, her face screwed up and she burst into tears. She had seemed like she was having a good time up until that point, despite being a little tense, but this was something new for me. Andy had not given me any advice about crying women, except that, when some women orgasm, that's what they do instead of twitching or screaming. What was I meant to do now?

'Hey, Gemma. What's wrong? Don't cry. Tell me what's wrong.' I cradled her in my arms, grateful that we were in a hotel room and not out on the street, attracting attention. Then, suddenly, my heart stopped. I had no Dictaphone. I had no way of proving that she had invited me up to her room or that I had not been the cause of her tears. I felt like crying myself as I realised how stupid I had been. I thought about what this would do to Chloe. My getting arrested and ending up in prison in Spain, for attempted rape, of all things.

But maybe it wouldn't get that far. Maybe she was just crying because she didn't want to pay. That was the other thing. I had been so flustered by arriving late that I hadn't even asked her for the money yet. But I knew I would rather walk out of there empty handed than have a rape allegation hanging over my head.

'I-I-I'm m-m-married,' she bawled.

'Is that all? I mean...' I winced, sometimes those things just come out under stress. 'Why are you upset?' I asked, regaining my previous compassion.

'He loves me. He'd never do this to me. What am I doing?'

'We don't have to do anything, we can just talk.'

'This was his idea.'

'Hiring an escort?' That was a first. If the husband was paying, in my experience, normally he at least wanted to be present to watch.

'No! Coming here, on holiday, alone. He thinks I just need a break.'

'Well, what do you need, Gemma?'

'I don't know... I just want him to... oh, I don't know.'

'You do. What do you want, Gemma? I don't know him or anyone else you know, so you can tell me.'

'I'm a terrible woman,' she repeated, over and over again.

'No, you're not. Don't say that. Why do you think that?'

'I want him to... I wish he'd pay me as much attention as... the kids.'

I felt terrible for this poor woman and, although she looked nothing like Chloe and we didn't have any children, I felt like this conversation had significance for my life. I asked her to explain and she cried some more and repeated what a terrible woman she was.

'He works all the time... and when he's not working it's always the four of us. The kids.'

Could this be another glimpse at one possible future? I thought. Would work ever become so important that I'd become blind to Chloe's needs and drive her into someone else's arms?

As Gemma cried into my chest, I saw that I had already started to carve a similar path to her husband. This was where Chloe and I would end up if I kept on doing what I was doing. Her seeking from someone else something she lacked at home and me blind to it, as I did what I thought was best for my family.

'Have you told him how you feel?'

'It's so hard. He does so much, it feels so wrong to ask him for anything more.' She dug around in her handbag and pulled out a packet of tissues.

'If you don't tell him what you need, Gemma, you can't expect him to read your mind.'

'I know. It's just sometimes I can't say. I can't... put it into words. It sounds so silly.'

'Are you happy, Gemma?'

She looked at me and her bottom lip quivered uncontrollably before she burst into tears again. 'I was going to leave him, but it doesn't seem right. He hasn't done anything wrong. I know it would kill him.'

'You've every right to feel how you feel. But, if you can't make him see how serious this is, how unhappy you are, then nothing will change.'

'How do I make him...?' she said, shaking her head.

We sat there on the bed and talked for hours about how he used to be with her, when they first met. How he used to remember all their special days, like their first kiss, their first 'I love you' and the like. He used to phone her from work more than once a day, just to see what she was doing, and whether she was asleep or not, on his way out in the morning, and before he went to bed each night, he would kiss her. But then, once the kids came along, all of that attention just got taken away from her and was devoted to them instead.

'I know I sound so selfish...'

'No, you don't. He needs to find a balance.'

Once we'd made a list of the things that her husband used to do, but didn't do any more, we talked about him.

'What does he love about you?'

Again, she burst into tears. 'I don't know any more. He used to love everything I did and he'd tell me that. My sense of humour, the way I ironed his shirts for him, leaving him good luck notes each time he went for an important meeting... he used to love it all.'

So we went through all of that stuff as well and, by the end, I was exhausted. It was past one o'clock and we were just about done, but then I got a sinking feeling as I was about to say goodbye.

'You are going to tell him all this, aren't you?' I asked.

'Well, I can't show him – it's your handwriting!' She was holding up the list we'd scribbled together.

'No, but please. Make sure you tell him.'

I felt that, as there was every possibility I would be in this man's shoes one day, I had to make sure she told him everything and didn't just carry on living an unhappy life. She nodded, but I wasn't convinced.

'Sod it, let's phone him,' I said, walking back to the phone on the bedside table.

'What? It's one o'clock. He'll be asleep.'

'It's only twelve there and, anyway, it's the weekend,' I replied, picking up the receiver and handing it to her.

'I couldn't wake him, I'd feel terrible,' she said, putting the receiver back down on the hook.

'If it was one of the kids phoning, if they were in trouble...?' I started to ask, picking up the receiver again.

'He'd answer it and go wherever he was needed,' she said, nodding, and reached for the phone.

As she dialled the number, a pleasant feeling washed over me. It was that same feeling I'd have got from giving up my seat or helping a woman with a pram at some stairs. I felt needed – useful, even.

'It's me. No, I'm fine. I just wanted to talk to you.'

I watched as she took her list and squinted at my hurried handwriting. She looked at me and I mouthed 'SORRY' and shrugged. She smiled and wiped her tears away with a tissue.

'Geoff, do you remember when you used to...' she began, and I felt that I had done at least one thing right that evening. For the first time in my escorting career, I'd made someone happy, rather than just given momentary pleasure.

Creeping out of the door, I hoped that maybe the karma bus would now save me from being in the same position as Geoff one day. Even when I remembered I hadn't been paid, I had no urge to go back and get my money, nor did I feel that I had lost out. I bet old Geoff would have paid much more than 400 euros to know what he had to do to make his wife feel loved and happy again, before it was too late. I'd just received a very important lesson, 25 years in advance, and that would last longer than the 400 euros would have. Seemed like a fair deal to me.

When I got home, I got undressed in the spare bedroom

and glanced over at my laptop, overcome by a strong urge to write down what had just happened. But then I knew I'd think of other things as well and end up staying there for hours, so instead I crept into the bedroom.

I slipped under the covers and snuggled up to Chloe's warm body, putting my hand on her belly. Her hand reached down through the fog of sleep, and fastened on to mine. I didn't have to write the night's events down. I had committed them to memory already and I knew that, in the morning, I would turn over a new leaf. Then, I thought, why wait till morning?

'Love you, babe. Night,' I whispered, kissing her head. It's something I'd always done when we first got together, but for some reason I'd stopped somewhere along the way.

Then I fell asleep with her in my arms.

Epilogue

'We come in alone; we go out alone. But in between, we just want some good company, whether we have to pay for it or not.' ANDY

On that same night in February 2006, I decided once and for all that my escorting days were over. The next day, I took the SIM card from my phone and threw it away, keeping a few numbers written down, just in case. The Merc had to go back to Brian anyway, as, without the money from escorting, I couldn't afford to keep it.

Giving up escorting for Chloe was not a hard decision to make because I knew that there was only so much any woman could take, and I had caused her enough pain already. Unfortunately, it wasn't enough. She eventually found out more about my gigolo days, and decided she couldn't trust me. And who could blame her?

The temptation to go back to escorting will always be there, I suppose, but for the moment I am going to concentrate on other things. There is more to life than money and work and, as long as I'm paying my own way, maybe how I earn a living doesn't matter that much. I'd like a proper job, eventually. When I say proper, I mean respectable. I want to be able to talk to the woman in my life about my work and not have to keep anything from her. I want to be someone my children can be proud of. When they ask me what I do for a living, I want to put them on my shoulders and take them with me to show them where Daddy works. Hardly appropriate in a few of my previous jobs, I think you'll agree.

I'm the last person to make judgements on anyone else, particularly those in the sex trade, as I think they provide a valuable service. But I have other options and I am capable of more. In the end, my decision comes down to what I want out of life. Despite my past, my goals are pretty conventional. I want a career (eventually), a wife and children. But, more specifically, I want to be a good husband, a good father and a good enough professional that I can put food on the table and keep a roof over our heads. Escorting was fun, but it's not going to get me the future I have in mind.

The last four years have been a hell of ride, full of great memories of family and friends, lovers and clients, and, of course, Chloe. My three years as an escort taught me a lot, not just about women, but also about life in general. Not that I'm an expert, or anything, but I've learned what I've needed to know, and that has always been enough. My role as an escort has helped me to understand women a lot better. Even though Chloe and I are no longer together, I think I was able to get closer to her because of what I learned from escorting. When I'm ready, I know I'll meet someone else, and I'll be able to use what I learned from escorting to be a better, more honest partner.

I consider myself extremely lucky for so many reasons. For having had the experiences I had while I was an escort and for being in a position to tell people about them. For having made mistakes, but none so bad that I couldn't learn from them and move on. For having been blessed with such a loving and forgiving family and for having such loyal friends. Who wouldn't feel grateful for all of that?

That's not to say my life is now a bed of roses! Apart from upsetting Chloe and my family, one of the other downsides to having been an escort is the way the job seems to rob life and love of its mystery. Maybe it's true that you can't judge a book by its cover – I have definitely been proven wrong on more than one occasion. But, in my experience, the gut feeling I get from the first few pages is often the right one. When you make a living from interacting with people, you begin to see the predictability of most humans and you begin to appreciate the random crazies a lot more!

Love, attraction, confidence... they are all just states, reproducible at will, under the right conditions. Recently, I read an article in the newspapers about an actor leaving his wife after falling for a co-star. It happens all the time, actors working together as on-screen lovers only to fall in love off-screen. Ever wondered why? Well, they are going through the motions, aren't they! Just as I had done as an escort. They are doing and saying the things that people in love or lust do and say, so why wouldn't they start to have those feelings? The problem for those actors is that, when the on-screen romance is over, unless their real-life characters are so suited anyway, the off-screen romance will also come to an end.

And that's how it is with most relationships I've seen. As soon as the honeymoon period's over, they stop saying and doing the things that make them and their partner feel loved, because they're waiting to feel the emotion first. But, if you always wait for the mood to take you to do things, you must expect to miss out on a lot in life. If you wait until you feel passionate, romantic or loving before you start acting that way for your partner, don't be surprised if they go elsewhere – whether that's with a friend, a colleague or an escort.

We all have needs and wants and the first thing we learn to do as babies is to communicate those to our parents. Then, for some reason, as we grow older and become involved in an adult relationship, we feel scared that asking for what we want or informing the other person of what we need will somehow ruin that relationship. Let me ask you something. If the person in whom you confide your wants and needs doesn't want to help you with those, why be in a relationship with them?

I'm not a mind-reader. With Chloe or any other woman I wanted to please, I had to play detective and find out what they wanted or needed. I had to ask them questions when the answers couldn't be deduced from other things. But most people see that as hard work, as opposed to an investment for which they will be rewarded with a happy bed- or life-partner.

Escorting also made me question myself and taught me a lot about my strengths and my weakness. It gave me an opportunity to push myself to see what I was capable of and helped me to grow and improve. Maybe it isn't for everyone but, like national service, I think a couple of years would do any young man some good. Some of the clients I met during my time introduced me to all sorts of fascinating subjects, from aromatherapy to Zen Buddhism and, with every conversation I had, I learned something I could use in my own life or perhaps with another client. None of them managed to convert me to politics, mind you, and, as soon as a conversation headed in that direction, I would play the dumb blond and change the subject as soon as possible.

I learned that physical beauty really does pale in comparison to a woman with a beautiful mind. As corny as that may sound, no one would deny that the way a person thinks, talks or acts can have an overriding influence on how we view them physically. When I started out, I was bogged down by a woman's age or physique, but I soon learned to look past the external and search for what was inside. Unfortunately, time is as cruel to some people's personalities as it is to their bodies, although thankfully I didn't meet too many of those!

I think the most important lesson I learned from being an escort is that happiness and pleasure are two different things. Happiness really is just an outlook on life, a way of travelling. It's something that you can learn with a little bit of effort and for free. Pleasure has always got a price tag and, if you can't see one, it'll probably cost you more than you can afford.

There is nothing wrong with that, but we have to realise that, if we don't work for our pleasures, we will have to pay somewhere else down the line.

Women who came to me seeking purely pleasure usually left satisfied, but there were others who were just merely unhappy and thought I would be their solution. These women might have found temporary satisfaction in spending time with an escort and, mistaking that pleasurable feeling for happiness, they returned again and again. It was my job to make them feel good and I felt good doing it, although almost anyone could have offered these women the same thing if they'd just asked, 'What can I do for you?'

Instead, most people just wait to be told what they're not doing and even then, sometimes, they put off fulfilling the other person's needs out of fear, or resentment, or a host of other negative emotions. It's very easy to let fear stop us doing things, or to let other emotions get in the way of potentially satisfying relationships. Unfortunately, people often don't realise that life is too short until it's too late. They hold grudges, they cut off old friends and they say and do things that they later regret.

I don't want any regrets, so I try not to let negative emotions get in my way. I don't regret having been an escort, although I do regret the pain it has caused some of those near to me. I think it's true that you can't please everyone all of the time and that, no matter what anyone says, you should go for what you want. But, after seeing the effect that my escorting had on my family and on Chloe, I decided I had to give it up. Pleasing my clients had taken over, when I should

have been concentrating on my loved ones. I've learned that lesson now and I will always put my family first.

But, other than my family, I have no reason to be in England. I have found my niche in Marbella and I have made a comfortable life for myself here. No underground system, no big city, no stressful office or overdemanding boss. At the moment, I still give private English lessons, walking along the beach to my classes in Puerto Banus, laughing with my students as we go for a drink afterwards. Life is a lot less stressful here now that I'm not an escort, and it has always been easier than England. They say that the grass isn't always greener; well, in Spain's case, I beg to differ. Everywhere has its good points and bad points, its heroes and its villains, but, for me, Marbella feels like home. Like good health, feeling 'at home' in a place is something you tend to take for granted, so every now and then I'll get out of Marbella for a while. But I'll always be back. I am a foreigner in Spain and, yet, I feel as though I fit in better here than in the UK. To me, it just feels as if there's more opportunity here. If you're willing to work for it, you can have a more than decent life. But, while I've learned the Spanish language and abide by their laws and customs, I'm still English and I'll never forget my roots.

And, whenever anyone mistakenly asks me which part of London I'm from, my answer will always be: 'Actually, I'm an Essex boy.'